KU-473-388

Ethel Jenner Rosenberg

*The Life and Times of England's
Outstanding Bahá'í Pioneer Worker*

by

Robert Weinberg

Robert Weinberg

Prayer revealed by 'Abdu'l-Bahá for
Ethel Jenner Rosenberg

O God, my God!
Fill up for me the cup of detachment from all things,
and in the assembly of Thy splendours and bestowals,
rejoice me with the wine of loving Thee.
Free me from the assaults of passion and desire,
break off from me the shackles of this nether world,
draw me with rapture unto Thy supernal realm,
and refresh me amongst the handmaids
with the breathings of Thy holiness.
O Lord, brighten Thou my face with the lights of Thy bestowals,
light Thou mine eyes
with beholding the signs of Thine all-subduing might;
delight my heart
with the glory of Thy knowledge that encompasseth all things,
gladden Thou my soul with Thy soul-reviving tidings of great joy,
O Thou King of this world and the Kingdom above,
O Thou Lord of dominion and might,
that I may spread abroad Thy signs and tokens,
and proclaim Thy Cause, and promote Thy Teachings,
and serve Thy Law, and exalt Thy word.
Thou art verily the Powerful,
the Ever-Giving, the Able, the Omnipotent.

GEORGE RONALD
OXFORD

George Ronald, Publisher Limited
46 High Street, Kidlington, Oxford OX5 2DN

© Robert Weinberg 1995
All Rights Reserved

British Library Cataloguing in Publication Data

A catalogue record for this book is available from the British Library.

ISBN 0-85398-399-2 pbk

Typesetting by ComputerCraft, Knoxville, Tennessee, USA
Printed and bound in Great Britain by
Biddles Ltd, Guildford and King's Lynn

Contents

List of Illustrations

Preface

It was in the summer of 1990 that a casual conversation with Dr Wendi Momen, chairman of the National Spiritual Assembly of the Bahá'ís of the United Kingdom, first alerted me to the extraordinary life of Ethel Jenner Rosenberg. Wendi and her colleague at George Ronald, Publisher, May Ballerio, in their great desire to give British Bahá'í women a strong sense of their rich spiritual heritage, suggested to me that the life of Ethel Rosenberg was a potentially inspiring story that had somehow slipped by the wayside and deserved examination. Thus the seed was planted.

I had previously heard of Ethel Rosenberg but I had never had any particular inclination to carry out detailed research into her life. Although I made no firm commitment to the idea of writing such a biography, it seemed that wherever I looked from that moment on I stumbled across the name of Ethel Rosenberg. Almost every Bahá'í history book I opened seemed to feature this remarkable women making her quiet but important contribution to its narrative. It appeared to me that whatever she did, she was always somehow a witness to, or often a key player in, the most important events in early western Bahá'í history. The comparative ease with which I found rare information about her artistic family background convinced me that she was a subject worth pursuing. More than four years later, this book is the result of that research.

In the opening minutes of the classic Orson Welles film *Citizen Kane*, the newsreel producer Charles Van Zandt spells out the challenge facing any would-be biographer. 'It isn't enough to show what a man did,' he tells his journalist employee. 'You've got to tell us who he was.' The difficulty in putting together this book, more than 60 years after the passing of Ethel Rosenberg, has been finding out exactly who she was. Only two souls in Britain remember meeting her and each gave quite different reports of her personality and manner. While Ethel left to posterity illuminating diaries, letters to friends, copious pilgrim's notes, as well as countless minutes from meetings that she attended, she gave very little of herself away. Her desire to transcribe accurately the happenings and conversations to which she was a witness necessarily meant putting her own personality to one side, although this fastidiousness and precision was naturally an important part of her character. If I may be so bold as to generalize, I feel she was essentially a product of late-Victorian England and was consequently not easily given to expressing – visibly or verbally – her emotions. To Ethel Rosenberg duty and correctness came first and duty to the Cause of Bahá'u'lláh and unswerving obedience to its central figures was the correct course to follow. From the outset, then, I apologize if the reader is disappointed at my inability to 'get inside the head' of Ethel Rosenberg. Given my own, very limited, historical, spiritual and gender perspective, I can do no more than leave the reader to draw his or her own conclusions about Ethel Rosenberg's private character and spiritual station from the events of this most significant life.

I offer this research to you in the hope that it will provide you, as it has me, with a deep admiration for the marvellous achievements of this extraordinary woman and a ceaseless wonder at how the Bahá'í Faith managed to survive its challenging first decades in the West thanks to – and sometimes in spite of – its early adherents. Most importantly perhaps, I hope you will discover that sense of history and heritage of which we must be proud as British Bahá'ís.

Many people are to be thanked for their support in the creation of this book. Grateful thanks are due to Wendi Momen and May Ballerio for planting the seed and for the inspiration and assistance they have lent this project from the beginning. Thanks must also go to the Research Department of the Universal House of Justice which rendered invaluable assistance with this work; the National Spiritual

Assembly of the Bahá'ís of the United Kingdom for giving me access to its archives; and Lewis V. Walker of the National Bahá'í Archives in Wilmette, Illinois for sending me more than 90 pages of correspondence and important documents relating to Ethel Rosenberg's life.

Alma Gregory and Rose Jones were the only living believers I could discover who remembered meeting Ethel Rosenberg. Despite the obvious difficulty in recalling meetings and events of 70 years ago, they provided me with moving and helpful descriptions. I am also grateful to Liz Emerson for her assistance in interviewing Alma Gregory.

I am grateful to David and Marion Hofman, Zebby Whitehead, Dr Moojan Momen and Rebecca Vickers for providing me with useful information and for their moral support. Jan Jasion managed to find me a copy of *A Brief Account of the Bahai Movement*, which was a great help to my research.

Stephen Chaplin, Archivist at the Slade School of Fine Art in London, and his assistant Annabel Osborne uncovered details of Ethel's courses at the school and directed me to useful publications. My gratitude also goes to Alexandra Fennel of the Portrait Miniature Department at Christie's in London; Daphne Foskett, FRSA, who has written definitive works on miniature painting and was most helpful on this subject; Claire Johnson of the National Art Library; Ron Parkinson, the Assistant Curator of the Paintings Section, Collection of Prints, Drawings and Paintings, Victoria and Albert Museum; and Susan Sloman, Keeper of Art, Bath City Council. Elizabeth Bevan, the Senior Assistant of Arts and Humanities at the County of Avon Community Leisure Department, and Colin Johnston, the City Archivist at Bath City Council, both provided useful historical information about the Rosenberg family's life in Bath. The Bath *Evening Chronicle* published my appeal for information about the Rosenberg family and I am grateful to Andrew Leach for lending me excellent materials related to the life of Tudor Pole. The London Borough of Merton sent invaluable information which helped in the search for Ethel Rosenberg's grave. I would further like to express my thanks to Counsellors Patrick O'Mara and Nabil Perdu, Dr Ridvan Moqbel, the Association for Bahá'í Studies English-Speaking Europe, the late Roger White, William Collins, Pamela Carr, Shahriar and Tiffani Razavi, Lindsey and Adam Thorne, Erica and Barney Leith, Sally and Derek Dacey and the Bahá'ís of Bath, Thelma Batchelor, Adam Robarts, Pieter-Bas Ruiter, Payam Beint, Howard Reeve, Ahlam Mirzai, Evren Celimli and Shirin Youseffian for their interest, encouragement and support as I carried out this work.

Last, and by no means least, my gratitude goes to the Bahá'ís of the United Kingdom and the Republic of Ireland – and, in particular, to two devoted and steadfast workers, my parents – who have given me my sense of Bahá'í history and to whom I dedicate this book with love.

Robert Weinberg
London, March 1995

1

The Rosenbergs of Bath

Like a queen enchanted who may not laugh or weep,
Glad at heart and guarded from change and care like ours,

Girt about by beauty by days and nights that creep
Soft as breathless ripples that softly shoreward sweep,
Lies the lovely city whose grace no grief deflowers.[1]
Algernon Charles Swinburne

Located at the point where the Cotswold and Mendip Hills meet with the Wiltshire Downs, the English city of Bath was extolled by the seventeenth century politician and diarist Samuel Pepys as 'the prettiest city in the Kingdom'.[2] Situated on an oolitic limestone belt which, in time, would give Bath its distinctive, coloured brick and whose caverns have yielded many important prehistoric remains, the city stands on land once inhabited by the Beaker people who arrived from the Rhineland around the year 2000 BC and whose name stems from the stone beakers that have been excavated at a number of their burial sites. It is believed that these people were responsible for building the remarkable stone circles which still stand at nearby Avebury and Stonehenge.

Bath's abiding distinction as a city, though, derives from its world-renowned hot springs. According to folklore, the bubbling natural waters were first discovered by Prince Bladud, supposedly the father of Shakespeare's King Lear. A legend tells of how the prince, who was banished from court on account of his leprosy, became a swineherd. One day, while tending to his animals close to the River Avon, he was astounded to discover that his pigs had been cured of their ailments after wallowing in a nearby steaming swamp. Immersing himself in the mire, he found to his amazement that his leprosy disappeared. Eventually, on acceding to the throne, Bladud established his seat in Bath and turned the swamp into a spa by building cisterns to retain the thermal waters.

Centuries went by and the attraction of the healing springs continued. Before the Romans invaded Britain in 43 AD, the springs were dedicated to the native Celtic god, Sul. Within fifty years of the invasion, a bathing complex named Aquae Sulis was established on the site. It included a forum, a theatre and a temple dedicated to Sul-Minerva, a combination of the Celtic and Roman gods. The baths were frequented by visitors from all over Europe for some three-and-a-half centuries but, following the Saxon invasion in the sixth century, the surrounding monumental buildings fell into neglect and were, in time, submerged by the swamp.

In 973 AD Edgar, who was crowned first king of all England at Bath, installed an order of Benedictine monks who would rule the city for over five hundred years. By the eleventh century the Bishop of Somersetshire, John de Villula of Tours, who was also the court physician, built himself a palace, a new abbey and the king's bath. This resulted in the city becoming once again a cynosure for people from all over Britain who sought to be cured by its natural elixir. Bath flourished under monastic rule, with wool and weaving as its main industries. However, in 1539 the monastery was dissolved at the order of King Henry VIII and sold. The member of parliament for Bath, Edmund Colthurst, bought the abbey and presented it to the people of the city. In 1574 Queen Elizabeth I sponsored a fund dedicated to its restoration.

As the weaving industry declined, the city once again was required to rely upon the spring as its main source of income. The baths, despite becoming an attraction for the sick poor and vagrants, nevertheless inspired influential doctors to recommend the water's curative properties to patients and a new bath was opened in 1576. The nude, mixed bathing was considered scandalous by some but many, including Samuel Pepys, were delighted by it.

In 1692 the then Princess Anne, later Queen Anne, paid a visit to the city and thus began Bath's history as a fashionable aristocratic resort. Anne's interest in Bath was subsequently maintained by succeeding monarchs, their courts and fashionable followers, but the city was poorly equipped to cater to their needs and interests. Its transformation from a teeming, dark and unpaved hive of pickpockets and beggars to a bright fashionable resort of worldwide fame was largely owing to the work of three men in the eighteenth century – Richard 'Beau' Nash, Ralph Allen and John Wood.

The young Nash, whose social skills established him as an influential high society figure, was able to set up funds for the cleaning, paving and lighting of the city's streets. He built the first Pump Room and in his Assembly House of 1708 introduced a card-room, a tea-room and, later, a ballroom and attractive musical concerts, making it the social centre of the city. Nash's influence also extended to the etiquette and behaviour of the gentry who called at his institutions. Duelling was forbidden, gambling controlled and, since Bath was a health resort, all balls had to end by eleven o'clock. Nash believed all social life should be communal and frowned upon private dinner parties and exclusive balls. His code of conduct became an established ingredient of taste throughout the entire country.

It was the entrepreneur Ralph Allen who was largely responsible for Bath's distinctive visual appearance by buying stone quarries at Combe Down. There the city's famous stone was mined to be fashioned into stately and imposing buildings by the architect John Wood. When it was first put to use, the Bath stone was almost white and some citizens complained of being blinded by the glare of the new edifices. The dazzling brightness would not remain for long, however, as atmospheric weathering rapidly turned the stone grey or black. John Wood's dream was to turn Bath into a second Rome with a royal forum, grand circus and imperial gymnasium. His plans, inspired by a revivalist interest in classical architecture, were quickly dismissed by the City Corporation, forcing him to take on private commissions in order to realize his vision, building by building, over several decades.

Wherever the aristocracy went, portrait painters followed and Bath became a prominent centre for portraiture. Thomas Gainsborough, one of England's greatest artists, arrived in the city in 1759, charging five guineas for a portrait. He stayed for fifteen years, by which time he could command a hundred guineas and was Bath's most sought-after painter. The well-groomed elegance of Bath's visitors and residents had a profound impact on Gainsborough's own artistic development. During this time, he began his well-known series of full-length, life-size portraits set in imaginary landscapes. Thomas Lawrence, later the president of the Royal Academy, would also begin his career in Bath in 1780.

Bath in its heyday spawned many innovations and discoveries. An invalid carriage widely used in its streets, though not invented in the city, came to be known as the Bath chair, while for the sweet-toothed connoisseur the city inspired the Bath bun and the chocolate oliver biscuit. Working from Bath in 1781, the German-born astronomer Sir William Herschel, who had come to Britain as a musician, discovered the planet Uranus. In the nineteenth century, Sir Isaac Pitman, also at work in the city, gave the world his method of shorthand writing. Bath was captured for posterity in great works of literature – by Sheridan in *The Rivals*, as well as in the works of Tobias Smollett and Jane Austen and by Charles Dickens in *The Pickwick Papers*.

Within a hundred years, by the end of the eighteenth century, Bath's population had grown from two thousand to 34,000 people. As the population grew, royalty and the aristocracy transferred their interests to other resorts such as Brighton. Despite the exodus of those who had originally made Bath the centre of attraction, architects and builders, motivated by the opportunity to benefit from such a rapidly expanding city, created new estates on its outskirts. In the confident climate of expansion, the Assembly Rooms were extended and the hot bath was rebuilt. Towards the end of the century, the Pump Room was redesigned and rebuilt.

It was to this overflowing and prosperous city that an Austrian-born portrait painter, a silhouette artist by the name of Charles Christian Rosenberg, came to set up business in the late 1780s. Rosenberg, born on 21 November 1745, had landed on the shores of Great Britain in 1761 as a page in the entourage of King George III's consort, Princess Charlotte of Mecklenburg-Strelitz. The King's reign, which had begun in 1760, would see the questioning of English power in both India and Ireland, as well as the loss of the American colonies. These were also the early decades of the industrial revolution which would transform England from a largely agricultural into a predominately industrial economy, beginning with the mechanization of the textile industry followed by mining and transport.

In the aristocratic circles of the day, Charles Christian Rosenberg was to rise to become one of Britain's most celebrated and successful silhouette artists. Taste for the silhouette as an art form was at its highest by the end of the eighteenth century. Society people flocked to have their profiles uniquely rendered, most commonly by way of a solid black outline or, alternatively, cut from paper. Rosenberg became known for an attractive and original technique, painting the profiles on a convex glass with a flat, pink-coloured background fixed away from the glass. Thus the profile would not only stand out but would also cast a soft shadow on the background.

On 11 October 1787 Rosenberg placed his first advertisement in the Bath *Chronicle*. At the time he was 41 years old and still a bachelor but he was already boasting a prestigious clientele.

Mr Rosenberg (from Vienna) at Mr Tucker's, St James' Street, Bath, having had the honour of taking the Likenesses of most of the Princes of Germany, as well as Their Majesties, the Prince of Wales, Duke of York, and the Princesses at Windsor, begs leave to acquaint the Nobility, Gentry &c. that he takes the most excellent LIKENESSES IN PROFILE, which he paints on glass, in imitation of stone, agate, &c., and so never to fade, in a manner superior to anything ever attempted in this country. He flatters himself to give satisfaction to all those who shall honour him with their Commands.

PROFILE LIKENESSES painted for Lockets, Rings, &c. Mr Rosenberg also acquaints the Inhabitants of Bath that he can accommodate them with the most Striking Likenesses of the Royal Family.

Any person may be taught, if unacquainted with drawing, on the most reasonable terms.[3]

On 4 February 1790, at the age of 44, Rosenberg married Elizabeth Woolley in Bath Abbey, the last vestige of the medieval city. The fact that the wedding was held in the abbey suggests that Rosenberg was either not of Jewish origin, as has previously been thought, or, if he was, that certainly from this time onwards, it would appear he was content for all of his children to be christened and raised in the Anglican Church. Elizabeth Woolley was descended from a family of still life and genre artists. Her father, Thomas Woolley, was a tailor and habit maker. In this union the die was cast for the artistic pursuits of the Rosenberg family for several generations to come. On 19 November of the same year the couple's first son, Thomas Elliot Rosenberg, the grandfather of Ethel Jenner Rosenberg was born.

By 1792 the master silhouettist had entered into a professional partnership with a pair of ivory sculptors, Stephany and Dresch, who would for the next five years embellish his work for snuff boxes, lockets and other items of jewellery. The three men worked from the same premises, with

Rosenberg offering to execute a silhouette in just one minute at prices ranging from seven shillings and sixpence to one guinea. The process of detailing and presenting the basic silhouette would then ordinarily take a further 24 hours. The North Parade studio also offered a 'very fashionable assortment of Trinkets, Toys, artificial Flowers, Jewellery, and French fancy feathers'.[4] By this time Elizabeth Rosenberg had given birth to another son, Charles, who would also become an artist of good repute.

The period of the French Revolution between 1789 and 1815 saw Europe engulfed by conflict, with France declaring war on England in 1793. Charles Christian Rosenberg took a keen interest in public and foreign affairs and closely watched the progress of the Revolution. When news reached Bath of the execution on 21 January 1793 of Louis XVI, Rosenberg's nationalist feelings came to the fore. He decided to prepare an effigy of the Duke of Orleans who had supported the Jacobins, members of the radical democratic club established in Paris in 1789. For a fortnight the effigy was exhibited in Rosenberg's Bath studio and then conveyed in a cart to a field where it was hanged from a gallows and set alight 'amidst the execration and groans of a great concourse of spectators'.[5] Rosenberg collected more than ten pounds during the exhibition of the effigy and donated the sum to the city's hospital. The Rosenbergs' first daughter, Elizabeth Maria Antoinette, named for Rosenberg's unfortunate countrywoman, was christened at Bath Abbey in January 1794.

Rosenberg's interest in the events of the day was reflected in his use of advertising. Often he would introduce an event of topical or fashionable interest in a humorous way into the advertising material he prepared to promote his business. On 12 June 1794 Bath received news of Admiral Howe's sea victory against France off Ushant. The celebrated event was marked by a public holiday complete with illuminations and fireworks. Earl Howe had been a frequent visitor to Bath since 1780 and its citizens competed with each other in decorating their houses with mottos and emblems. Rosenberg installed three illuminated transparencies with mottos and portraits into the window of his shop, lit from behind by lamps and candles.

Rosenberg, it would appear, always seemed to be searching for extra sources of income and by 1796 had once again expanded his business to include a 'curious assortment of WORK, WRITING, and other BOXES, most elegantly worked in Straw'[6] as well as an exotic range of elasticated braces manufactured by himself. A later development in the studio was the introduction of a 'well-regulated *Weighing Machine*' and a '*Measure*, where Ladies and Gentlemen may ascertain their weight and height at One Shilling the Season'.[7] In the summer of 1796 the Duke of York revisited Bath to be cured of his 'spasmodic affections'.[8] The visit coincided with the birth of the Rosenberg's third son and the boy was christened Frederick, after the Duke, who was to become the child's godfather and who agreed to sponsor his young namesake by proxy.

As the eighteenth century came to an end, Charles Christian Rosenberg disbanded his partnership with Stephany and Dresch, gave up his extra lines of income and moved his family and his collection of some three thousand profiles to a new address:

No. 14, GROVE, BATH.

CHARLES ROSENBERG, Profile-Painter to their MAJESTIES and all the ROYAL FAMILY, respectfully informs the Nobility and Gentry, that he is removed from the North Parade TO THE ABOVE HOUSE, where he takes the most perfect LIKENESSES in his usual and approved style; and where the largest Collection of PORTRAITS of the most celebrated Characters in the kingdom is exhibited *gratis*.

C.R. having declined every other business, means to apply himself solely to a profession in which he has given universal satisfaction; – assiduity, constant attendance, and gratitude, shall render him deserving of the future favours of his friends.

All the likenesses which C.R. has taken, during ten years residence in this city, have been and will continue to be carefully preserved for the satisfaction of relatives, &c, who may wish to have copies.

Time of sitting One Minute only - price from 7s.6d. to one guinea, frames included.

The very excellent, genteel and airy LODGINGS, in the above House, to be let, furnished or unfurnished, at an easy rent.[9]

The nineteenth century began with a new development in the Rosenberg's lives, as another advertisement placed in the Bath *Chronicle* of 25 April 1804 reveals:

We have pleasure to inform the respectable inhabitants of this city, that in compliance with the wishes of several ladies, Mrs. Rosenberg has been prevailed upon to open a Day school for children. Those who know Mrs. R's attention to her own family, will say how capable she is to undertake this:

Delightful task! To rear the tender thought
To teach the young idea how to shoot
And pour fresh instruction o'er the Mind.[10]

As if the task of opening and maintaining a school was not enough, Elizabeth Rosenberg also gave birth to two more children during this period. Ann and Samuel were christened together in March 1805. In the meantime, Elizabeth's husband continued to capture the likenesses of royalty and the landed gentry, among them Louis XVIII of France, who had taken refuge in England in 1807 following the Napoleonic Wars. As Bath lost its appeal to the upper classes, Rosenberg chose to spend extensive periods of time away from the city. He visited some of the newly fashionable resorts – including Harrogate, Brighton and Ramsgate – in order to capitalize on their expanding markets for portraiture. The Rosenberg's lives would continue in much the same manner for the next eight years, with Elizabeth running the school while raising her own five children and Charles going away to profit from the seasonal trade in Britain's major towns and cities. In 1812 Thomas Elliot Rosenberg, by now a promising young artist, joined his father in the business.

Tragedy struck the family in 1815 with the untimely death of the Rosenberg's third son, Frederick, who was just eighteen years old. Charles Christian Rosenberg, now 70, left his family in Bath and returned to the Royal Court. On 28 April 1816 he was appointed King's Messenger to George III. Three years later, on 15 April 1819, he was dismissed from the job but was reinstated by the following July. There is a suggestion that during the intervening three months Rosenberg was naturalized. The King himself was not in power at the time owing to his mental instability, now attributed to the genetic disorder porphyria. It would seem that Rosenberg's post was largely a nominal one, reinstated for the reign of King George IV as well as after the accession of King William IV in 1830.

In 1834 Rosenberg, then aged 89, retired on an allowance of 140 pounds a year. He remained at Court to see the early years of the record 64-year reign of Queen Victoria, who called him 'Rosie'. It is even reported that the old man took a likeness of the young Queen.[11] Charles Christian Rosenberg died eight days short of his ninety-ninth birthday in November 1844, having outlived his eldest son, Thomas Elliot, by nine years.

As an era ended for one of the foremost artistic families of the time, another era – of world-shaking consequences – was just beginning in far-off Persia. In the person of Ethel Jenner Rosenberg, Charles Christian Rosenberg's great-granddaughter who would be born fourteen years later, these two vastly contrasting worlds would find a mysterious point of connection.

Thomas Elliot Rosenberg clearly inherited his father's artistic gifts. By the time Thomas was in his early twenties he was assisting in the production of silhouettes. He studied with an artist named Burgers and in the Bath Directory of 1812 there is a listing for 'Rosenberg & Son, Profile Paint-

ers'. It is thought that some of the more accomplished silhouettes painted in that period to which Charles Christian
Rosenberg's trade labels are attached are in fact the work
of Thomas. Among his sitters were members of the Royal
Family – Queen Charlotte, King George IV, his daughter
Princess Charlotte and her husband Prince Leopold. The
visit of Leopold to Bath in 1830 caused controversy as the
future Belgian King believed he was complimenting the city
by declaring it similar in style to an Italian one. The Bath
Chronicle dismissed the Prince's remarks out of hand and
proclaimed Bath's absolute uniqueness amongst the world's
cities. It could not be denied, however, that Bath's rapid
expansion had slowed down and that the mood – once described as gay-spark and macaroni – had become somewhat
more sombre, with the Palladian style giving way to Gothic
revival.

Thomas Elliot Rosenberg's particular specialities were
landscape and miniature painting as well as teaching. The
latter provided his family with its main source of income. For
the duration of his adult life, Thomas taught drawing and
practical perspective in Bath. Works by Thomas's younger
brother, Charles, also remain. Although apparently not a
professional artist, Charles drew in a mannered style typical
of the period.

As a landscape painter, Thomas Elliot Rosenberg's subjects were usually locations in the west of England and his
paintings were considered comparable to the work of his
contemporary Peter De Wint, who enjoyed great success by
specializing in capturing the flat countryside around Lincoln.
Thomas's work was not limited to country landscapes,
however. He also became known for his clearly detailed
urban scenes. Drawings of Bath and Hastings as well as a
portrait of his daughter Frances remain in the collection of
Bath's Victoria Art Gallery to this day.

Thomas Elliot Rosenberg excelled in miniature painting
– a medium which would later be favoured by his granddaughter Ethel – but few of his works have survived. The

tradition of miniature painting, usually showing a portrait
of some kind, had always enjoyed a special position in British
art. The format traces its origins back to the medieval illuminated manuscript, and just as their precursors had done,
sixteenth century miniaturists often worked on vellum, their
paintings usually replete with allegories and symbolism. By
the seventeenth century miniatures had become more common in style and technique with the use of oils. In the following century, with the introduction of ivory into miniatures,
a dramatic change of character occurred. Works would often
be painted in watercolour directly onto a plain white background.

In February 1817 Thomas married Mary Wood, a local
woman, who took over the running of the Ladies School
founded thirteen years earlier by her mother-in-law. The
marriage of Thomas and Mary Rosenberg spawned an artistic dynasty. The couple's first child, a daughter, also christened Mary, was born in 1819. From the girl's childhood it
was Thomas's intention that she should become a flower
painter. Plans were made for her to become a pupil of a noted
artist, William Davis, while she continued her education at
her mother's school. The idea failed owing to the sudden
death of Davis. Mary was taken on by one of Davis's pupils,
and at the age of fourteen she was awarded the silver medal
of the Institute of the Society of Arts for a study of a flower
from nature. Her early years were spent at the family home
at 6 New King Street, Bath, from where by 1841 she also
taught flower and landscape painting. She exhibited fruit and
flower paintings at the Second Exhibition of Living Artists
in Quiet Street in 1838 as well as landscapes of Conway
Castle and Hastings Beach and European views, including
a scene of Emerick on the Rhine.

On 28 February 1850 Mary married William Duffield, an
acclaimed painter of fruit and game. Duffield's determination
to paint accurate representations of game ultimately led to
his own sudden death. He is believed to have died after
contracting an illness from the corpse of a stag which he had

been keeping in his studio so he could capture its likeness accurately.

In 1860 Mary Duffield was elected to the New Watercolour Society, of which she eventually became the oldest living member, surviving until the age of 94. Her death on 14 January 1914 at Stowtin Rectory in Hythe, Kent, was recorded in *The Times*. Mary Duffield exhibited 393 paintings in total between 1848 and 1912, including 341 at the New Watercolour Society and 12 at the Royal Academy. In addition, she published a treatise on flower painting, which went into several editions, and had work reproduced in a number of magazines and periodicals.

When Mary was three years old her mother gave birth to another daughter, Frances Elizabeth Louisa. She too adopted flower painting as her speciality, exhibiting some 142 works – 139 at the New Watercolour Society and 3 at the Royal Academy – from 1845 until her death in 1873. In November 1846 she became the wife of a Bath jeweller and from that time on exhibited under the name of Mrs John Dafter Harris. Another sister, Ellen Manners Rosenberg, born in 1831, would also devote her creative talents to capturing flowers and still life subjects, becoming a constant exhibitor in London and the provinces, in Bath and the West of England.

It was, however, the son of Thomas Elliot and Mary Rosenberg, George Frederick, father of Ethel Jenner Rosenberg, who made the greatest impact on the artistic circles of his day, if only because of his exemplary and upright character.

2

A Most Valued Citizen

*A good character is, verily, the best mantle for men
from God. With it He adorneth the temples of His loved
ones. By My life! The light of a good character sur-
passeth the light of the sun and the radiance thereof.
Whoso attaineth unto it is accounted as a jewel among
men.*[12]

Bahá'u'lláh

Thomas Elliot Rosenberg died after a serious illness on 17
June 1835 at the age of 44. During his brief life, spent exclusively in the city of Bath, Britain had changed dramatically,
becoming one of the world's wealthiest countries through its
industrial and economic prowess. On the human scale,
however, the victories of progress were outweighed by the
suffering of a populace enslaved by the technological revolution. There had undoubtedly been positive moves towards
alleviating the pain of existence for large numbers of people.
The slave trade had been abolished in 1807 and slavery was
outlawed throughout the Empire in 1833. Yet at home the
prevailing image of the country for the masses of working
people was characterized by poverty and the miseries of child
labour, long working days and slum conditions.

George Frederick Rosenberg, the third child and only son
of Thomas Elliot Rosenberg, would have known little of this
suffering. He was born in Bath on 9 March 1825, by which
time his father was already a successful teacher and practis-
ing artist. Owing to the early death of his father, George was
an almost entirely self-taught artist who, just as his sisters
had done, became a proficient flower and still life painter. His

own obituary some 44 years later recorded how 'early in life,
left with a widowed mother and orphaned sisters looking to
him for guidance and help, he was called upon to exhibit the
steady perseverance, the high sense of honour, the true
unselfishness which distinguished him throughout life'.[13]

George had much in common with his late father. Both
excelled as painters as well as teachers of drawing and
painting. In 1846 one of George's drawings, entitled *Fish*,
was shown at the Royal Academy in London. In addition to
the sale of his own works, he earned in the region of an extra
five hundred pounds a year for his tuition 'in colleges and
schools of the best class',[14] a large sum of money for the time.

It was during this period that a good number of societies
devoted to promoting art emerged in Bath and George Frederick Rosenberg actively encouraged local talent. The Bath
Society for the Encouragement of Fine Arts, founded in
1836, held large annual exhibitions at the Assembly Rooms
and offered prizes. In the 1846 exhibition works by the late
John Constable were exhibited.

The following year, in an unprecedented move, the Old
Watercolour Society, one of the most exclusive of British art
institutions, welcomed George as an Associate. His election
was an unusual and unexpected accolade for such a young
painter. Initially, George made noticeable contributions to
the Society's department of fruit, flowers and still life painting. However, by the mid-1850s he made a conscious switch
from depicting domestic subject matter to capturing mountain landscapes. This move led commentators of the time to
note that his name of Rosenberg curiously foreshadowed a
change that subsequently took place in his line of art: beginning with flowers, he ended with mountains. Thus, between
1848 and 1870 George Frederick Rosenberg exhibited constantly with the Old Watercolour Society, showing some 228
works including 150 at the Society's summer exhibitions. For
the first seven years of his membership of the Society he
exhibited a modest range of subjects, mainly fruit, dead game
and fish, and a few views near Bath. It was in 1855 that he

introduced one or two studies of buildings in Wales and Shropshire, and in the following year his *Scene in Glencoe* led the way to the fascination with mountains and peaks that would continue for the rest of his life. Between 1857 and 1860 George exhibited views of Switzerland as well as the Scottish Highlands. After 1861 views of Norway became his most common and characteristic subjects, showing his great skill and interest in accurately capturing a landscape.

In 1853 George published an octavo handbook, *The Guide to Flower Painting in Watercolours*, illustrated by his own pen. While moving in the high-powered artistic circles of the Old Watercolour Society, he remained a keen promoter of art in his own neighbourhood, exhibiting at the first meeting and exhibition of the Bath Sketching Club on 7 April 1853. Two years later, two paintings *Seashore* and *Fruit* were shown at the Exhibition of Fine Arts in Widcombe's Temperance Hall. This interest in promoting local arts is reflected in letters written in 1854, 1856 and 1863 in which George made appeals for the loan of drawings to exhibit at the Bath Fine Art Society, which he defined as a 'Graphic Society on a large scale'.[15]

Also in 1853, George was appointed Drawing Master at Bath Proprietary College. The Bath and Cheltenham *Gazette* of 15 November advertises a lecture by George at Grosvenor College. The college prided itself on its discipline, 'strict without severity',[16] which led to many of its students registering for 'Academical first-class distinctions'[17] and five of them receiving the Victoria Cross.

On 8 July 1857 in Dorrington, Wiltshire, George Frederick Rosenberg married Hannah Fuller Jenner, believed to be a descendant of Edward Jenner, the discoverer of vaccination. Following in the footsteps of his father and grandfather, George was content to establish his home and artistic base in Bath. The Bath Directories indicate that 'George Rosenberg, artist' lived at 6 New King Street, the home of his father and mother, until around 1864, some eight years after his marriage, when he moved his own young family to

3 Brunswick Place. His first child, Ethel Jenner Rosenberg, was born on 6 August 1858. Another daughter, Gertrude Mary, and a son, also named George Frederick, followed, although George senior would not live long enough to see the birth of his son. He would, alas, only have some 12 years to enjoy married life and a bright, young family.

There is no doubt that the Rosenberg children had a privileged infancy encouraged by parents who valued moral uprightness as well as academic and artistic excellence. At an early age Ethel Jenner Rosenberg became a knowledgeable student of the Old and New Testaments and gained a thorough knowledge of French. Her mother, Ethel often later recalled, counselled her to 'watch for a great teacher sent from God'.[18] Ethel's younger sister, Gertrude, went on to exhibit work at the Royal Academy as well as in the West Country where she settled in the area around St Ives. Their brother George, while also an accomplished painter, opted for a career in education, studying at Cambridge and subsequently working as a schoolmaster at Rockhampton in Queensland, Australia, and ultimately as headmaster of a London school.

George Frederick Rosenberg's success as an artist and teacher continued as he watched his two daughters grow up. He was well-respected in the artistic circles of the day for his exemplary character. It is recorded that he was 'of a modest and amiable disposition'.[19] In a letter of 17 April 1858, he asked 'without a trace of irritation, and in a manner strongly contrasting with that of some other similar requests received by the Secretary [of the Old Watercolour Society], whether a drawing of his not hung by the committee had been rejected for want of merit; saying, "I value the criticisms of brother artists of note *very much* more than any others."'[20] In April 1867 George exhibited a selection of watercolour paintings at Paris and received a bronze medal.

On 17 September 1869 George took his wife and Ethel to Norway where he intended to build up a body of new work. Tragically, the journey had a sad conclusion for the family.

On his return home, after a short but severe illness, George died from the effects of a chill contracted sitting down 'while overheated to sketch a glacier'.[21]

The Bath *Chronicle* of 23 September 1869 reported:

> It is with much regret that we have to record the loss of another of our most valued citizens, Mr George Rosenberg, who recently returned with his wife and eldest child from a trip to Norway, whence he had brought a number of beautiful but alas unfinished drawings, died on Friday last at his house 3, Brunswick Place . . . For many years an Associate of the Old Watercolour Society, he is well known to the world as an accomplished artist, in whose works they have admired the earnestness of purpose and scrupulous veracity with which all he undertook was impressed. His generous and all efficient aid in the management of the Graphic and Quartett Societies and the rare kindliness and ability he evinced in the discharge of the daily duties of his professional life, have made him widely known and esteemed by the inhabitants of Bath and there can be few indeed who, in any of these ways have been brought into contact with him, who do not feel that in him we have lost a man of sterling worth and great usefulness . . . [22]

The three hundred or more drawings and sketches that George left behind at his passing were sold at Christie's Auction House on 12 and 14 February of the following year.

Entering into her teenage years, Ethel Jenner Rosenberg worked hard to perfect her inherited artistic gifts and began to pursue a calling as an artist in her own right. It was probably unthinkable that she should follow any other career. It was common at that time for a young woman hailing, as Ethel did, from an illustrious artistic family to follow the profession of her forebears. Women were 'led to the cultivation of art through the choice of parents or brothers. While nothing has been more common than to see young men embrace the profession [of art] against the wishes of their families, and in the face of difficulties, the example of a woman thus deciding for herself is extremely rare.'[23] Families in the middle classes often expected their women to work, and especially between the 1840s and 1870s, the death of a male provider was frequently the reason for a woman to decide to become a professional artist. Whereas young men commonly trained as artists in specialized institutions, women learned their craft by working as assistants to their relatives. Having lost her father at an extremely young age, Ethel found in her two aunts, Mrs Duffield and Mrs Harris, fine examples and teachers. They, like the majority of women artists of their time, specialized in the still life genre whereas their male counterparts concentrated on landscapes and figure paintings. This was a common practice in a period when more vigorous outdoor pursuits were considered the lot of men. Painting fruit and flowers were seen as 'divine appointment the property of ladies'.[24] Such subjects were deemed decorative and not intellectual and thus, to the Victorian mind, suitable for women artists.

While it might be thought that a typical girl of Ethel's age would contemplate married life, wherein it was considered proper for a woman to give up her own concerns and independence for the serving of others, it was not unusual for female artists of the Victorian period to opt for a life of spinsterhood. Those women artists who were able to pursue their careers as well as being married were usually in the situation of having committed themselves to a life with another artist where a creative and business-oriented partnership sustained their relationship. For a large number of women artists, however, spinsterhood represented a positive identity. Being unmarried was increasingly being seen as one of the highest forms of womanhood. One commentator of the time noted that 'the higher a woman's nature is, the more likely it is that she will prefer to forgo marriage altogether, than surrender herself to a union that would sink her below her own ideal'.[25] A contemporary art historian has stated that in 'electing spinsterhood women artists not only chose independence, but they harnessed their art practice to those moral principles of feminine purity which were perceived as

unique to their class and their sexuality'.[26] Spinsters, after
all, were responsible for their own earnings or their family
inheritances. By the 1880s there were large networks of such
women in the more artistic boroughs of London, who rented
or bought their own studios and socialized in a largely female
community. The Slade School, meanwhile, was known to
offer the best fine art training for women as, unusually for
the time, it offered fair and equal opportunities to both sexes.
It was for this world and for this school in particular that
Ethel Jenner Rosenberg chose to leave Bath at the age of
nineteen.

3

The Young Artist in London

*It hath been revealed and is now repeated that the true
worth of artists and craftsmen should be appreciated,
for they advance the affairs of mankind.*[27]

Bahá'u'lláh

In 1877 Ethel Jenner Rosenberg left her mother's home in
Bath and ventured to London to study at the Slade School.
Bath had changed dramatically since the heady days of
Palladian splendour which her forefathers had known. No
longer frequented by royalty, its mood was now influenced
by an influx of social climbers, fortune hunters and those
who had recently acquired wealth – the *nouveaux riches*. It
was a period when Britain under the leadership of Benjamin
Disraeli was feeling the effects of his commitment to social
reform and his devotion to furthering the Empire. Queen
Victoria had been proclaimed Empress of India and scientific
discoveries around the world were being made at remarkable
speed. Alexander Graham Bell had recently patented the
telephone and Edison the gramophone. Similarly, in the
world of fine arts, the 1870s were years of change and experimentation as women began to emerge onto the capital's art
scene and new methods were tried out. The revolution in the
visual arts brought about by the Impressionists in France
was just beginning to touch British shores.

The Slade School, where Ethel Rosenberg studied for four
years, had been founded by the art connoisseur and collector
Felix Slade who had, in his will, endowed three universities
– Oxford, Cambridge and London – with Professorships in
Fine Art. While at the first two these posts had consisted

exclusively of lecturing chairs, in London it was decided to
raise extra money and establish a Fine Art school. The first
section of the new institution was completed in 1871 and is
still standing today.

At the time of the Slade's opening, art in England had
reached a particularly low point. The Royal Academy was
frequented by painters who were badly trained and showed
an indifferent attitude to art outside of their own country.
One French critic said of the English Academicians: 'It would
seem as though their studios were closed by a portion of the
Great Wall of China. They keep up a continual Continental
blockade but it is against themselves. European art is a
sealed book to them.'[28] Similarly, the standards of art education had little to recommend them. Since the 1850s the
prestigious art schools at South Kensington had been losing
their direction, with students following an eight-year course
which largely involved drawing from antique plaster casts.
Drawing from a life model was introduced only towards the
end of a student's training.

There were, however, two small revolutions in English art
circles that posed a challenge to the conventional methods.
One was the influence felt from the Pre-Raphaelite Movement – Dante Gabriel Rossetti, William Holman Hunt, John
Everett Millais and, later, William Morris and Edward
Burne-Jones – which evolved an original style challenging
pictorial conventions, combining a stylistic treatment of
mythological subjects with elaborate symbolism and a strong
decorative element. The other development concerned a
circle of artists who had gathered around James Abbott
McNeill Whistler. These artists had known each other in
Paris in the 1850s. In this latter group, Edward Poynter,
who was to become the first Slade Professor, could be found.

At the time of his appointment, which lasted five years,
Poynter was in mid-career. Each year of his professorship
was launched with an ambitious address, demonstrating his
attachment to French methods of studio teaching. In his first
lecture, delivered in 1871, he attacked the English art

schools and the lack of experience English artists had of
drawing from life. In France, a student would work alongside
his teacher, working with a model for four hours a day for
a whole week. Older students would help the younger and
when the latter had acquired sufficient proficiency in drawing to understand the meaning of forms, then he would begin
to paint from the model. Working from the antique would
only be introduced after students demonstrated a grasp of
form acquired by working from life. Poynter's philosophy was
summed up in his statement that he would 'impress but one
lesson upon the students, that constant study from the life-
model is the only means they have at arriving at a compre-
hension of the beauty in nature, and of avoiding its ugliness
and deformity; which I take to be the whole aim and end of
study. . . Your work from the models . . . is not only to enable
you to paint what you desire with ease and skill, but is to
have a better result than this in forming your ideas of the
beautiful, and enabling you to distinguish good from bad; for
the study of nature is not the end of art, but merely a means
of enabling you to express your ideas.'[29]

By 1875 the Slade School was highly efficient and the
number of pupils attending it were all that could be accommodated. When Poynter moved on from the Slade he proposed that one Alphonse Legros should succeed him. Legros
hailed from the Parisian realist movement. His work, while
belonging to a tradition of nineteenth century painting that
depicted an idealized world of peasants working – closely
studied by the young Vincent Van Gogh – also involved a
certain modern approach to composition and tonality which
was influenced by photography.

Legros had settled in England in 1863 and had entered
Whistler's flamboyant circle of friends but the friendships
and the inspiration of these artists were not maintained.
Legros, who spoke poor English, taught through demonstra-
tion. There were two responses to his methods. Some
stressed his serious and demanding approach to draughtsmanship and his devotion to studying the old masters. Oth-

ers – who were closer to the Impressionistic revolution happening in France – thought his method dangerously conceived. One of Legros' pupils recalled how, 'if he did interest himself in a pupil, he managed to instil . . . not merely a feeling for style . . . but a feeling for that quality best expressed by the French epithet *noble* . . .'[30] To begin with, Legros followed Poynter's philosophy and encouraged his students to travel; but later it appears that he lost interest and relied on more conventional methods. Nevertheless, by the mid-1880s an entirely new mood existed in London's art schools owing to the revolution that had begun at the Slade.

The 1870s also saw the growth in the number of art courses open to women. A French master opened an art school for 'ladies' in London, teaching life drawing three days a week. Attached to the Society of Female Artists was also another school for women students of whom there were some 150, but few women enjoyed the fame of their male counterparts. It was generally believed that art would never take a woman 'out of her natural sphere, or tempt her to abandon the enjoyments of home, or interfere with the household duties which are, as they ought to be, woman's privilege, pride and reward'.[31] Notwithstanding the prevailing attitudes of the time, art schools for women began to open in a number of London suburbs. At the Academy schools at the beginning of the decade there were 23 women students. In certain quarters it was urged that there should be separate classes, for it was not considered seemly that 'young females should study from the nude side by side with young men, in an evening atmosphere where flirtations were inevitable'.[32] By 1873, however, the South Kensington art schools had some 331 women students on their registers in comparison to 392 men.

In the midst of this intense atmosphere of change, Ethel Rosenberg enrolled in a full year's Fine Art course at the Slade for the 1877-8 academic year. The course cost 19 pounds 19 shillings. The young and eager artist from such

a distinguished family of painters studied hard and clearly
demonstrated a strong attention to detail, a quality common
to all the previous Rosenbergs' work and one which would
be instrumental in her later decision to work in portrait
miniatures.

Ethel's devotion to her studies was rewarded when she
received a certificate for coming fifth equal in her drawing
from antique class. The following year she enrolled once
again for Fine Art and records still kept at the Slade School
show that she began to excel at drawing from the life model.
At the end of the year she was awarded a certificate for being
the second best student in life drawing as well as fourth
equal in etching. In 1879 Ethel registered for just one term,
paying seven pounds seven shillings. In this year her work
reached a standard where she felt confident to begin exhibiting. The Bath *Chronicle* of 18 September reports that her
paintings were on show at the Devon and Exeter Fine Art
exhibition.

The end of the decade saw increasing opportunities arising
for artists to show their work to ever expanding audiences.
The first Summer Exhibition to be held at the Royal Academy under the residency of Sir Frederick Lord Leighton as
President was staged in 1879. Leighton – a sculptor as well
as a painter – was a dominating man, with catholic taste and
excellent judgement. His period as president marked a peak
in the Academy's relationship with the general public and
established for it an impressive standing. Ethel Rosenberg's
work – when she began to exhibit in London – enjoyed the
continually expanding audiences at the Academy under
Leighton's leadership. His first summer exhibition attracted
more than 391,000 paying visitors, while almost six-and-a-
half thousand works were submitted for entry.

Ethel occasionally journeyed back to Bath to visit her
mother, who had moved into a house at Spencers Belle Vue,
some four streets away from the Brunswick Place home
where Ethel had grown up. Bath was enjoying yet another
wave of popular interest following the finding of the Roman

Great Bath in 1878 by the City Engineer Major Davis, who
had been investigating a leak in the Kings Bath at the time
of the chance discovery. In the years that Ethel had been in
London, Bath had become a haven for retired professional
people and had undergone quite a radical transformation
since Ethel's childhood. New standards and technological
developments meant the city now had a clean water supply,
sewerage, gas, electricity, trams, public parks, new schools
and three railways. Some of the imposing Georgian houses
had been knocked together to make hotels, and department
stores were beginning to open. Ethel's mother was not to
stay much longer in the city, choosing to spend her final
years with her youngest daughter in the more tranquil
setting of Cornwall. In the summer of 1880 Ethel painted a
picture of her mother's house at Spencers Belle Vue.

Ethel's devotion to her studies took her back to the capital
and in 1881 she returned to the Slade, attending one term
of Fine Art training. From this time on, Ethel set up a permanent residence in London, soon afterwards moving into
a house at 25 Albany Street just off Regents Park from where
her career as a portrait painter and miniaturist began to
prosper. Between 1883 and 1909 Ethel exhibited seven
pictures at the Walker Art Gallery in Liverpool, three at the
London Salon, 17 at the New Gallery, three at the Royal
Miniature Society and, most importantly, 30 at the Royal
Academy. One observer of her work described her red chalk
head drawings as quite remarkable. She also drew portraits
in the style of John Downman, who had enjoyed success
around the turn of the nineteenth century with his small
portraits, often on copper, rendered in pencil and charcoal
and delicately tinted with watercolour.

Ethel Rosenberg had little time for, or interest in, experi-
menting with the new, liberating methods of the Impressionists or the more fantastic symbolism of the Pre-Raphaelites.
Her miniature work was well-executed and precise with a
tendency towards soft colours and lines. It was a style which
by its very nature flattered the sitter and appealed greatly

to the upper echelons of London society. Ethel, it seems, had no problem receiving commissions for portraits from prominent society figures. In 1883 she exhibited a likeness of *An Italian Boy* at the Royal Academy; the following year she exhibited a portrait of *Daisy* and the next year *Dorothy*. In 1887 the Royal Academy received 8,686 entries for its Summer Exhibition. Ethel's work successfully came through the stringent reviewing procedure and she was able to show a portrait entitled *Nicola*. In subsequent years, on several occasions, more than one of Ethel's paintings enjoyed a showing at the Academy and, judging by the list of names of her sitters, it appears that her skill at rendering gently drawn likenesses was very much in demand by the cream of London society. *Edith, Daughter of Colonel Stanley Clarke*; *Master John Jenkins in Fancy Dress* and *Miss Madeline Stanley* were all shown in the Academy in 1888. *Master Dick, son of R. Bell Davies Esq.*; *The Late Colonel Sir Edward Fitzgerald Campbell, Bart.* and *Miss Alexandra B. Kitchin* were displayed in 1889. The next year saw the Royal Academy hanging Ethel's portraits of *John Venn Esq. FRS* and *Mrs Edward Campbell*. In 1891 *Ida, Daughter of J. H. Wheatley Esq.* and *The Rev. Canon Aubrey Moore* graced the gallery walls. Other subjects in subsequent years included *Alice, daughter of Sir Gurney Buxton*; *Lady Scourfield*; *The Hon. Bridget Astley, daughter of Lord Hastings*; *Augusta Spottiswoode* and *Lady Lilford*.

By 1896, when Ethel exhibited *Elinor, daughter of Dudley Drummond, Esq.* and a portrait of one *Mrs Massingberd*, the Academy was attracting some 12,500 works for display. Only two thousand could be shown, so Ethel's portraits were clearly considered accomplished against such enormous competition.

The works hung at the Royal Academy were not only enjoyed by members of the public but also members of the royal family and distinguished visitors. An annual dinner on the Saturday before the opening day of the exhibition was inevitably attended by the Prince of Wales, later to become

King Edward VII. The popularity of the Academy exhibitions caused a railing to be placed in front of particular pictures in order to prevent possible injury from the crowds of people who swarmed to view them.

During this period Ethel changed her address a number of times, moving from Albany Street to 20 Walpole Street, off Kings Road in Chelsea, to 41 New Bond Street and, finally, to 5 Grafton Street in Piccadilly. These were all comparatively expensive parts of London, indicative of the considerable success Ethel enjoyed in her career as a portrait painter of London's aristocracy. The large number of works she executed and subsequently exhibited meant that she also enjoyed the financial rewards of her chosen field of work.

At 40 Ethel Jenner Rosenberg thus continued her family's tradition of artistic excellence and financial success. However, in the final months of the nineteenth century, among her circle of rich and influential friends she met one woman who was to change her destiny for all time: Mary Virginia Thornburgh-Cropper.

4

The Bahá'í Movement

*Verily I say, this is the Day in which mankind can
behold the Face, and hear the Voice, of the Promised One.*[33]
Bahá'u'lláh

Mary Virginia Thornburgh-Cropper, an American by birth,
was, by the final years of the nineteenth century, perma-
nently resident in London. She was slightly younger than
Ethel Jenner Rosenberg and by the time the two women met,
Mrs Thornburgh-Cropper's husband, Colonel E. D. Cropper,
had already passed away.

A portrait of the young Mary painted by the celebrated
Royal Academician George Frederic Watts shows a delicate,
sympathetic woman, well-groomed yet not ostentatious in
her tastes, with strongly defined features and deep-set,
heavy-lidded eyes which suggest a patient and compassionate
disposition. Although Watts's best known works were large
allegorical pictures, he earned his living as a portrait painter.
It is well recorded, though, that he made a genuine attempt
to convey more than a superficial likeness of his sitters and
strove to convey their whole character, personality and
appearance, choosing only to paint people he could like or
admire. That admiration is more than evident in his portrait
of Mrs Thornburgh-Cropper.

Mary was a life-long friend of the American heiress
Phoebe Apperson Hearst. Mrs Hearst had been raised in a
family of prosperous slave-owners and had, at the age of 20,
eloped with a man 21 years her senior. George Hearst was
a wealthy businessman who settled with his young wife in

San Francisco. In 1863 Phoebe gave birth to William Randolph Hearst who would later become the foremost newspaper publisher in the United States and one of the country's most controversial figures. Mrs Hearst was an extremely generous woman who would, in the ensuing decades, donate enormous amounts of money to worthy causes. She was instrumental in founding the first Homeopathic Hospital in San Francisco and aided in the establishment of seven kindergartens. In 1886, when George Hearst was appointed a United States Senator, the family moved to Washington DC where his wife swiftly took on more philanthropic duties, assisting the needy or hosting impressive receptions for charity. After her husband's death in 1891, she divided her time between San Francisco and Washington and occasionally travelled to Europe. It was during one of her return trips to her west coast home that Mrs Hearst received a visit from a woman some 30 years her junior, Louisa Moore Getsinger. This was the first occasion on which Mrs Hearst heard about a new spiritual belief that was beginning to take root in the United States, the Bahá'í Movement.

Soon afterwards Mrs Thornburgh-Cropper received a letter from Mrs Hearst telling her about the wonderful new religious teaching that she had encountered. Mrs Hearst told her friend that she felt it would be of great interest to her and promised to tell her all on a forthcoming visit to London. A short time later, Mrs Thornburgh-Cropper was searching in an encyclopaedia for some information about King David, about whom she had had an argument. Turning the pages, her eye was caught by the name 'Bab' and she felt herself drawn to reading more about a Messenger of God who had been martyred in Persia having proclaimed a new revelation. The heroic and tragic story so moved Mrs Thornburgh-Cropper that she was prompted to go to the British Museum to search for more information about the Báb and His teachings.

It is not recorded whether Mrs Thornburgh-Cropper had manifested a strong inclination towards religion or spirituality before this time, though it may be assumed that a woman who had an argument about King David and whose friends wrote to her about religious teachings possessed more than a passing interest in such matters. Something about the story of the Báb appealed to her, however, and captured her imagination. Aside from the industrial, social and artistic reforms of the period, she may well have been aware of the changing spiritual climate in Britain at that time. The nineteenth century had seen the emergence of an enormous number of independent spiritual teachers around the world. It was a period when churches were suffering from a tremendous decline in their fortunes and popularity. They were attacked from outside by Darwinists, materialists and atheists as well as being internally racked by arguments between reformers and the old guard. Independent sects had sprung up within all forms of religious tradition. Often these revivals identified true spirituality with mysticism or occultism, allowing seekers a means by which they could protect their sense of spirituality from the corruption of religious institutions. Another identifiable preoccupation of the century was the quest for an ultimate, single answer to the mysteries of existence. With knowledge of other spiritual paths becoming more available and the accepted Christian explanations of existence being questioned, there was a widespread desire to find a unity in the diversity and a sense of ultimate authority. The earlier part of the century had seen a period of messianic expectation in the Islamic world as well as in Christianity. In Persia, doctrines emerged which stated that the appointed deliverer and successor of the Prophet Muḥammad was about to appear. This sense of expectancy was also apparent in Christianity, as groups such as the Millerites prepared for the return of Jesus Christ.

The Báb ('Gate' in Arabic), whose story so attracted Mrs Thornburgh-Cropper, was a young Persian descendant of the Prophet Muḥammad by the name of Siyyid 'Alí-Muḥammad. While still working as a merchant, He claimed in 1844 that

He was the Promised One of Islam. He taught His disciples
– known as Bábís – that He had been sent to prepare the way
for 'Him Whom God shall make manifest', a Supreme Messenger from God expected by the followers of all religions to
establish His Kingdom on earth. The Báb's teachings attracted a widespread following and caused a great commotion
in Persia. The country's religious leaders launched a campaign of bitter persecution against the Bábís and, after six
years of fierce opposition, the Báb Himself was publicly
executed. Thousands of Bábís were subsequently tortured
and killed. Among the surviving followers of the Báb, one
figure emerged who won over the hearts of the dispirited and
sorely oppressed community. His name was Mírzá Ḥusayn
'Alí, entitled Bahá'u'lláh ('the Glory of God'), a Persian
nobleman renowned for His acts of charity and great learning who had renounced His wealth and the offer of a position
in the court of the Shah to devote His energies to defending
the Cause of the Báb. Imprisoned – where He experienced
an extraordinary vision of His forthcoming mission – and
then banished to Baghdad for His open allegiance to the new
religion, Bahá'u'lláh continued to guide the group of exiles
in Iraq. In 1863, after a decade of rebuilding the shattered
Bábí community while demonstrating extraordinary perception and revealing profoundly mystical as well as inspira-
tional writings containing spiritual and social guidance,
Bahá'u'lláh announced publicly that He was in fact 'Him
Whom God shall make manifest' and the Promised One
foretold by the Messengers of the past. He explained that the
Covenant that God had made with humankind always to
protect and guide His creation had never been broken. He
was, He said, a 'Manifestation of God', sent to provide the
latest chapter of divine revelation between the Creator and
His creation, set forth in previous centuries by Abraham,
Krishna, Moses, Jesus Christ, Muḥammad, Zoroaster and
countless others. Thus Bahá'u'lláh's revelation – found in
some one hundred volumes of His writings – essentially
unveiled and updated eternal spiritual truths and was tai-

lored to suit the new conditions of humanity, at a time when the outmoded institutions of the past were no longer able to deal effectively with the challenge of a scientifically and intellectually advanced world. Bahá'u'lláh's revelation took the theme of unity as its cornerstone. The day was approaching, He taught, when the human race would, either through an act of collective will or out of dire necessity, put aside war and conflict once and for all and establish a world brotherhood and civilization. For this message, which He proclaimed to the unheeding ears of the kings and rulers of His time, He endured 40 years of imprisonment and exile at the hands of the Persian authorities and the Turkish Ottoman Empire.

Shortly before He passed away in the Holy Land in 1892, Bahá'u'lláh received a visit from the distinguished Cambridge orientalist, Professor Edward Granville Browne. Browne had taken a keen interest in the origins and growth of the Bábí community and had devoted a large part of his early life to studying it. He had presented and published papers on it, to the dismay of his contemporaries who wondered why he spent so much of his time studying what they considered to be an insignificant sect of Shi'i Islam. However Professor Browne saw in the history of the new religion similarities to the birth of other great religious systems and chose to record for posterity the heroism which the followers of the Báb displayed. The effect of the personality of Bahá'u'lláh on Professor Browne was recorded in one of the few pen-portraits of the Manifestation. Browne described Him as a 'wondrous and venerable figure' whose 'piercing eyes seemed to read one's very soul; power and authority sat on that ample brow . . . No need to ask in whose presence I stood, as I bowed myself before one who is the object of a devotion and love which kings might envy and emperors sigh for in vain!'[34]

On the same night in 1844 that the Báb had declared His mission in the Persian city of Shíráz, Bahá'u'lláh's wife had given birth to a baby boy named 'Abbás, who would become known as 'Abdu'l-Bahá ('the Servant of Bahá'). From the age of nine years 'Abdu'l-Bahá shared in the sufferings of His Father, spending 55 years as a prisoner and an exile. Bahá'u'lláh Himself gave 'Abdu'l-Bahá the title of 'Master', along with the task of protecting the new Faith – now identified as Bahá'í rather than Bábí – from its enemies and helping its growth. The Master's special qualities were also recorded by Edward Granville Browne who said of Him:

> Seldom have I seen one whose appearance impressed me more. A tall strongly-built man holding himself straight as an arrow, with white turban and raiment, long black locks reaching almost to the shoulder, broad powerful forehead indicating a strong intellect combined with an unswerving will, eyes keen as a hawk's, and strongly-marked but pleasing features . . . One more eloquent of speech, more ready of argument, more apt of illustration, more intimately acquainted with the sacred books of the Jews, the Christians, and the Muhammadans, could, I should think, scarcely be found even amongst the eloquent, ready and subtle race to which he belongs . . . About the greatness of this man and his power no one who had seen him could entertain a doubt.[35]

'Abdu'l-Bahá was recognized in the community as the model of Bahá'í behaviour. Despite His extraordinary spiritual perception, He did not have the station of a Prophet or Divine Messenger; rather He was understood to be the perfect human exemplar of Bahá'u'lláh's teachings. In His Will, Bahá'u'lláh appointed 'Abdu'l-Bahá as the 'Centre of the Covenant' to whom all the Bahá'ís must turn for guidance. Those in the community who rejected 'Abdu'l-Bahá's authority and actively worked to undermine it – among them His scheming and envious half-brother Mírzá Muḥammad-'Alí – were expelled from the community as 'Covenant-breakers'. All the believers were forbidden to associate with them as their disruptiveness and poisonous behaviour was the antithesis of everything that Bahá'u'lláh had sought to achieve.

'Abdu'l-Bahá's pronouncements, interpretations and

writings were given the same authority as Bahá'u'lláh's own. His exemplary moral character, his gentle and kindly 'Christ-like' manner, and his spiritual authority were of immense importance to the followers of the new Faith as it emerged from the Middle East and established its roots further afield.

The Bahá'í Movement – initially it was never called a 'faith' or 'religion' – began to spread to the West under 'Abdu'l-Bahá's leadership shortly after the passing of Bahá'u'lláh. It was mentioned at the Parliament of Religions held in conjunction with the 1893 Chicago World's Fair when a Christian speaker concluded his paper with the words that Bahá'u'lláh had addressed to Professor Browne. Around that time also a Syrian by the name of Ibráhím George Khayru-'lláh, who had become a believer in Cairo, began classes for 'truth seekers' in the Chicago area. By 1897 Khayru'lláh had enrolled hundreds of believers in Chicago and Kenosha, Wisconsin. These believers were encouraged to write directly to 'Abdu'l-Bahá, who remained a prisoner in the Holy Land, to express their faith in the teachings of Bahá'u'lláh and to seek the Master's blessing. The first prominent figure to emerge from Khayru'lláh's converts was an insurance executive named Thornton Chase, designated by 'Abdu'l-Bahá as the 'first American believer'. Another was the talented and energetic Louisa Moore Getsinger.

This history of triumph over adversity which coloured the Bahá'í Faith's 'heroic age' would probably have been, more or less, the terms in which Louisa Getsinger – known as Lua – would have introduced the Bahá'í Movement to Phoebe Hearst, for there was little published material available to the early Bahá'ís and no authorized translations of scripture. The millionairess philanthropist was deeply moved by what she heard and in 1898 decided to visit 'Abdu'l-Bahá. In her usual spirit of generosity she invited others to accompany her and put together a travelling party that included her servant Robert Turner, who had also declared himself a believer, Lua and her husband Edward Getsinger, another of their 'converts' Ella Goodall and her friend Nellie Hillyer, and Dr

Khayru'lláh. In Paris Mrs Hearst's nieces Miss Pearson and
Miss Apperson joined the group along with May Ellis Bolles,
a young American woman who would return to establish the
first Bahá'í centre in Europe. Khayru'lláh's daughters and
their grandmother joined the party in Egypt.

Having learned about the Báb from her own research at
the British Museum, Mrs Thornburgh-Cropper received a
visit from some of Mrs Hearst's friends who were passing
through London on their way to the Turkish prison colony
of 'Akká where 'Abdu'l-Bahá was being held along with His
family. This group was going on ahead to make arrangements for the party. When Mrs Thornburgh-Cropper heard
more about 'Abdu'l- Bahá's life and sufferings, as well as
about the station of Bahá'u'lláh, she too eagerly began
arrangements to accompany the group. Only at that point
did she understand that Bahá'u'lláh was the Promised One
whom the Báb had foretold. She also persuaded her mother,
Mrs Thornburgh, who was then staying in London, to join
them. Late in November of 1898 they joined Mrs Hearst and
nine other pilgrims in Paris. An uncomfortable sea journey
followed, exacerbated by a primitive steamer ship and fero-
cious storms at sea. Arriving in Egypt, the group – now
numbering fifteen – divided into three smaller groups to
travel separately to the Holy Land, as 'Abdu'l-Bahá's situation was at that time still precarious. Although there was no
visible guard enforcing the Holy Family's incarceration,
'Abdu'l-Bahá was not allowed to leave the premises without
permission from the Turkish authorities.

Mrs Thornburgh-Cropper later described how she took
a 'small, miserable boat to Haifa. There was a storm here
also, and we were beaten about unmercifully in our all too
inadequate steamer. Upon arrival we went to an hotel, where
we remained until nightfall as it was too dangerous for us,
and for 'Abdu'l-Bahá, Whom we were to visit, for strangers
to be seen entering the city of sorrow.'[36] It was 10 December
1898. After night fell, the small party, which also included
Lua Getsinger and Mrs Hearst, took a carriage and drove

along the hard sand leading to the gates of the prison city.
There arrangements were made by the driver for them to
enter. They arrived at the House of 'Abdu'lláh Páshá where
'Abdu'l-Bahá had been living since the end of 1896, a large
house formerly the main building of the Governorate, adja-
cent to the prison where Bahá'u'lláh had spent more than
two years incarcerated. They started up the uneven stairs
that led to 'Abdu'l-Bahá's quarters. Someone went ahead of
them with a small piece of candle which 'cast strange shad-
ows on the walls of this silent place'.[37]

Mrs Thornburgh-Cropper, in an account written at the
very end of her life, described the experience of being among
the first Western pilgrims ever to encounter the Master face
to face:

> Suddenly the light caught a form that at first seemed a
> vision of mist and light. It was the Master which the candle-
> light had revealed to us. His white robe and silver, flowing
> hair, and shining blue eyes gave the impression of a spirit,
> rather than a human being. We tried to tell Him how deeply
> grateful we were at His receiving us. 'No,' He answered,
> 'you are kind to come.' This was spoken in a very careful
> English.
>
> Then He smiled, and we recognized the Light which He
> possessed in the radiance which moved over His fine and
> noble face. It was an amazing experience. We four visitors
> from the Western world felt that our voyage, with all its
> accompanying inconvenience, was a small price to pay for
> such treasure as we received from the spirit and words of
> the Master, Whom we had crossed mountain and seas and
> nations to meet.[38]

The subsequent days were spent in the company of 'Abdu'l-
Bahá, who used the unique opportunity of the visit to explain
clearly many of the teachings of Bahá'u'lláh to His new
followers. On the 16 February 1899 the second group of
pilgrims arrived, including May Bolles, Mrs Thornburgh and
Robert Turner. The effect of the Master's personality on Mrs
Hearst's servant was tremendous. He dropped down onto his

knees and exclaimed, 'My Lord! My Lord! I am not worthy
to be here!'[39] 'Abdu'l-Bahá embraced him as if he were a
member of the Master's own family.

One evening at dinner the conversation turned to the
subject of kindness to animals. 'Abdu'l-Bahá told the group
that they should be kind and merciful to every creature, that
cruelty was sin and that human beings should never use any
living creature for pleasure, vanity or hunting. Mrs
Thornburgh asked permission to tell a story of a little boy
who had stolen a bird's nest full of eggs. A lady meeting him
on the road stopped him and rebuked him: 'Don't you know
it is very cruel to steal the nest? What will the poor mother
bird do when she comes to the tree and finds her eggs all
gone?' The little boy looked up at the lady and said, 'Maybe
that is the mother you have got on your hat!' 'Abdu'l-Bahá
laughed and said, 'That is a good story and a clever little
boy!'[40] May Bolles recorded how in the house of 'Abdu'l-
Bahá, despite its effectively being a prison for its occupants,
she had never seen such happiness or heard such laughter.
The Master, she said, seemed to 'sound all the chords of our
human nature and set them vibrating to heavenly music'.[41]

Mrs Hearst described her pilgrimage as 'the most memo-
rable days of my life'.[42] Speaking of the Master, she enthused,
'He is the Most Wonderful Being I have ever met or ever
expect to meet in this world. Tho He does not seek to impress
one at all, strength, power, purity, love and holiness are
radiated from His majestic, yet humble, personality, and the
spiritual atmosphere which surrounds Him and most power-
fully affects all those who are blest by being near Him, is
indescribable . . . I believe in Him with all my heart and soul,
and I hope all who call themselves Believers will concede to
Him all the greatness, all the glory, and all the praise, for
surely He is the Son of God – and 'the spirit of the Father
abideth in Him'.[43] In another letter, she wrote, 'Without a
doubt 'Abbás Effendi is the Messiah of this day and generation and we need not look for another.'[44]

The first visit of Western pilgrims was a highly significant

step in the history of the Bahá'í Faith in the West. 'Abdu'l-
Bahá's personality made an immediate and powerful impression on His visitors, who returned to their homes filled with
enthusiasm to spread the teachings of Bahá'u'lláh. As demonstrated in the tributes from Mrs Hearst, many of them
believed that in 'Abdu'l-Bahá they saw the spirit of Jesus
Christ in the world, placing the Master's station far above
that which Bahá'u'lláh had assigned to Him. However,
'Abdu'l-Bahá swiftly and forcefully dismissed such pronouncements, stressing His humility and nothingness, His
selfless devotion to the Cause of the Manifestation,
Bahá'u'lláh, and His desire to be nothing else but a servant
to the entire human race.

Mrs Thornburgh-Cropper, elevated by her profound
religious experience in 'Akká, returned to London where she
set about gently conveying the teachings that she had received. For Ethel Rosenberg, who had been told many years
before by her mother to watch for a great teacher sent from
God and who was deeply schooled in both the Old and New
Testaments, such teachings must have had an immediate
appeal. There are, alas, no available records to describe how
Ethel first responded to the news of the Revelation nor how
she might have 'declared' her belief, although it is likely that
she sent a letter of supplication to 'Abdu'l-Bahá. It is widely
accepted, however, that by the summer of 1899 she had
become the first Englishwoman in her native country to
recognize Bahá'u'lláh as the Manifestation of God. She and
Mrs Thornburgh-Cropper then began the task of spreading
the good news to anyone who cared to listen.

5

Afire with the Love of God

*O thou handmaid afire with the love of God! . . . know
thou that delivering the Message can be accomplished
only through goodly deeds and spiritual attributes, an
utterance that is crystal clear and the happiness reflected from the face of that one who is expounding the
Teachings.*[45]

Tablet of 'Abdu'l-Bahá to Ethel Rosenberg

Adopting and attempting to promote the universal Bahá'í
message of peace, tolerance and harmony at a time when
Britain was embroiled in the Second Boer War in South
Africa was a formidable task for Ethel Rosenberg and Mrs
Thornburgh-Cropper as they undertook their unique mission. Regardless, however, of the lack of actual published
material which they had at their disposal, their hopes and
spirits were high, and with the love of the Master in their
hearts they began the process of telling others of the teachings they had encountered.

The early Bahá'ís almost certainly never referred to
themselves as belonging to a 'religion' in the formal sense
of the word. This, for them, would have carried the suggestion of exclusivity and dogma. Rather, as Ethel Rosenberg
later wrote in one of her own pamphlets, they saw the Bahá'í
Cause as a 'widening of the basis of [their] faith'.[46] Many still
considered themselves to be Christians who, while under no
compulsion to eschew their connections with their previous
forms of worship or religious activities, had accommodated
a broader, more modern interpretation of doctrine. 'Abdu'l-
Bahá openly extolled and glorified the station of Jesus Christ
in His correspondence with them and in the Master's charac-

ter and life many early Western Bahá'ís believed they saw the spirit of Christ in the world. In time, Ethel would take on a most important role in the British Bahá'í community, clarifying for the Bahá'ís the true nature of the Master's station and mission.

Until 1901 Ethel's working life as a miniaturist and portrait painter continued. She remained resident at 5 Grafton Street in Piccadilly and continued to exhibit her works in a number of galleries.

Interestingly, what might be termed as Bahá'í themes began to emerge in her work at this time. At Mrs Thornburgh-Cropper's request, Ethel painted a delicate, miniature portrait of 'Abdu'l-Bahá which explicitly depicted Him as Jesus Christ. Ethel was yet to meet the Master and she had never seen a likeness of Him, for there were no photographic images available to the believers. Ethel based her likeness on the description of the Master that she had received from Mrs Thornburgh-Cropper as well as on a photograph she had of what was known as the 'original portrait of Christ', an image of a face engraved on a gem in the reign of the Roman emperor Tiberius. The portrait greatly satisfied Mrs Thornburgh-Cropper and Ethel went on to copy it several times for Bahá'í friends in the United States.

A third woman, Mrs Scaramucci, entered the Movement in Britain around this time. Little is known about her except that she identified herself as a Bahá'í for the next two decades and in 1911 wrote an introductory pamphlet entitled 'The Bahá'í Revelation'. Bahá'í community life as it is known and experienced today, when there are over one hundred thousand Bahá'í centres in some two hundred countries, must have been inconceivable for Ethel and her friends in those early days. There was as yet no formal registration procedure to become a Bahá'í nor any administrative structure to establish and consolidate. However, what was to become a truly worldwide religion with its own divinely-inspired, elected international governing body, the Universal

House of Justice, was already having the effect of uniting souls on different continents and from diverse cultures. Bahá'ís began to communicate with each other around the world, often as a result of meeting while on pilgrimage to 'Akká. In the case of the British Bahá'ís, a close relationship developed with the Bahá'í community that was evolving in Paris around May Ellis Bolles. Ethel herself began to make a number of journeys across the English Channel and, assisted by her excellent command of the French language, developed lasting friendships with her compatriots in the French capital. May Bolles, who had shared that first historic pilgrimage with Mrs Thornburgh-Cropper, was 30 years old at the turn of the century and had obeyed 'Abdu'l-Bahá's instruction to return to Paris to establish the first Bahá'í centre in Europe. During this period – and significantly for the history of the relationship between the Bahá'í Faith and the British Isles – May was instrumental in introducing a young Englishman named Thomas Breakwell into the Bahá'í Cause.

Thomas Breakwell was born on 31 May 1872 in the small market town of Woking in Surrey. His father, Edward, was an ironmonger and a herbalist who, at some point during the 1860s, had joined the non-conformist Christian sect known as the Primitive Methodists and subsequently held evangelical meetings in the family home. Thomas, the youngest of five children, was educated at an ordinary state school before his family emigrated to the United States. He found a responsible and well-paid job in a cotton mill, which at that time was run with child labour, in one of the southern states. His high salary enabled him to spend long summer vacations in Europe. During the summer of 1901 Thomas, now aged 29, was crossing to France on a steamer ship when he encountered a friend of May Bolles, Mrs Milner, who noted Breakwell's apparent interest in Theosophy and informed him of a group of friends in Paris who were interested in similar esoteric subjects.

May Bolles had remained in Paris despite her mother's

wish for her to spend the summer with the family on holiday in Brittany. Mrs Bolles resented her daughter's work for the Bahá'í Cause and closed the family home, leaving May to find accommodation with another believer, Edith Jackson. The first Frenchman to become a Bahá'í, Hippolyte Dreyfus, and several others received the teachings at that time. It was to this apartment that Mrs Milner brought Breakwell.

May Bolles described this first encounter, saying: 'I shall never forget opening the door and seeing him standing there. It was like looking at a veiled light. I saw at once his pure heart, his burning spirit, his thirsty soul, and over all was cast the veil which is over every soul until it is rent asunder by the power of God in this day.'[47] Breakwell was 'of medium height, slender, erect and graceful, with intense eyes and an indescribable charm . . . a very rare person of high standing and culture, simple, natural, intensely real in his attitude toward life and his fellowmen'.[48]

Their conversation lasted about half an hour and centred around Theosophy and the details of Breakwell's life. As he was leaving, he expressed an interest in hearing about the teachings that Mrs Milner had mentioned to him and an appointment was made for another meeting the following day. When Breakwell returned, May Bolles noticed a profound difference in his character:

> He arrived the next morning in a strangely exalted mood, no veil of materiality covered this radiant soul – his eyes burned with a hidden fire, and looking at me earnestly he asked if I noticed anything strange about him. Seeing his condition I bade him be seated, and reassured him, saying he looked very happy.
> 'When I was here yesterday he said [sic] I felt a power, an influence that I had felt once before in my life, when for a period of three months I was continually in communion with God. I felt during that time like one moving in a rarefied atmosphere of light and beauty. My heart was afire with love for the supreme Beloved, I felt at peace, at one with all my fellow-men. Yesterday when I left you I went

alone down the Champs Élysées, the air was warm and heavy, not a leaf was stirring, when suddenly a wind struck me, and whirled around me, and in that wind a voice said, with an indescribable sweetness and penetration, "Christ has come again! Christ has come again!"'

With wide startled eyes he looked at me and asked if I thought he had gone crazy. 'No,' I said smiling, 'you are just becoming sane.'[49]

Within three days Breakwell received and accepted the Bahá'í Message from May Bolles. In a written supplication to 'Abdu'l-Bahá, he begged, 'My Lord! I believe; forgive me. Thy servant, Thos. Breakwell.'[50] That same evening when May Bolles went to collect her post she found a cablegram that had just arrived from 'Abdu'l-Bahá, saying she could now leave Paris to rejoin her mother.

Thomas Breakwell immediately planned to visit 'Akká with a young Bahá'í friend, Herbert Hopper. The two sailed for Port Said and then on to Haifa. When they arrived at the House of 'Abdu'lláh Páshá, they were ushered into a room to await their first encounter with the Master. Seeing a group of oriental believers, Hopper's face lit up with the joy of instant recognition but Breakwell, unable to sense 'Abdu'l-Bahá's presence in the group, felt ill and disillusioned. Suddenly, a door opened and 'Abdu'l-Bahá entered. Breakwell immediately sprang to his feet, all doubts dispelled on seeing the Master approach, surrounded by what seemed to be dazzlingly intense, white light.

Breakwell was spiritually transformed by his meeting with 'Abdu'l-Bahá. The Master urged him to cable his resignation to the cotton mill where he worked and to return to Paris. Dr Yúnis Khán Afrúkhtih, 'Abdu'l-Bahá's secretary, recalled, that

the fervour and the faith of this young man were so sublime in character that his blessed name shall ring throughout centuries, and shall be remembered with deep affection in many chronicles. Verses from the Gospels which attest to the glories of the Kingdom were always on his lips, His

sojourn was too short, but so intense was his love, and so
ardent his zeal that he touched the depths of the hearts of
those who heard him . . . We were all in tears when we bade
farewell to him.[51]

On his return to Paris Breakwell imbued new spirit into the
activities of the embryonic Bahá'í community there, despite
suffering a condition of poor health which rapidly developed
into consumption. Working in the daytime as a stenographer,
he lived in a cheap *arrondissement* of Paris, walking miles
to meetings to save his money to give to the Bahá'í funds. He
showered love upon all he met, particularly the mother of
May Bolles who was yet to recognize the Cause her daughter
had enthusiastically embraced. Breakwell's father, who had
disowned his son for rejecting Primitive Methodism, arrived
in Paris with his wife to persuade him to return to England
to convalesce. Breakwell's unfailing devotion to 'Abdu'l-Bahá
also succeeded in persuading his father to write a letter of
supplication to the Master.

In a letter to Dr Yúnis Khán Afrúkhtih written just days
before Breakwell died, he spoke of his pain:

> Suffering is a heady wine; I am prepared to receive that
> bounty which is the greatest of all; torments of the flesh
> have enabled me to draw much nearer to my Lord. All agony
> notwithstanding, I wish life to endure longer, so that I may
> taste more of pain. That which I desire is the good-pleasure
> of my Lord; mention me in His presence.[52]

May Bolles recalled:

> He seemed to have no care for his future, burning like a
> white light in the darkness of Paris, he served his fellow-
> men with a power and passion to the last breath of his life
> . . . He burned with such a fire of love that his frail body
> seemed to be gradually consumed; he in the deepest sense
> shed his life for the Cause by which he was enthralled, and
> in a few brief months shattered the cage of existence and
> abandoned this mortal world.[53]

Thomas Breakwell died on 13 June 1902 aged 31. His passing came as a heavy blow to 'Abdu'l-Bahá, who mysteriously knew about the death without having received notification of it. Dr Yúnis Khán reports how one evening the Master suddenly turned to him and said, 'Have you heard? Breakwell has passed away. I am grieved, very grieved. I have written a prayer of visitation for him. It is very moving, so moving that twice I could not withhold my tears, when I was writing it. You must translate it well, so that whoever reads it will weep.'[54]

There was some puzzlement as to how 'Abdu'l-Bahá could have known about Breakwell's death, as any communication of it in English or French would have first passed through Dr Yúnis Khán's hands. Two days later, he received the Master's Tablet to Breakwell for translation. He could not hold back his tears. It was initially translated into French and then later, with the help of Lua Getsinger, into English. One year after Breakwell's passing, 'Abdu'l-Bahá called for Dr Yúnis Khán to translate a number of letters that had arrived from all over the world. While examining the envelopes, which were still sealed, 'Abdu'l-Bahá suddenly picked one out saying, 'How pleasing is the fragrance that emanates from this envelope. Make haste, open it and see where it comes from.'[55] Dr Yúnis Khán opened the envelope which contained a solitary flower – a violet – and a coloured card with the words, 'Not dead, but liveth in the Lord's Spiritual Kingdom' in gold lettering. On the other side were the words, 'In loving memory of Thomas Breakwell, who departed this life on June 13th 1902, aged 30 years. Blessed are those who die in the Lord.'[56] To this, hand-written, was added, 'This flower was picked from Breakwell's grave' and on an enclosed letter, 'Praise be to the Lord that my son left this world for the next with the recognition and love of 'Abdu'l-Bahá.'[57] When Dr Yúnis Khán informed the Master of the content of the message, 'Abdu'l-Bahá immediately rose up, took the card and put it to his forehead, tears flowing down His cheeks. Thomas Breakwell's grave was leased for five years after which time, as no surviving members of his family kept up the payments on the plot, his bones were disinterred, cleaned, bundled and numbered, and placed in the cemetery's charnel house. The section where Breakwell's bones are stacked has long since been sealed and other sections built against it which in turn have been filled. It is unlikely that Ethel Rosenberg would have met Thomas Breakwell, so brief was the period during which he had contact with the Bahá'ís in Paris. Yet she would certainly have heard his mysterious story from the close friends she was beginning to make in the city and she would have no doubt derived inspiration from the tale of her fellow countryman who had displayed such spirituality and devotion to the Cause.

o

In January 1901 Ethel followed in the footsteps of her 'spiritual mother' Mrs Thornburgh-Cropper and made the gruelling sea journey to visit 'Abdu'l-Bahá in 'Akká. The wisdom which she would hear from His lips and carefully take note of, coupled with the intimate way in which His family welcomed her into their fold, would result in her becoming the central focus of Bahá'í activities in England for the next three decades.

At the time of Ethel's journey, 'Abdu'l-Bahá was still residing at the House of 'Abdu'lláh Páshá where two years previously He had received that first momentous visit from the West. In a memoir of such a pilgrimage entitled *In Galilee*, Thornton Chase described how the pilgrims entered through an

arched, red brick entrance to an open court, across it to a long flight of stone steps, broken and ancient, leading to the highest story and into a small walled court open to the sky, where was the upper chamber assigned to us, which adjoined the room of Abdul-Baha. The buildings are all of stone, whitewashed and plastered, and it bears the aspect of a prison.

Our windows looked out over the garden and tent of Abdul-Baha on the sea side of the house. That garden is bounded on one side by the house of the Governor, which overlooks it, and on another by the inner wall of fortification. A few feet beyond that is the outer wall upon the sea, and between these two are the guns and soldiers constantly on guard. A sentry house stands at one corner of the wall and garden, from which the sentry can see the grounds and the tent where Abdul-Baha meets transient visitors and the officials who often call on him.[58]

Mary Hanford Ford, a believer from Chicago who first heard of the Bahá'í Movement a few months after the arrival of Ethel Rosenberg in 'Akká and who later became a devoted friend of hers, described the room in which guests stayed and where 'Abdu'l-Bahá spoke with them as having a floor

covered with matting, the narrow iron bed and the iron wash stand with larger and smaller holes for bowl and pitcher were of that vermin-proof description with which I had become familiar. Everything was scrupulously clean, and there was an abundant supply of sparkling water for bathing and drinking. A wide window looked over the huge town wall upon the blue Mediterranean and before this stretched a divan upon which 'Abdu'l-Bahá sat when He came to see me.[59]

During this period 'Abdu'l-Bahá's unfaithful half-brother Mírzá Muḥammad-'Alí had been plotting to undermine the Master's authority. He had persistently attempted to create a widespread schism in the Bahá'í community with little success. He did, however, manage to plant suspicion in the mind of the Governor of Beirut, who was taken in by Muḥammad-'Alí's wild accusations and false rumours. This seditious stirring would result in harsh restrictions being placed on 'Abdu'l-Bahá's movements and activities shortly after Ethel's visit. The rumours centred around a building project which the Master had embarked upon and which Mírzá Muḥammad-'Alí alleged was the construction of a fortress from where 'Abdu'l-Bahá was planning to overthrow the Turkish regime. In fact, the edifice that 'Abdu'l-Bahá had begun to construct in 1899 on Mount Carmel, just across the bay from 'Akká, was to be a permanent mausoleum to house the remains of the Báb. Eight years previously, 'Abdu'l-Bahá had been requested by Bahá'u'lláh to transfer the sacred remains to a befitting tomb on 'the mountain of the Lord'. In 1898 'Abdu'l-Bahá had sent detailed instructions to Persia to arrange for the remains, which had been hidden for almost fifty years, to be sent to the Holy Land. Those remains were discreetly hidden until the Master's personal situation made it possible to inter them in 1909. Ethel Rosenberg would not have been aware of the presence of those remains in the house where she was staying, though she did spend some days across the bay in Haifa with the Master, noting with interest the construction of the building, every stone of which He was raising and placing in position with 'infinite tears and at tremendous cost'.[60]

Having such a small amount of literature on the Movement with which they had associated themselves meant that the early believers came to rely heavily on the written notes that pilgrims took whilst in the Master's presence. These, along with the communications which individuals received from 'Abdu'l-Bahá – known as Tablets – were often typed and re-typed or carbon copied and widely circulated around the world. As the communities began to grow and became more financially self-supporting, books of such notes were formally compiled and published. 'Pilgrims' Notes', as they are known, are not considered by Bahá'ís today as authoritative scripture as they are, by their very nature, merely records of what the early believers heard (usually through translators), or what they understood they had heard. They cannot therefore be viewed as accurate but at the time they were all that 'Abdu'l-Bahá's followers had to guide them.

During her months in 'Akká, Ethel assiduously began to write down all that she heard from the Master's lips, knowing that this material would be priceless guidance for her

friends in London and further afield. Day after day throughout January, February and March 1901 Ethel listened with
rapt attention to the Master's expositions and carefully wrote
them down in her notebooks. It is known that she had taught
herself Persian. Whether she had already started on this
remarkable venture at such an early stage in her Bahá'í life
is difficult to say but the experience in 'Akká must have done
much to motivate her to understand better 'Abdu'l-Bahá's
words in His own tongue, so hungry was she to familiarize
herself with the knowledge He imparted to the pilgrims who
gathered about Him. The precise attention to detail and
accuracy that she had displayed in her artistic works was
now put to use in recording the Master's teachings.

'Abdu'l-Bahá was keen for His followers to understand
the concept and station of the Manifestations of God so that
they might comprehend the nature of the relationships
between these Divine Messengers and God on the one hand
and the world of creation on the other. He told them how the
Manifestations have two characteristics – the spiritual and
the material. In their spiritual condition, He explained, they
reflect entirely the bounties of God and His perfections.
These perfections are given freely as gifts to the people
without there being any hope of a return to themselves.
'Abdu'l-Bahá urged his listeners to consider how the sun
shines, the rain falls and the breezes blow upon a growing
tree. The earth then gives its strength to the tree and it
grows and lives. The tree, in turn, gives this power to the
twigs, branches and leaves which grow strong and flourish.
In time, blossoms and fruits appear. So it is with the Messengers of God who give their perfections and graces to people,
to make them grow strong and live.

The Master then pointed Ethel to references in the Bible
concerning the coming of Muḥammad and spoke of how
these Great Prophets are devoid of sin. He dismissed the
existence of a devil as some great entity in the world. He said
every great prophet had an active opponent or 'satan' which
shows forth the opposite characteristics, for example, Abra-

ham and Nimrod, Jesus Christ and Caiaphas, and even He, 'Abdu'l-Bahá – while not counting Himself a Great Prophet – had to contend with His half-brother. Anything, He said, that causes man to become heedless of God is his satan. Some of the Manifestations only had the power to sway and subdue one country, others had the power to influence many more. In this day, He announced, Bahá'u'lláh has the power to sway and subdue them all as well as all prophets and all religions. Two of the signs of the Manifestation of God, the Master added, were the preaching and acceptance of the religion of God and that people should be endowed with the characteristics of God. He believed the first sign was now apparent and He hoped and prayed that the second sign would also be fulfilled. Many of the advances of the nations and humanity were caused by the presence of this Revelation without humanity knowing the reason for the advance.

People, 'Abdu'l-Bahá commented, were always inquiring why, if this religion was such a great one, did not more people hear of it in the lifetime of Bahá'u'lláh, forgetting that in the time of Jesus Christ even the people of 'Akká even had not heard of Him and when He died His followers had numbered only about 120. 'Abdu'l-Bahá spoke of the letters which Bahá'u'lláh had addressed to the kings and rulers of His time and how they had failed to recognize His station or heed His warnings.

Much of the material in Ethel's notes dwells on biblical themes and interpretations which were clearly her concerns at the time and the major interest of the predominately Anglican or Roman Catholic 'seekers' she would meet in London. Ethel's deep knowledge of the New Testament provided 'Abdu'l-Bahá with many fascinating questions to answer. She asked Him the meaning of a passage in the Gospel according to St Luke where it is written, 'Be not afraid of them that kill the body, and after that have no more that they can do. But I will forewarn you whom ye shall fear: Fear him, which after he hath killed hath power to cast into hell; yea, I say unto you, Fear him.'[61] 'Abdu'l-Bahá explained to Ethel that this meant that the death of the body is of no importance and not in the least to be feared because a spiritual soul lives forever. The thing to be feared, He stressed, is the death of the spirit.

The resurrection and miracles of Christ also provided Ethel with many questions. 'Abdu'l-Bahá explained the symbolic interpretations of such events, explaining the resurrection to be the disciples' realization of the divine power that was still amongst them. All miracles, He explained, have their mystic and hidden meaning enfolded within them. The disciples of Jesus', Ethel noted, 'attempted to sail over the Sea of Creation and Existence in the Ark of Argument and Reasonings, finding great difficulty and danger in proving the Truth by so doing. But when Christ, the Light of the World, who knew all things by the Light of the inner spiritual illumination, came to them in their boat, walking by His Knowledge over the Ocean of Existence, and having no need of the Ark of Argument, then *immediately* they were at their desired haven.'[62] Thus 'Abdu'l-Bahá explained the symbolic meaning of the incident of Christ's miracle of walking on the water.

Questions were asked about the justice and mercy of God. The pilgrims wanted to know whether people who had committed great evil in this present life and had died in their sin would be hopelessly lost or destroyed. 'Abdu'l-Bahá responded by saying that while those who commit evil suffer and are punished for it, mercy is by far the greatest of the divine attributes and, owing to this, those who die in their sins are not left without the possibility of attaining to life. Hellfire and punishment are not sufferings inflicted by God but are rather the state of being deprived from the sight of His beauty. 'Abdu'l-Bahá employed the analogy of physical blindness saying that when a man is blind it is said that it is the greatest possible affliction that he can have. But this affliction and suffering does not consist in any torture inflicted upon the person, it merely consists of the absence of a great blessing and this is his affliction.

The Master's talks were not limited to matters of theology or religious doctrine. He took the opportunity to elucidate on how the friends should live the Bahá'í life. In the early days of the Faith, He insisted, it was of the first importance for the believers to have the right qualities and to show the right attributes. One unconquered fault could cast one down, in a single moment, from the highest station to the lowest. Bad qualities had to be changed into good ones. Quick temper had to be transformed into calmness, laziness into activity, pride into humility, falsehood into truth, deceit into frankness. The Master said there were three kinds of belief – first, to confess with the lips only; second, to confess with the mouth and believe with the heart in sincerity but not to do according to one's belief; third, to confess and truly believe, and also to live as the heart believes. He described how all atoms and particles were united by the power of attraction and cohesion and if it were not for this, everything would immediately be dissolved and annihilated. The life of creation depends upon this power. Similarly, spiritually everything is united by the love of God which is the only power able to unite hearts. The power to unite hearts is one of the signs of the true Prophet. 'Abdu'l-Bahá said it was almost beyond belief to see so many pilgrims from the most distant parts of the earth assembled together and that this was one of the most wonderful works of God to bring unity. He stressed the imperative necessity of absolute union and harmony among the believers by likening them to the construction of the hand. 'When all the fingers are joined to the hand,' He explained, 'what a wonderful instrument it is and how useful. But if the fingers are cut off and torn apart from each other – in separation they are absolutely useless.'[63] He spoke of the unity and harmony existing between the believers in Persia, Paris and London and said that this was but the dawn of what would be the case in the future. In time to come, one believer would represent all because the believers manifest the oneness of God.

He urged His visitors to pray and to make particular use

of one of three daily obligatory prayers of varying length
revealed by Bahá'u'lláh. These prayers, 'Abdu'l-Bahá emphasized, were between the believer and God, while other
prayers, including those chanted, were acceptable in the
company of other believers. He forbade any set form of public
worship. He also discouraged the believers from taking
alcoholic drinks, saying it did no permanent good. He compared those who drank to urging a horse to full speed by
whipping it, the whip representing the effect of wine on the
drinker's body.

Reference was often made to tests and difficulties as the
means by which men gain spiritual powers. 'Had not Joseph
been sold as a slave,' He said, 'never would he have become
the mighty ruler of Egypt.'[64] However 'Abdu'l-Bahá also
warned his listeners about opposition to the Bahá'í Cause
coming, in the future, from historians and the Christian
Church in particular. He spoke about the unfaithful members of his own family, saying that the Cause of God is like
the sea which refuses to accept or contain a dead body within
it. It will only contain the living.

'Abdu'l-Bahá encouraged Ethel to teach the Cause with
discretion and to use common sense and good judgement
when speaking of it, as it was still little known in England.
He illustrated how there were two types of good people –
those who are naturally good and those who attain to it after
receiving the gift of the Holy Spirit. He said all will accept
the truth when it is presented to them but as it takes some
fruits much longer to ripen than others, some will accept it
immediately and others after a long time of gradual ripening
in the sun. 'Abdu'l-Bahá warned that it was a great sin to
reject these teachings and that it was the duty of the Bahá'ís
to persuade and teach people to embrace the truth. But if
they should reject it, He said, the rejection must be borne
with patience and that person should be treated exactly as
before.

'Abdu'l-Bahá also stressed the importance of teaching
children, saying that they should be familiar with the attrib-

utes of God and be good. Their hearts and minds should be prepared to receive the Truth as soon as they are old enough to be taught. No infant is ever born bad – all infants are born alike, good. But their education and surroundings and their individuality make them become what they afterwards are.

During her visit Ethel also witnessed the qualities of 'Abdu'l-Bahá's life which made Him the perfect exemplar of Bahá'u'lláh's teachings – His perfect kindness and generosity to young and old, rich and poor alike; His charitable acts in the streets of 'Akká towards the downtrodden and penniless; the unusual yet harmonious combination of majestic authority and pious humility.

On one occasion Ethel was present at a conversation between the Master and the English Consul, where 'Abdu'l-Bahá's skill at turning a potentially confrontational conversation around to make a spiritually illuminating point was clearly demonstrated. The Consul was proudly remarking that all the inventions and improvements of civilization had come from the West. Patiently and lovingly 'Abdu'l-Bahá explained how the Western nations had dedicated themselves a great deal more to the pursuit of material improvement and civilization than the Eastern nations. However, on the other hand, He explained, since the earliest times no Prophet had ever appeared except from the East. God had divided His gifts, 'Abdu'l-Bahá remarked, giving to the West the power of inventions and material improvements and to the East, spiritual civilization. The Consul noted that in ancient times the Eastern nations were far more advanced and were of far higher character. 'Abdu'l-Bahá agreed and said that this was because the Easterners depended entirely upon their spiritual leaders for their inspiration and advancement. During the days of these leaders great progress was made but this gradually died out. It took the coming of a new Prophet, He concluded, to give these cultures a fresh start.

Apart from the priceless opportunity of receiving enlightenment from 'Abdu'l-Bahá Himself, Ethel met and became deeply attached to the women of His household. She encountered 'Abdu'l-Bahá's only sister, Bahíyyih Khánum – known as the Greatest Holy Leaf and later designated as 'the outstanding heroine of the Bahá'í Dispensation'[65] – who was two years younger than the Master and had shared in all of the sufferings and exiles of the family. 'Abdu'l-Bahá's wife Munírih Khánum, known as the Holy Mother, was also a prominent figure in the household, along with their four daughters, in order of age, Díyá'iyyih, Túbá, Rúhá and Munavvar. Díyá'iyyih had married Mírzá Hadí Shírází, a descendant of the Báb's own family – known as Afnán – and they had three sons: Shoghi Effendi (who 'Abdu'l-Bahá would designate Guardian of the Bahá'í Cause on His passing), Husayn and Riyád, and two daughters, Rúhangíz and Mihrangíz. Túbá married another Afnán and had three sons and a daughter. Rúhá married Mírzá Jalál, son of one of Bahá'í history's most renowned martyr heroes, and had two sons and three daughters. Munavvar and her husband Mírzá Ahmad Yazdí had no children. After her return to England, Ethel would embark on a loyal and devoted correspondence with 'Abdu'l-Bahá's daughters.

The women would often join the Master for His talks with the pilgrims, assisting with translation and adding their own insights to the proceedings. On one such occasion a believer raised the question as to whether a person who was highly spiritually developed would ever be capable of overcoming extreme physical pain and hardship. Díyá'iyyih explained that while the body was conscious of human sufferings such as hunger and thirst, the perfect spirit was so strong that it was always happy and did not let these sufferings appear outwardly. She illustrated this point with stories from the past. She spoke of the night that Bahá'u'lláh, the Holy Family and the believers with them reached 'Akká and how they were kept entirely without food by the soldiers who guarded them. Two sentries were placed at the door and they were forbidden to go to the market to buy anything. The mothers, through not having eaten, had no milk for their infants, the young children were famished and the sufferings

Ethel Rosenberg
6 August 1858 — 17 November 1930
'England's outstanding Bahá'í pioneer worker'

2. *A portrait of the young Mary Virginia Thornburgh-Cropper,*
painted by the celebrated Royal Academician George Frederic Watts.

3. Mrs Phoebe Apperson Hearst
who introduced the Bahá'í Faith to Mrs Thornburgh-Cropper and
who arranged the first pilgrimage of Westerners to 'Akká in 1898-9.

4. Louisa Moore 'Lua' Getsinger
who introduced the Faith to Phoebe Hearst.

5. *Mary Hanford Ford*
American Bahá'í teacher who taught the Bahá'í Faith in London,
York and Liverpool.

6. *Thornton Chase*
designated by 'Abdu'l-Bahá the 'first American believer'.
Ethel Rosenberg and Chase often corresponded.

7. May Bolles Maxwell
who established the first Bahá'í centre in Europe.
Ethel often travelled to Paris and made lasting friendships with the
Bahá'ís there.

8. ʻAbduʼl-Bahá
*As well as being the recipient of several Tablets, Ethel was one of
the few Western Baháʼís able to translate the Tablets of ʻAbduʼl-Bahá
into English.*

of all of them were very great. Nevertheless they were so happy in spite of all their miseries. Bahíyyih Khánum especially had laughed so much that Bahá'u'lláh had sent a messenger to warn them in case the soldiers considered them to be foolish people who enjoyed themselves and laughed although they had nothing to eat. The following day the Governor sent them some very bad rice which was unwashed and full of stones. The children were very happy and crowded round the tables but when it was cooked it was so black and filthy that it made them ill and they could not eat it. Then Bahá'u'lláh told them not to cry and lovingly gave each one of them a sugar plum. When they had eaten these they all went to sleep quite peacefully and contentedly. Again, when 'Abdu'l-Bahá's young brother, Mírzá Mihdí – known as the Purest Branch – fell through the roof of the Prison and was killed, the believers were not allowed to bury him. Soldiers took the body away and the Holy Family did not know for two years whether it had been thrown into the sea or what the soldiers had done with it. His mother in her 'human' nature was terribly sad and grieved at his death and this sorrow made her so ill that it afflicted her heart. For a long time she was confined to bed. However, when Bahá'u'lláh told her that it was for His sake that this had come upon Mihdí, and that he had borne a sorrow and trouble that had been coming to Bahá'u'lláh, from that day no one ever saw her weep and she was always quite happy and cheerful. This was because of her faith and the strength of her spirit.

For Ethel, the days spent in the company of the Master and His family were filled with joy and quiet wonder. In common with the other early believers who had attained His presence, it was impossible for her to describe adequately the effect which His luminous personality had on her life.

'Abdu'l-Bahá's dealings with His early Western followers were very subtle. He refrained from insisting on too many laws or regulations and He certainly did not urge them to relinquish the diverse range of spiritual or religious beliefs they held. In instances where a fundamental principle of

Bahá'u'lláh was being broken or challenged, such as racial equality, then He would be firm and unswerving, but in secondary matters He allowed the believers freedom and flexibility for He knew they were but tiny children in the Cause and were as yet unready to take on board the deeper and more spiritually strenuous aspects of His Father's teachings. But from the beginning it must have been apparent to the Master that Ethel Rosenberg was by nature a serious and reliable person who wanted to convey the teachings in their purest and most accurate form. He lavished His attention on her and called upon her to undertake important teaching missions on His behalf. For her part, Ethel wanted to be able to preserve His precise spiritual and social guidance for the benefit of the believers and her acquaintances back home in England.

o

After the summer during which Ethel exhibited a portrait of *James Bernard* at the Royal Academy, the end of 1901 saw her travelling overseas once again to fulfil one of the tasks with which 'Abdu'l-Bahá had entrusted her. This time she made the long sea voyage to the United States to visit some of the American believers with whom she had begun to correspond.

The American Bahá'í community had been through severe tests since the first group of pilgrims had gone to visit 'Abdu'l-Bahá some three years previously. Their chief teacher Khayru'lláh had defected from the orthodox Bahá'í position and had allied himself with 'Abdu'l-Bahá's unfaithful half-brother Muḥammad-'Alí. There are varying accounts of how this defection came about but it seems most likely that Khayru'lláh had grown proud of his position in the community, having brought in hundreds of converts, and envisaged that he might become an equivalent figure to 'Abdu'l-Bahá for the Bahá'ís of the West to turn to and emulate. However, in contrast to the perfect example set by the Master, Khayru'lláh's private life and character left

much to be desired. As differences in the understanding of
doctrine arose, Khayru'lláh found a sympathetic ear in the
Covenant-breakers who, in turn, saw an opportunity to
undermine 'Abdu'l-Bahá's special place in the hearts and
minds of the Western Bahá'ís. Just as the Master had told
Ethel that the Cause of God is like the sea which refuses to
accept or contain a dead body within it, the spiritual father
of the American Bahá'í community found himself shunned
by the very people he had brought into the fold. One of
'Abdu'l-Bahá's solutions to the crisis that developed was to
send a succession of experienced and knowledgeable Persian
Bahá'í teachers to guide the Western believers towards a true
understanding of Bahá'í doctrine. At the time of Ethel's visit
to the United States, the greatest and most erudite of Bahá'í
scholars, Mírzá Abu'l-Faḍl-i-Gulpáygání, had arrived, staying
some three-and-a-half years, travelling and lecturing extensively around the country. Hearing this great man share his
knowledge of the Bahá'í writings made a great impact on
Ethel's own growing knowledge of the teachings.

Unfortunately, little information remains of Ethel's first
journey to the United States, although it is known she stayed
with Phoebe Hearst in California. Mrs Hearst had a home
in Pleasanton, San Francisco which was known as the Haci-
enda. From there she conceived and directed many of her
philanthropic and charitable endeavours. During this visit
Ethel would have met many of the outstanding Californian
Bahá'ís, such as Ella Goodall Cooper. Mrs Hearst presented
Ethel with a beautiful large-format picture book containing
hand-coloured photographs of the Bahá'í Holy Places in
'Akká. Inside she wrote, 'To Ethel Rosenberg with love
Phoebe A. Hearst Sept 17th 1901'.[66] The book is now kept
in the United Kingdom Bahá'í Archives.

This journey was not Ethel's only visit to the United
States. She would return in later years to undertake teaching
missions and renew her old acquaintances. On a later visit
to Chicago, 'Abdu'l-Bahá sent her a most inspiring and
valuable Tablet, urging her to selflessness and new heights

of devotion:

> O thou handmaid afire with the love of God! I have consid-
> ered thine excellent letter, and thanked God for thy safe
> arrival in that great city. I beg of Him, through His unfailing
> aid, to cause this return of thine to exert a powerful effect.
> Such a thing can only come about if thou dost divest thyself
> of all attachment to this world, and dost put on the vesture
> of holiness; if thou dost limit all thy thoughts and all thy
> words to the remembrance of God and His praise; to spread-
> ing His sweet savours abroad, and performing righteous
> acts; and if thou dost devote thyself to awakening the heed-
> less and restoring sight to the blind, hearing to the deaf,
> speech to the mute, and through the power of the spirit,
> giving life to the dead.
>
> For even as Christ said of them in the Gospel, the people
> are blind, they are deaf, they are dumb; and He said: 'I will
> heal them.'
>
> Be thou kind and compassionate to thine enfeebled
> mother, and speak to her of the Kingdom, that her heart
> may rejoice.
>
> Give thou my greetings to Miss Ford.* Convey to her the
> glad tidings that these are the days of the Kingdom of God.
> Say unto her: Blessed art thou for thy noble aims, blessed
> art thou for thy goodly deeds, blessed art thou for thy spiri-
> tual nature. Verily do I love thee on account of these thine
> aims and qualities and deeds. Tell her further: Remember
> the Messiah, and His days on earth, and His abasement, and
> His tribulations, and how the people paid Him no mind.
> Remember how the Jews would hold Him up to ridicule, and
> mock at Him, and address Him with: 'Peace be upon thee,
> King of the Jews! Peace be upon thee, King of Kings!' How
> they would say that He was mad, and would ask how the
> Cause of that crucified One could ever spread out to the
> easts of the world and the wests thereof. None followed Him
> then, save only a few souls who were fishermen, carpenters,
> and other plain folk. Alas, alas, for such delusions!

* Mary Hanford Ford

And see what happened then: how their mighty banners were reversed, and in their place His most exalted standard lifted up; how all the bright stars in that heaven of honour and pride did set, how they sank in the west of all that vanisheth – while His brilliant Orb still shineth down out of skies of undying glory, as the centuries and the ages roll by.

Be ye then admonished, ye that have eyes to see! Ere long shall ye behold even greater things than this. Know thou that all the powers combined have not the power to establish universal peace, nor to withstand the overmastering dominion, at every time and season, of these endless wars. Ere long, however, shall the power of heaven, the dominion of the Holy Spirit, hoist on the high summits the banners of love and peace, and there above the castles of majesty and might shall those banners wave in the rushing winds that blow out of the tender mercy of God.

Convey thou my greetings to Mrs. Florence,* and tell her: The diverse congregations have given up the ground of their belief, and adopted doctrines that are of no account in the sight of God. They are even as the Pharisees who both prayed and fasted, and then did sentence Jesus Christ to death. By the life of God! This thing is passing strange!

As to thee, O handmaid of God, softly recite thou this commune to thy Lord, and say unto Him:

O God, my God! Fill up for me the cup of detachment from all things, and in the assembly of Thy splendours and bestowals, rejoice me with the wine of loving Thee. Free me from the assaults of passion and desire, break off from me the shackles of this nether world, draw me with rapture unto Thy supernal realm, and refresh me amongst the handmaids with the breathings of Thy holiness.

O Lord, brighten Thou my face with the lights of Thy bestowals, light Thou mine eyes with beholding the signs of Thine all-subduing might; delight my heart with the glory of Thy knowledge that encompasseth all things, gladden Thou my soul with Thy soul-reviving tidings of great joy, O

* Possibly Florence Breed, a Boston believer who married Mírzá Abu'l-Faḍl's translator Ali Kuli Khan

Thou King of this world and the Kingdom above, O Thou
Lord of dominion and might, that I may spread abroad Thy
signs and tokens, and proclaim Thy Cause, and promote Thy
Teachings, and serve Thy Law, and exalt Thy Word.

Thou art verily the Powerful, the Ever-Giving, the Able,
the Omnipotent.

As to the fundamentals of teaching the Faith: know thou
that delivering the Message can be accomplished only
through goodly deeds and spiritual attributes, an utterance
that is crystal clear and the happiness reflected from the
face of that one who is expounding the Teachings. It is
essential that the deeds of the teacher should attest the
truth of his words. Such is the state of whoso doth spread
abroad the sweet savours of God and the quality of him who
is sincere in his faith.

Once the Lord hath enabled thee to attain this condition,
be thou assured that He will inspire thee with words of
truth, and will cause thee to speak through the breathings
of the Holy Spirit.

Thus 'Abdu'l-Bahá gave Ethel Rosenberg a method by which
she could live her life, teach His Cause and, consequently,
realize her full spiritual potential.

How far she had come! What contrasts she had experienced – from the mid-Victorian splendour of Bath to the
atmosphere of experimentation pervading the English art
establishment; from the company of London's high society
figures to the dusty, vermin-infested streets of a Turkish
penal colony; from the simplicity of 'Abdu'l-Bahá's household
to the palatial splendour of Mrs Hearst's Californian residence. A transformation had occurred in the life of Ethel
Rosenberg that would ultimately lead her to put aside her
art and devote all her energies and time to the promotion of
the Cause of God.

6

Questions and Answers

. . . the honour and exaltation of man must be some-
thing more than material riches. Material comforts are
only a branch, but the root of the exaltation of man is
the good attributes and virtues which are the adorn-
ments of his reality.[67]

'Abdu'l-Bahá

Shortly after Ethel's return to London news reached her that
the machinations of the Covenant-breakers had resulted in
'Abdu'l-Bahá, His family and followers being strictly confined
within the city limits of 'Akká. The worst of all these deprivations was the fact that the Master was now prohibited from
visiting the Shrine of His Father. In addition, He had been
subjected to long hours of official questioning. But 'Abdu'l-
Bahá's serene composure and kindly manner had won over
the hearts of the officials who interrogated Him and gradually they became loathe to restrict Him further and, in some
instances, even encouraged Him to give them guided visits
to the Holy Shrine. This development enraged the Covenant-
breakers and, in their desire to circulate false representations
of the Master's character, they stepped up their destructive
activities. Nevertheless, 'Abdu'l-Bahá's arduous work in
constructing the Tomb for the Báb progressed and His
correspondence with His followers around the world dramatically increased as their numbers swelled.

In Britain there was increasingly a sense of a new age
beginning. Apart from the fact that a new century had
begun, Queen Victoria had passed away in 1901 after a
monumental 64-year reign, while Gladstone had died three

years earlier. The Victorian era and its preoccupations now seemed worlds away. The more affluent members of society began to invest in electric light, telephones, typewriters, gramophones and automobiles. Meanwhile, attempts were being made to address the critical social problems arising from poverty.

In London, Ethel and Mrs Thornburgh-Cropper hosted a series of meetings in their homes and at the Higher Thought Centre in Kensington and began to attract a small but increasing number of spiritual seekers who were intrigued by the Bahá'í message. Ethel's marvellous experiences in the Holy Land and in the United States had done much to fortify their teaching efforts and the greater availability of literature enabled them to convey the Bahá'í message with more authority and accuracy than ever before. Her personal study of the Persian language, which by now was well under way, also helped in this process and she found herself in the unique position of being able to translate the Master's Tablets and many of the writings as and when they became available. Thanks to London's burgeoning developments in the field of communications, Ethel often found herself being used as an intermediary for messages directed from 'Abdu'l-Bahá to the West and vice versa.

The London believers, however, found the process of spreading the teachings of Bahá'u'lláh very slow and difficult and Ethel expressed her frustration in correspondence with the Master and the Holy Family during 1902. 'Abdu'l-Bahá assured Ethel in His letter to her that He constantly remembered her in His prayers and asked the Almighty to strengthen and confirm her by the fire of His love and plenteousness. In another letter, dated 7 October of that year, the Master's youngest daughter, Munavvar, assured Ethel that prayers would be said, imploring God to strengthen and encourage her efforts and to give her the power to turn the hearts of people so 'that they may be guided by the radiance of the Sun of Truth'.[68] 'O dear friend,' Munavvar wrote, 'summon all your courage and endeavour to show the people their blindness and ignorance by teaching them the true religion and showing them the light of it.'[69] Such blessings and encouragement from the Holy Family were a source of great strength to Ethel and she found that there were indeed some sincere souls who showed more than a passing interest in the Movement. For example, Ethel told the Holy Family in one letter of a young Australian woman who had shown great receptivity during this time.

Ethel's extended journeys away from England and the energy she put into promoting the Bahá'í Movement naturally resulted in a reduction of the professional commissions she received and a serious deterioration in her level of income. This problem was exacerbated by increasingly poor health, including bronchial asthma, chest problems and an astigmatism of the eyes which reduced the number of miniatures she was able to paint. Her difficult situation touched the hearts of the Holy Family, who constantly assured her in their letters of their love. Regardless of her living circumstances, Ethel returned their affections and in a spirit of selfless generosity regularly sent them gifts. She had learned from the Master that one's physical restrictions and limitations should not become a barrier hindering one's service to humanity.

Through their correspondence, Ethel's relationship with 'Abdu'l-Bahá's daughters Rúhá and Munavvar deepened. The women came to address Ethel as their dearest 'Rosa', 'Roser' or 'Rosie' – a true friend and a spiritual sister. Among the many gifts Ethel sent was a handkerchief to Rúhá which was warmly appreciated, as well as English books, toys for the Master's grandchildren, electric lamps and items of clothing, particularly a seemingly continual supply of corsets which the women of the household no doubt would otherwise have had difficulty obtaining in their circumstances. The women expressed their deepest joy and surprise at her willingness to offer these items as gifts and not accept payment for them. A succession of compassionate letters from Rúhá, penned in beautiful handwriting, stressed how she always remembered Ethel and hoped to see her again in the Holy Land. Ethel's news brought joy to the Holy Family at a time when they were suffering the deprivations of being prisoners once more. In one letter, Munavvar mentioned how touched they were to hear from Ethel, saying that it 'breathed forth your true and sincere love to all of us, which is indeed very acceptable'.[70] Munavvar hoped Ethel would be strengthened and enabled to teach and spread 'His holy truth among the people who are desiring to know Him. Can there be any better prayer to pray for you than this?' asked Munavvar.[71]

> Oh, may your tongue become eloquent with His praise. May your mind become brilliant with His knowledge and your heart illuminated with the light of His love! Do not be discouraged at anything, even should you see all of the people denouncing this great cause. It is the cause of God, and at last it will overcome and surmount all obstacles and opposition! Only try my dear friend to teach the truth and proclaim the good news to all![72]

One seeker after truth whom Ethel met towards the end of 1902 was the Countess de Canavarro, also known as Sister Sanghamitta. She had arrived in London on her way to the Holy Land from the United States before teaming up with Myron H. Phelps, a member of the New York Bar who would later record their visit to 'Akká in his book *The Life and Teachings of Abbas Effendi*. The Countess had been an ardent Buddhist and had spent large sums of money promoting Buddhism. Already middle-aged, she had applied for permission to visit 'Abdu'l-Bahá after having made a deep study of Sufism and other spiritual traditions. It fell upon Ethel's shoulders to make contact with the Countess as she stayed in London awaiting official confirmation of her pilgrimage. This came addressed to Ethel, who duly forwarded the letter.

The Countess had been staying at an address in Dulwich but had fallen ill and was delayed in London before making the journey to 'Akká which she planned for the end of October. She wrote a letter, inviting Ethel to lunch with her, in which she outlined her own peculiar perspective of spiritual matters:

> It is not permitted that we shall be martyred more than once in a life time, and as I have gone through a greater martyrdom than death in the cause of Truth, I must rest here and not defy God's injunctions by rushing into danger. Please don't think that I am weak in Faith. If I were beside the Master – for His life, mine I would freely give – or if he bade me do that which would surely bring death to me – nevertheless I would do his behest . . . The greatest sacrifice that I can now bring to a cause is to live for it and I must not tempt providence by rushing into the danger of a quarantine which would be nearly fatal to me at present.[73]

Ethel accepted the invitation and paid a number of visits to the Countess as she recovered from her illness. The Countess was a powerful if not eccentric personality who followed a spiritual path which at times sounded almost masochistic to Ethel, struggling as she was in straitened circumstances. In one of their conversations Ethel was told by the Countess that she had made the choice to suffer. Ethel was shocked at the statement but the Countess justified herself by saying that when she had made up her mind to undergo suffering she recalled the material condition of things and put on the armour of patience, endurance and the knowledge that the mind can span space and ride over all. Whatever their disagreements on spiritual matters, Ethel followed the example of 'Abdu'l-Bahá and showed great love to the Countess. The effect of Ethel's personality on this particular seeker was enormous. By the end of October the Countess, who was leaving England from Liverpool to make her pilgrimage, wrote a last letter to Ethel praising her for her kindness and hospitality.

> I am afraid I am thinking now of you more than I am of the Master. I suppose this will horrify you but if it is so why not say it! . . . You have interested me as none other ever has and I think I follow the working of your mind. I have gone

over in my mind all the gifts you have apparently bestowed
upon me and I realize that each and every one is an offering
of your heart on the sacrifice altar of your great *lover*,
objectivized in the Master at Akka, expressed in the gifts
and through me as a medium. It is wonderful and sublime.
It is greater than all gifts, and is the greatest of all miracles
. . .[74]

The Countess's pilgrimage turned out to be a testing one for
all concerned as at times she showed a reluctance to let go
of her own esoteric ideas when hearing the answers that
'Abdu'l-Bahá had to offer. She also became frustrated and
angry in having to wait for answers to be translated. 'Abdu'l-
Bahá's secretary, Dr Yúnis Khán Afrúkhtih, reported how
when abstruse concepts began to be discussed, a fracas broke
out with the Countess attacking what she heard shouting,
'You people of the East, why should you be in the forefront
of religion, in view of the fact that you are not all that advanced and why should we Westerners need to receive our
ideas from you?'[75] 'Abdu'l-Bahá, in His inimitable style,
managed to win over the Countess by explaining the truth
with the utmost patience and tolerance.

o

The following year Ethel resumed some of her artistic activities and began to answer the requests of Bahá'í friends for
copies of portraits. The miniature of 'Abdu'l-Bahá that she
had executed for Mrs Thornburgh-Cropper was in much
demand from the friends she had met in the United States.
In a letter to Helen Goodall of California, she wrote:

> It has been a great pleasure for me to paint for you a minia-
> ture of the head of Christ (as the Master). The original one
> which I did for our dear Mrs Cropper was copied in the main
> outline from a photo of what is called the 'original portrait
> of Christ' engraved on a gem in the reign of Tiberius. I
> painted it long before I had seen our beloved Master. The
> price of the miniature is, to you, fifteen guineas – I mention
> this because Mrs Cropper asked me to write and tell you . . .
> I do not expect to be in London more than another month

or so – as I am endeavouring to let my house. It was a very
great disappointment to me not to have met you when I was
in California – but I hope to have that happiness at some
future day.[76]

A month later, another letter to Mrs Goodall refers to this
artistic enterprise:

> Your most kind letter (and enclosing money orders) has
> been sent onto me in the country where I am now staying
> in order to paint the miniature of a sweet little baby boy 2
> and a half years old. I am rejoiced to think that you have the
> miniature safely, and that it gives you so much happiness
> to have it. I do myself think that it bears a most wonderful
> likeness to our beloved Master – but I hope you will forgive
> me if I recall to you once more the fact that the original was
> painted before I ever saw Him. And I do hope that in show-
> ing it to believers you will be so very kind as to explain this
> fully. My reason for asking this so urgently is that as you
> no doubt know, he does not allow anyone to paint His
> portrait nor does He wish a photograph even to be taken.[77]

One other 'Bahá'í' work painted by Ethel during this time
was a miniature portrait of the Greatest Holy Leaf. She
showed this widely to her Bahá'í friends and promised finally
to send it on to the Master's household in 'Akká.

Ethel's financial concerns came to a head in November
1903. She wrote to the Holy Family saying that she had been
forced to rent out her home in Albany Street off Regent's
Park where she had been hosting meetings. Fortunately the
loving counsel from the Holy Land continued to sustain her.
Munavvar told her not to worry, saying she thought it was
right 'to suffer a little this year and taste a drop of the sea
of calamity which our brothers and sisters so willingly took
for the sake of their Lord so that we could be a little sympathetic with those real pure and sincere servants of God the
Almighty'.[78] Munavvar prayed at the Holy Tomb that
Bahá'u'lláh would enable Ethel to serve Him under all
circumstances and would open the door of success to her face.
'Abdu'l-Bahá too advised Ethel not to be sorry about any-

thing that came to her. There was in it, He said, a great wisdom, of which she was not cognizant. He exhorted her to be happy and to be sure that all the difficulties she had would benefit her very much in the long term. He told her there was no joy or happiness for man save in serving God – all joy and gladness aside from this is a mirage. While her living conditions had become difficult, 'Abdu'l-Bahá urged her nevertheless to continue with her art, saying it was very necessary for her means of livelihood and that she should not neglect it.

It should not be thought that Ethel only wrote to the Holy Family about her personal difficulties. Her great appetite for knowledge was manifest in dozens of letters asking specific questions relating to history and doctrine. In one example, she asked 'Abdu'l-Bahá about the meaning of the 'seven churches' mentioned in the book of Revelation. 'Abdu'l-Bahá replied that the seven spirits and the seven stars mentioned in the Apocalypse refer to the seven letters of the alphabet that constitute the Most Great Name (in Arabic and Persian, the title Bahá'u'lláh as well as the name Ḥusayn-'Alí consist of seven letters each) – and that the seven churches refer to the holy souls who were ignited with the fire of the love of their Lord. Regarding a question about the number of the 'Beast', also mentioned in Revelation, 'Abdu'l-Bahá informed Ethel that the number 666 referred to the year when the Umayyad ruler Mu'áwíyyih arose to oppose the Imamate. Ethel also had questions relating to pilgrimage and the visiting of Holy Places. 'Abdu'l-Bahá replied:

> You have asked about visiting holy places and the obser-
> vance of marked reverence toward these resplendent spots.
> Holy places are undoubtedly centres of the outpouring of
> Divine grace, because on entering the illumined sites associ-
> ated with martyrs and holy souls, and by observing rever-
> ence, both physical and spiritual, one's heart is moved with
> great tenderness. But there is no obligation for everyone to
> visit such places, other than the three, namely: the Most
> Holy Shrine, the Blessed House in Baghdád and the vener-

ated House of the Báb in Shíráz. To visit these is obligatory if one can afford it and is able to do so, and if no obstacle stands in one's way. Details are given in the Tablets. These three Holy Places are consecrated to pilgrimage. But as to the other resting places of martyrs and holy souls, it is pleasing and acceptable in the sight of God if a person desires to draw nigh unto Him by visiting them; this, however, is not a binding obligation.[79]

'Abdu'l-Bahá's correspondence with Ethel was always filled with loving encouragement. He referred to her as a 'firm and steadfast leaf'[80] and hoped that by the boundless favour of God she would increase daily in her firmness and steadfastness and become the cause of the illumination of humanity. In one Tablet He exhorted her to even greater detachment:

> O Thou handmaid of God, I pray God that He may raise up sanctified, pure and spiritual souls in the countries of the West and the territories of the North, and make them signs of His guidance, ensigns of the Concourse on High and angels of the Abhá Kingdom. Then wilt thou witness the West as the dawning place of lights shining from those regions, even like unto moons. Then will the earth become a portion of the heavenly realm, and the showers of divine bounty will rain down upon it from the most exalted heights, and will cause the soil of those regions to be stirred, and the blossoms of divine wisdom and utterance, and the flowers of understanding and certitude to grow and flourish.
>
> Rest thou assured, O thou handmaid of God that the light of this divine grace will shed its radiance upon the West, and God will raise up those souls, invested with spiritual powers, heavenly confirmations, exalted motives, shining faces, heavenly hearts, and uplifted spirits blessed by the bounty of His inspiration. Thy God, verily, is the All-Powerful, the Almighty. The most effective means to attain these lofty stations is through spiritual purity and sanctity, detachment from the world, and forgetfulness of everything save God.[81]

The summer of 1903 saw a new wave of persecutions sweep

through the sorely-tried Bahá'í community of Persia. Dissatisfaction with the prime minister Amínu's-Sulṭán, who had been in power for more than a decade, led to clergy-inspired outbreaks of violence against foreigners, Jews and Zoroastrians. In the south of the country the Bahá'ís were made the scapegoats for the people's troubles and a wave of violent madness swept through Isfahan and Yazd. People rampaged in the streets of Yazd for two days hunting out the Bahá'ís. Reports of the massacres reached London via articles in *The Times* through which the believers attempted to spread the news of the atrocities. Ethel wrote an article for circulation to draw the attention of important people to the horrors. She sent a copy to 'Abdu'l-Bahá for His correction.

The Master was deeply distressed and fully occupied trying to relieve the sufferings of His followers in Persia. Munavvar wrote to Ethel saying that the Shah was almost powerless, as the clergy, who virtually ruled the state, had risen against the Bahá'ís determining to annihilate them. 'Our friends and brothers are being killed in the most horrible manner,' she wrote. 'Some are cut to pieces with meat axes, some are nailed to trees and burned while others are thrown into red hot ovens and baked to death. They take little children and cut them to pieces before their parents or worse still leave them to wander homeless and helpless after depriving them of their father and mother.'[82] Ethel learned that for nearly two weeks 'Abdu'l-Bahá was so sad that He had scarcely slept at all. He told His daughters that the tree of the Cause of God had ever been and ever will be watered by human blood and that He was sad that His own blood had not been spilled in the way of God. 'Of course,' Munavvar wrote to Ethel, 'you can imagine what an effect such words from his lips have upon our hearts. We are just like dead people walking around without any aim or object in life for you see we cannot speak to a single soul about our sorrow while the people come to us and we are obliged to sit and talk with them as though nothing had happened. Oh blessed you are that you are free and can speak to everybody about this blessed truth and write about it too!'[83]

Another source of news from the Holy Land which Ethel greatly appreciated was the Master's secretary Dr Yúnis Khán. In one letter he also shared news of the martyrdoms in Persia and reported how glad they were at Haifa to receive notification that the government had arrested some of the clergy who had excited the populace to carry out such acts against the Bahá'í Cause in the land of its birth. Dr Yúnis Khán's letters contained assurances that 'Abdu'l-Bahá remembered and prayed for the London Bahá'ís and promised them great results as a consequence of the calamities besetting the Persian believers: 'Indeed the holy blood of these souls has watered and refreshed the plants of the garden of the Divine Cause and new blossoms are going to bloom in this splendid Orchard.'[84]

Despite the steady progress made in promoting the Bahá'í Cause in London, Ethel Rosenberg longed to share once again in the spirit of 'Abdu'l-Bahá 's household. Her wish was fulfilled in 1904 when from 21 April until 24 December she was able to return to 'Akká as His guest. The year was another painful one for 'Abdu'l-Bahá, who had been subjected to even more tribulations. Mírzá Muhammad-'Alí and his circle had created fresh confusion and unrest within 'Akká, resulting in hostility from some of the newly appointed officials. As a result of an indictment drawn up against 'Abdu'l-Bahá by the Covenant-breakers, a Commission of Inquiry arrived from Constantinople. Spies were planted around the Master's house and, fearing for the safety of His followers, 'Abdu'l-Bahá, assisted by a financial loan from an American Bahá'í living in Paris, was able to help some 70 of the Bahá'ís to leave 'Akká for Egypt. On several occasions the Master was forced to appear before the Inquiry, answering its questions with great majesty and refuting the accusations with such eloquence that the Commission had no choice but to dismiss the case and return to Turkey.

It was during these painful and testing periods of His life that 'Abdu'l-Bahá left a legacy to His followers unique in the entire history of religion. Ethel Rosenberg was privileged to witness the Master revealing answers to specific questions posed to him by her friend Laura Clifford Barney. Laura had come from a distinguished American family of artists and scholars. May Bolles had introduced her to the Bahá'í revelation while Laura was completing her education in France. From then on, her whole life was devoted to promoting human cooperation, bringing people from different walks of life together. It was during one of many frequent visits to see the Master, while Ethel was also present in 1904, that Laura began writing down the expositions made by Him at His table talks to the pilgrims.

Dr Yúnis Khán later recalled how the Master would sit at the head of the dinner table while Laura sat on His left and Ethel took the seat next to her. Usually some eight or nine other pilgrims were present. Dr Yúnis-Khán would sit beside the Master facing Laura, first rendering her questions into Persian and then translating the answers given by the Master into English, while Ethel noted down both the questions and answers in English. The answer in its original language was also written down by a Persian believer. 'Since the nourishment of the spirit,' wrote Dr Yúnis Khán, 'was given priority over that of the body, it often happened that eating was delayed.'

> The Master when elucidating the problems used to speak in such a manner that the hearer would be enchanted. One day when He was insisting that I should first eat and then speak, and I was deeply engrossed in the subject under discussion, He asked Laura what was the English for 'mutarjim'; she said 'interpreter'. Again he asked what was the word for 'gorosneh'. She said 'hungry'. Thereupon 'Abdu'l-Bahá, pointing at me, exclaimed: 'Hungry inter-preter! Hungry interpreter!'[85]

These recorded expositions of the Master's wisdom have since become known throughout the world as the book *Some Answered Questions*.

One day as He rose from the table, Laura wrote that 'Abdu'l-Bahá told her that He had given her His tired moments.

> As it was on this day, so it continued; between the hours of work, His fatigue would find relief in renewed activity; occasionally He was able to speak at length; but often, even though the subject might require more time, He would be called away after a few moments; again, days and even weeks would pass, in which He had no opportunity of instructing me. But I could well be patient, for I had always before me the greater lesson – the lesson of His personal life.[86]

It was not initially Laura's intention to publish 'Abdu'l-Bahá's talks, which she had the bounty to hear between 1904 and 1906. Rather, she had hoped simply to preserve them for her own future study as the questions strongly reflected her interests and understanding at that time. But after deciding they would be of value to the growing community of Bahá'ís around the world, the questions were classified for the convenience of other readers. 'Abdu'l-Bahá granted His permission for their publication, reading the transcriptions and sometimes changing a word or a line.

Being present at such momentous gatherings gave Ethel and the other pilgrims who heard 'Abdu'l-Bahá tremendous new insights into the Cause. 'Abdu'l-Bahá dealt with the vast eternal questions about the nature and existence of God, the universe, the life of the soul, and the relationship between science and religion. He spoke about esoteric matters – immortality, predestination, free will and reincarnation – as well as practical aspects of the Bahá'í teachings concerning labour and capital, law and order. Most importantly perhaps for Ethel, He dwelt on Christian subjects, the fulfilment of prophecies and explanations of biblical themes. Ethel's notebooks filled with His insights provided her with a rich source of materials for public lectures in the years to come.

Ethel was, however, most distressed to see the severe

conditions and pressures that the Holy Family was now living under. She asked 'Abdu'l-Bahá why He, who was so perfect, should have to endure such sufferings. He answered, 'How could they (God's teachers) teach and guide others in the way if they themselves did not undergo every species of suffering to which other human beings are subjected.'[87] He spoke to Ethel about life after death and how important it was to pray for those who had departed this world. He told her that to pray for the dead had not been given as a special religious command before the coming of Bahá'u'lláh but that now the progress of the soul in another world was a revealed truth and that souls could benefit from the supplications and intercession of others.

On 29 April the pilgrims gathered to celebrate the Bahá'í Holy Day known as the Ninth Day of Riḍván, marking the occasion in 1863 when 'Abdu'l-Bahá and the Holy Family had joined Bahá'u'lláh in the Garden of Riḍván in Baghdad shortly before their departure for Constantinople. All the believers and visitors were served in shifts in the Master's house. On a table covered with roses and other fragrant flowers 28 places were set, and that number of guests was again seated after each successive sitting had finished.

'Abdu'l-Bahá did not sit down with His visitors but rather stood and directed the proceedings and assisted with the serving of the food. He then addressed the gathering saying that He desired to stand and serve them all as Bahá'u'lláh was looking down upon them from His Kingdom. There were many gatherings and banquets in the world for different purposes, the Master said, some for friendships, others for showing honour and reverence to distinguished people, and again others for business. Many luscious feasts were held but it was a wonder, He observed, to have such a gathering in a prison! 'Abdu'l-Bahá told the meeting that is was for the love of God alone. It was His teaching and their love for Him that had enabled them to gather together from all parts of the world – from Russia, India, Burma, Persia, America, France and England – and from different faiths – Zoroastrian, Muslim of different sects, Christian and Jewish.

We are all assembled under one tent, and in our midst is
hoisted the banner of the love of God. We are all breathing
one atmosphere, drinking from one cup and sailing upon one
sea. All the prophets of the World have said the same thing,
have taught the same truths of brotherhood . . . but the soil
of the hearts was not ready to receive their Divine Teachings. But now, thank God, the soil is prepared, so that the
good seed which has been sowed by the hands of the Divine
Farmer Himself has sprung up and we now see the effect
of His words. It is a very marvellous thing that such a
glorious meeting should be held here in the very centre of
a prison; and it is one of the great signs of the Divine Manifestation. We must speak of it everywhere and never forget
it.[88]

The climate in the Holy Land suited Ethel's fragile health
very well, so it must have been something of an upheaval –
both physically and spiritually – to return to an English
winter after eight months of the Mediterranean climate and
in the incomparable company of the Master and His family.
Her poor health would have a seriously debilitating effect on
her activities for the next couple of years, but in spite of this,
her widespread correspondence continued, meetings were
resumed on Sunday afternoons and Ethel was instrumental
in arranging for the first few publications of Bahá'í literature
in English to be produced or circulated in the United Kingdom. Her extensive pilgrim's notes became the main substance of all the London meetings where she would also
relate stories of the Master's life in 'Akká, conveying how He
seemed to be absolutely without self in any shape or form.
She recalled how all the inhabitants of 'Akká went to Him
in their difficulties and trouble and how high He set the
example for the services of His followers.

Shortly after Ethel's return the Bahá'ís in London lost one
of their staunchest supporters with the death of Mrs
Thornburgh, the mother of Mrs Thornburgh-Cropper. Ethel
had been having Sunday lunch with them and noted that

Mrs Thornburgh was very bright and happy. However she fell ill the following day and passed away almost immediately. It was a terrible shock to Mrs Thornburgh-Cropper but, as Ethel reported to Helen Goodall in a letter, the most wonderful look of peace and happiness transfigured Mrs Thornburgh's face five minutes after the death and her daughter felt it was a perfect benediction to look at her. Mrs Thornburgh-Cropper herself collapsed after her mother's funeral and was confined to bed for a few days before leaving London to stay with friends in South Wales where the atmosphere suited her better. The lessons learnt in 'Akká were uppermost in Ethel's mind and she reflected on what she had learned about the immortality of the soul.

Ethel's curiosity to know more of, and understand better, the teachings of Bahá'u'lláh led to her questioning 'Abdu'l-Bahá about one of Bahá'u'lláh's most widely circulated Tablets, the *Lawḥ-i-Ḥikmat* or the Tablet of Wisdom. This document, revealed in Arabic, presents Bahá'u'lláh's view of philosophy, referring to ancient Greek thought as well as explaining the influence of the Word of God and the cause and origin of creation and nature. In a letter dated 6 April 1906 Ethel questioned 'Abdu'l-Bahá about the fact that Bahá'u'lláh's account of the Greek philosophers differed from other historical documents. In the Tablet, Bahá'u'lláh states that 'the essence and fundamentals of philosophy have emanated from the Prophets',[89] asserting that the ancient philosophers believed in God and acquired their wisdom from the Prophets of Israel.

'Abdu'l-Bahá offered a lengthy reply to Ethel's question which was widely circulated and published in Persian. This communication became known as the Rosenberg Tablet and an authorized translation is published here for the first time:

He is God!
O thou dear handmaid of God!
Thy letter dated 6 April 1906 hath been received. Thou hast written that Mrs . . . hath regained her health. God be praised, this daughter of the Kingdom hath attained unto

spiritual health. A disaster to the body, when spiritual health is present, is of no importance. That is the main thing. God be thanked, she hath attained that great bestowal; she hath taken on immortal life.

It is to be regretted, however, that her husband is still wrapped in the veils of his idle imaginings. If her dear daughter ... be trained according to the instructions of God, she will grow to be a peerless plant in the garden of the heart. It is incumbent upon the father to choose for his daughter the glory that dieth not. Nevertheless, this is up to him; he may educate her in any way he desireth.

As to what thou didst ask regarding the history of the philosophers: history, prior to Alexander of Greece, is extremely confused, for it is a fact that only after Alexander did history become an orderly and systematized discipline. One cannot, for this reason, rely upon traditions and reported historical events that have come down from before the days of Alexander. This is a matter thoroughly established, in the view of all authoritative historians. How many a historical account was taken as fact in the eighteenth century, yet the opposite was proved true in the nineteenth. No reliance, then, can be placed upon the traditions and reports of historians which antedate Alexander, not even with regard to ascertaining the lifetimes of leading individuals.

Wherefore ye should not be surprised that the Tablet of Wisdom is in conflict with the historical accounts. It behoveth one to reflect a while on the great diversity of opinion among historians, and their contradictory accounts; for the historians of East and West are much at odds, and the Tablet of Wisdom was written in accordance with certain histories of the East.

Furthermore the Torah, held to be the most ancient of histories, existeth today in three separate versions: the Hebrew, considered authentic by the Jews and the Protestant clergy; the Greek Septuagint, which is used as authoritative in the Greek and other eastern churches; and the Samaritan Torah, the standard authority for that people. These three versions differ greatly, one from another, even with regard to the lifetimes of the most celebrated figures.

In the Hebrew Torah, it is recorded that from Noah's flood until the birth of Abraham there was an interval of two hundred and ninety-two years. In the Greek, that time-span is given as one thousand and seventy-two years, while in the Samaritan, the recorded span is nine hundred and forty-two years. Refer to the commentary by Henry Westcott [the transliteration of this name is not certain] for tables are supplied therein which show the discrepancies among the three Torahs as to the birthdate of a number of the descendants of Shem, and thou wilt see how greatly the versions differ one from another.

Moreover, according to the text of the Hebrew Torah, from the creation of Adam until Noah's flood the elapsed time is recorded as one thousand six hundred and fifty-six years, while in the Greek Torah the interval is given as two thousand two hundred and sixty-two years, and in the Samaritan text, the same period is said to have lasted one thousand three hundred and seven years.

Reflect thou now over the discrepancies among these three Torahs. The case is indeed surprising. The Jews and Protestants belittle the Greek Torah, while to the Greeks, the Hebrew version is spurious, and the Samaritans deny both the Hebrew and the Greek versions.

Our purpose is to show that even in Scriptural history, the most outstanding of all histories, there are contradictions as to the time when the great ones lived, let alone as to dates related to others. And furthermore, learned societies in Europe are continually revising the existing records, both of East and West. In spite of this, how can the confused accounts of peoples dating from before Alexander be compared with the Holy Text of God? If any scholar expresses astonishment, let him be surprised at the discrepancies in Scriptural history.

Nevertheless, Holy Writ is authoritative, and with it no history of the world can compare, for experience hath shown that after investigation of the facts and a thorough study of ancient records and corroborative evidence, all establish the validity of God's universal Manifestation; once His claim proveth true, then whatsoever He may choose to say is right and correct.

The histories prior to Alexander, which were based on oral accounts current among the people, were put together later on. There are great discrepancies among them, and certainly they can never hold their own against Holy Writ. It is an accepted fact among historians themselves that these histories were compiled after Alexander, and that prior to his time history was transmitted by word of mouth. Note how extremely confused was the history of Greece, so much so that to this day there is no agreement on the dates related to the life of Homer, Greece's far-famed poet. Some even maintain that Homer never existed at all, and that the name is a fabrication.

It is my hope that through the favour and grace of the Abhá Beauty, thou wilt fully recover thy health, and engage in serving the Cause with all thy might. I am aware that thou art much afflicted, and in extreme distress; but if we taste a drop from affliction's cup, the Blessed Beauty drank down a sea of anguish, and once we call this to mind, then every hardship turneth into peaceful rest, and toil into merciful bliss. Then will a draught of agony be but refreshing wine, and the tyrant's wound only a friend's most gentle balm. Greetings be unto thee, and praise.[90]

Ethel's poor health – particularly concerning her chest and her eyes – was now indeed causing her extreme distress. She was forced to cancel her meetings for teaching the Cause and at one stage was even taken into hospital for an operation. The Holy Family were most concerned and in several letters assured her of their thoughts and prayers. Ethel had hoped to accompany Laura Barney on a trip to Persia but her physical condition would not allow it. Munavvar particularly sympathized with Ethel's frustration and expressed how hard it was to

be so caged up as we are and be prevented from doing which you like best to do and the most interested in (sic). But perhaps it has to be so for some wisdom which we do not know. Of course how can the limited mind of man know the mysteries of the great wisdom of God. Therefore we must willingly accept everything He prepares for us for we believe that He is the wise Doctor so we must happily take the things He gives us and if we do otherwise we are only satis-fying our desire and harming ourselves.[91]

The health of many of the Bahá'ís in the Holy Land was also poorly as a smallpox epidemic had swept through 'Akká and Munavvar and most of the family had been forced to leave for Haifa. Munavvar told Ethel how anxious she was about her when she heard she had been in hospital and undergoing an operation. She wrote:

> I am sure, dear, you must have felt my prayers at the time of your suffering. I cannot tell you how I felt with you as I have always done in your physical troubles and all kinds of difficulties you go through. Do not think dear Roser that I do not realize them for indeed I do more than you know I do. I cannot express in words how I wish to be able to help those whom I really love and are dear to me.[92]

Unable to move about as freely as she would have liked, Ethel began a strong correspondence with Thornton Chase, the first American believer, whom she had met earlier in Chicago. Ethel contacted Chase after she encountered an American by the name of Mr Kellogg who seemed most receptive to the Bahá'í teachings. In a letter of 16 March 1906 Chase mentions meeting Mr Kellogg to whom Ethel had introduced him via a letter the previous February.

Ethel learnt from Chase that the believers in Chicago faced somewhat different problems in teaching than those experienced by the English Bahá'ís. Chase told Ethel that in America the main barrier to teaching was that there were so many fads, cults and ideas so that although it was easy to meet people and talk of such things, the Movement was always being placed in such categories and not appreciated for what it truly was. In England the whole issue of raising the matter of the Faith in conversation was a more delicate and difficult process entirely.

Details of an unusual phenomenon that plagued the early believers also emerge in the correspondence between Ethel and Thornton Chase. It would appear that less than honest or occasionally mentally unstable individuals often appeared in their midst who sought to take advantage of their generosity and kindness. One such figure encountered by Ethel was a Mr Lazarus about whom she warned Thornton Chase prior to the former's decision to go to America. The American Bahá'ís at that time had experienced the confidence tricks of Abraham Haddad, the brother of the prominent New York teacher Anton Haddad. Abraham had, under the claim of Bahá'í brotherhood, sold goods and borrowed money. Another such trickster was Miss Carrie Rogers who had been encountered first in the Chicago area and later made contact with the Bahá'ís in London. Thornton Chase warned Ethel to be careful of Miss Rogers, saying she was not always well balanced and could not be relied upon for matters of importance, a characteristic which the friends attributed to an unsettled mental condition rather than to any deliberate mischief-making. Despite the warning, Miss Rogers managed to secure a considerable amount of money from the Bahá'ís in London.

Thornton Chase was intimately involved with the pioneering developments in Bahá'í publishing. The believers around Chicago had legally incorporated a Bahá'í Publishing Society which set about publishing new translations of Bahá'u'lláh's and 'Abdu'l-Bahá's writings. These were sent to Ethel and included a translation of the *Hidden Words*, arguably Bahá'u'lláh's most popular and accessible work, which encapsulates the essence of all religious truth in a collection of short, powerful and poetic verses. The greater availability of literature – in both English and French – inspired Ethel to try her own hand at preparing an introductory pamphlet on the Movement entitled *Behaism*. The leaflet was well-received and, while Ethel later substantially reworked it and published it under the title of *A Brief Account of the Bahai Movement*, Thornton Chase remarked that this first effort was an 'excellent presentation to interest the seeking ones'.[93]

As a result of her correspondence with Thornton Chase, Ethel now found herself as a kind of way station for correspondence between the friends in the United States and the Master, passing on Tablets and providing the Bahá'ís in return with literature that was prepared in England. London itself was increasingly becoming a stopping-off point for many Bahá'í travellers who were passing between America and the Holy Land. Among the visitors was Sidney Sprague, a young man who had travelled widely for the Faith in India and Burma. He had caught typhoid fever in Lahore and a Bahá'í of Zoroastrian background had come to care for him. After a few days the man caught cholera and died. Sprague was seen as the first occidental Bahá'í for whom an oriental Bahá'í had sacrificed his life. He was a noted author, lecturer and composer who had studied in Paris and had, as a freelance journalist, covered the trial of Captain Dreyfus and the funeral of Emile Zola. He was also credited with teaching music to the daughter of the Shah of Persia and introducing Persian music to the West.

One Persian believer who also visited London during these days was Dr Amín Faríd who was indirectly related to the Holy Family: his mother was the sister of 'Abdu'l-Bahá's wife. His father, Mírzá Asadu'lláh, had been charged by 'Abdu'l-Bahá to take the remains of the Báb to the Holy Land. 'Abdu'l-Bahá paid a great deal of attention to Faríd's education and sent him to America to study medicine. Coincidentally, both Sprague and Faríd would later be influenced by their dealings with the Covenant-breakers and would come to be known as enemies of the Bahá'í Cause, although Sprague was readmitted to the religion towards the end of his life.

By the end of 1906 Ethel had sufficiently regained her strength to begin travelling again. Her destination was Paris and in prospect was a meeting which, although she did not know it, would have major consequences for the prestige and profile of the Bahá'í Movement in Britain.

Encountering Lady Blomfield

The names of handmaidens who are devoted to God are
written and set down by the Pen of the Most High in the
Crimson Book. They excel over men in the sight of
God.[94]

Bahá'u'lláh

Ethel Rosenberg could not have imagined that by the end of
her 1907 visit to Paris she would have encountered another
Englishwoman with whom she would be intimately con-
nected for the rest of her life. Her main reason for venturing
to the French capital was to continue her collaboration with
Laura Clifford Barney in preparing the book of 'Abdu'l-
Bahá's table talks which would, the following year, become
available throughout the Bahá'í world as *Some Answered*
Questions. Apart from the necessary encumbrances of travel,
Ethel would no doubt have been armed with her precious
notebooks, filled with the English transcriptions of 'Abdu'l-
Bahá's priceless expositions which she had herself recorded
in 'Akká three years previously.

In the middle years of the first decade of the twentieth
century, Paris remained in the throes of the artistic revolutions which had characterized its cultural life for the previous four decades, ever since the as-yet-unlabelled Impression-
ist painters had staged their first exhibition in 1874. Since
the turn of the century, the French capital had become the
Mecca of young artists of many nationalities who thronged
to the city to soak up its atmosphere of experimentation and
controversy and for them the city provided the opportunity
to display their new creations to an audience which was, by

now, accustomed to – but nonetheless occasionally scandalized by – cultural and intellectual challenges.

To Ethel's artistic sensibilities, schooled as she was in the demanding draughtsmanship of the Old Masters, it must have been surprising to hear of, if not to view first hand, the works of Henri Matisse and his companions, dubbed *Les Fauves* (the Wild Beasts) by their critics. Since 1905 they had been evolving a form of painting that entirely shunned realism in favour of the expression of emotional responses to a subject in violent colours and distorted, flattened forms. Other developments in the world of the arts at that time drew heavily on the visual motifs of so-called 'primitive' cultures which had become more-widely known and accessible to European audiences. Georges Braque and Pablo Picasso were beginning their ground-breaking experiments in Cubism, with Picasso's *Demoiselles d'Avignon* causing a great furore when it was first exhibited in 1907, owing to its revolutionary analysis and separation of forms into component shapes.

Aside from witnessing the overturning of well-established traditions in the arts world, France itself had been rocked by the resurgence of an age-old conflict between the church and the state and by the Dreyfus Affair. Captain Alfred Dreyfus, who was an Alsatian Jew, had been accused of treason on account of his alleged supplying of military secrets to Germany. His conviction was later discovered to have been based on forged evidence, concocted by military leaders who were highly anti-semitic. The affair had the effect of uniting and bringing to power the French left wing who rallied behind Dreyfus, in spite of their being monarchists. Army leaders and the church were both discredited and Dreyfus won his freedom in 1906. The upheaval signalled the final separation of church and state in France.

France was also still firmly committed to continuing colonial expansion, a policy which brought it into conflict with both Britain and Germany. Georges Clemenceau, a radical known as 'the Tiger', had become prime minister in

1906. His terms in office were marked by attempts to restrain a growing strike movement as well as violent attacks on the socialists. It would not be until 1917 that Clemenceau would enjoy the circumstances that would enable him to unite the country in the face of war when he became prime minister again in November of that year.

The wild experimentation and the challenging of accepted, time-honoured rules and aesthetics in the arts world; the loosening of the church's hold on people's minds; and the striving towards greater rights and freedoms for ordinary, working people – all of these developments must have been observed with great interest by the steadily growing number of supporters of the Bahá'í Movement in Paris as indications of the upsetting of the world's equilibrium brought about by the revelation of Bahá'u'lláh. Since the establishment of the first European Bahá'í centre in Paris by May Bolles, many of the outstanding figures in early Western Bahá'í history had learned of the new Revelation in the French capital. Among those drawn to the magnetic personality of 'Abdu'l-Bahá through May Bolles's own purity, simplicity and devotion to His teachings were Edith MacKaye, Charles Mason Remey, Helen Ellis Cole and Agnes Alexander. Later the strength of the group was reinforced by the painter Juliet Thompson and captivated by the visits of the Faith's most outstanding scholar, Mírzá Abu'l-Faḍl, accompanied by his translators Anton Haddad and Ali Kuli Khan.

Ethel Rosenberg had naturally developed close friendships with the first French believer, Hippolyte Dreyfus, and Laura Clifford Barney. They were effectively counterparts of each other, pioneer workers engaged in the same important task, separated only in body by a narrow stretch of sea. The age-old barriers of language were not a problem for them, as Dreyfus understood English well, Barney was an American and Ethel's own mastery of French, should she have needed it in France, was impeccable. Dreyfus and Laura were not yet married at the time of Ethel's visit although a close working relationship was developing between them. Laura was putting the finishing touches on the manuscript of *Some Answered Questions* and Dreyfus was so impressed by the remarkable text that he offered to undertake its translation into French. Collaborating on the translation, the two realized how well they could work together and were finally married in 1911. Their lives – both before and after marriage – were filled with tireless activities, carried out as a partnership. They travelled at the request of 'Abdu'l-Bahá to Máh-Kú, the prison fortress where the Báb had been kept captive for nine months, and to other parts of Persia; to 'Ishqábád in Russian Turkistan where the first Bahá'í House of Worship had been built; and to areas of Indo-China and eastern Asia.

Paris, which had played such an important role in bringing together those souls who were destined to become some of 'Abdu'l-Bahá's most distinguished followers, was now about to be the setting for a meeting between Ethel Rosenberg and Sara Louisa, Lady Blomfield who was visiting the French capital with her daughter, Mary.

Lady Blomfield was born in Ireland to a Protestant mother and a Roman Catholic father, Matthew John Ryan. The family lived at Knockanevan in Borrisoleigh, some 30 miles north-east of Limerick, in the south of the country. Young Sara Louisa's childhood was thus spent in an atmosphere of religious conflict. Her maternal grandmother was so scared that the young girl would be taken from her and sent to a distant convent where she would be lost forever, that she took Sara away to England.[95]

Despite the religious confrontations which characterized her early years, Sara was always careful to be loyal to both her parents. Several decades later her daughter recalled how Lady Blomfield's inborn sense of justice meant that she could understand the views of both a sincere Catholic and a fearless Protestant so long as they lived piously up to the light inherent in their paths of worship. This early experience of religious intolerance, however, had a deep effect and inspired in Lady Blomfield a lifelong quest for spiritual truth. She

9. *Thomas Breakwell*
'the fervour and the faith of this young man were so sublime in
character that his blessed name shall ring throughout centuries, and
shall be remembered with deep affection in many chronicles'.

10. Hippolyte Dreyfus
the first Frenchman to become a Bahá'í and translator into French of
Some Answered Questions.

11. Laura Clifford Barney
seen here at the Wilmette Temple site in 1909.
Ethel collaborated with Laura in the preparation and
translation into English of Some Answered Questions.
Laura Barney married Hippolyte Dreyfus in 1911.

12. Ethel Rosenberg's first pilgrimage, 1901
From left to right, standing: *Charles Mason Remey (arrived in 'Akká February 1901), Sigurd Russell, Edward Getsinger (arrived September 1900), Laura Barney*
Seated: *Ethel Rosenberg (arrived January 1901), Madam Jackson, Shoghi Effendi, unknown (identified in* Bahá'í World *volumes 3 and 4 as Mrs Thornburgh, although she is only known to have been in 'Akká in 1899; some sources identify her as Mary Virginia Thornburgh-Cropper, who was in 'Akká only in 1898 and 1906), Lua Getsinger, Claudia Coles.*

13. Bahíyyih <u>Kh</u>ánum, the Greatest Holy Leaf
Ethel painted a miniature portrait of her in 1903.

14. Munírih Khánum, the Holy Mother
Ethel regularly sent letters and gifts to the members of the Holy Family.

15. Bahá'í women in 'Akká

Members of the Holy Family are seated in the second row: Second from left is Munavvar <u>Kh</u>ánum, then Túbá <u>Kh</u>ánum, the Greatest Holy Leaf, Munírih <u>Kh</u>ánum, Díyá'íyyih <u>Kh</u>ánum and Rúhá <u>Kh</u>ánum

16. An early view of the Shrine of the Báb.

made a point of teaching her daughters – Mary Esther and
Rose Ellinor Cecilia – both Catholic and Protestant aspects
of Christianity and endeavoured to hide from them the
bigotry that divided the two churches. When her daughters
were old enough to ask questions about such bitter prejudices, she would answer them wisely and truly. Fearing,
however, that she had over-emphasized the errors of Catholi-
cism, she decided to send the girls to a French convent where
she hoped they would learn to appreciate the truth and
beauty of the Catholic faith and, in addition, improve their
French. Her efforts in the first instance were, to her shock,
more than successful. After one year, Mary wrote to tell her
mother that she was to be received as *un enfant de Marie*.
By the middle of the term Lady Blomfield had swiftly removed both girls from the school.

Lady Blomfield was a loving wife to a husband some 30
years her senior, Sir Arthur William Blomfield. Their daughter Mary would remember him as a youthful man at heart
in spite of his greying curls, dignified appearance and mono-
cle. Sir Arthur, the son of a former Bishop of London,
Charles James Blomfield, was an architect who had been
educated at Rugby and Trinity College, Cambridge. In his
professional life, he enjoyed great distinction, establishing
his offices in Adelphi Terrace in 1856. By 1861 he was
President of the Architectural Association, becoming a fellow
of the Royal Institute of British Architects in 1867 and its
vice-president in 1886. He was associated with the building
of London's Law Courts in 1881, and two years later he was
architect to the Bank of England. Among other buildings of
note which he designed were Sion College Library on the
Thames Embankment, Queen's School at Eton College, the
scheme for Church House at Dean's Yard in Westminster
and many churches in England and abroad. He carried out
important restoration work at the cathedrals of Salisbury,
Canterbury, Lincoln and Chichester.

From their tall, old-fashioned house in London's
Montague Square, the Blomfields led the conventional life

of London society in the late 1890s. Before attending count-less functions dressed in her shimmering frocks and jewels, Lady Blomfield – herself a gracious and hospitable hostess – made it her habit to go up to the nursery to hear her daughters pray and to wish them a good night. It is indicative of the transformation that was to occur in Lady Blomfield's life that those jewels would later be sold for the benefit of a philanthropic cause.

Among the Blomfield's friends who influenced her think-ing at that time was Sir Edwin Arnold, the poet, journalist, translator and traveller, whose 'Light of Asia', an epic poem concerning the life of the Buddha, revealed the truth at the heart of Buddhism to Lady Blomfield. Another acquaintance was Sir William Crookes, whose experiments in psychic research were seen at the time to shed a new light on myste-rious phenomena. Although she respected the work of Crookes, Lady Blomfield refused to practise spiritualism, believing that to seek communication with the other world disturbed those who had departed. Her instincts were born out in later years when she discovered the Bahá'í teachings on this subject.

An incident from the Blomfield daughters' childhood well illustrates one of their mother's impressive qualities: her immense courage and sense of self-abnegation when required to assist others. One day the family was walking in the Cotswolds when a runaway pony was spotted racing down a hill towards them, a little girl clinging to its mane and screaming in terror. Having had two bad accidents, Lady Blomfield was in fact afraid of horses. Nevertheless in this instance she chose to forget her own safety and rushed to grab hold of the pony, seizing the bridle. Dragged off her feet, she managed to stop the animal just before it reached a rough stone wall. The child's life was saved.

Another story indicates her moral courage and lack of concern about what others thought of her. Whenever the Athanasian Creed was read in church, she remained seated when everyone else in the congregation rose to their feet. She later explained that although hellfire might be everlasting, it was blasphemy to say that God the Father would punish a man forever for a sin he had committed in a moment of depravity, or even for a lifetime of sin, which however long it lasted was but temporary. There was ultimate salvation, she believed, even for the more dire sinner.

Lady Blomfield was not afraid of causing controversy for dignitaries of the church or political leaders. In her early days, before encountering the Bahá'í Movement, she had taken an interest in politics. Her husband was a light-hearted Conservative but Lady Blomfield identified herself as a Liberal up until the Women's Suffrage campaign when she was so ashamed by the government's treatment of the suffragettes that she left the party and never joined another. She came to deplore labels and believed that party politics were in effect holding up necessary reforms.

When Sir Arthur died at the age of 70 in 1899, Lady Blomfield and her two daughters went to live at their country house in Broadway, Worcestershire. There, as in London, they enjoyed the company of an interesting circle of friends. Among their many visitors were Frank Millett, an American artist who would later go down in the Titanic disaster, heroically giving his place in the boat to another; the English actress, Mrs Patrick Campbell, for whom the part of Eliza Doolittle in Shaw's *Pygmalion* was especially written; the composer Maud Valerie White; and Lady Maud Bowes Lyon, an aunt of the future Queen Elizabeth who is now known in Britain as the Queen Mother.

Those early years of being a young widow were the turning point in Lady Blomfield's life. She was beginning to lose her enthusiasm for the society circles which she had been accustomed to frequenting and, instead, found great happiness exploring the worlds of thought and spiritual contemplation. A study of Theosophy naturally followed on from her interest in Eastern religions awakened by Sir Edwin Arnold. She avidly read the books of Annie Besant, A.P. Sinnett and others and whenever she was in London she would attend lectures and meet the authors.

The Theosophical Society had been founded by Madame Helena Blavatsky, a Russian occultist, and Henry Olcott, an American Freemason, some 25 years previously. Madame Blavatsky's personal history is obscured by the stories which grew up around her apparently to substantiate her claims as a mystic. It would appear that she was born in 1831, the daughter of a Russian aristocrat, and that her early years were spent living a bohemian life, including a spell as a spirit medium. She claimed she had been contacted by a Tibetan sage by the name of Master Morya who taught her about the divine hierarchy that rules the cosmos. It was claimed that Morya, who was only visible to initiates, was a member of a Great White Brotherhood of Masters who were immortal and invisible. Among the members of the Brotherhood were Buddha, Moses, Plato and various other enlightened Teachers. An important element of their message for that particular period in history was that Darwin was mistaken in thinking man had descended from apes; rather, the human race had come from spirit beings who had arrived on earth via other planets.

When the Theosophical Society was founded its aims were to follow an unlimited inquiry after truth, encapsulating both religion and science and drawing on myths and traditions from both East and West. The Society aimed to be free from religious dogmas and adopted the slogan 'There is no religion higher than truth'. Feminist historians have noted that the mid-to-late nineteenth century taste for spiritualism was largely a female preoccupation. It has been suggested that, finding most organizations male-dominated, the woman medium, having been barred from the accepted institutions of power, created an alternative, higher source of authority. Many of Theosophy's leaders and financial backers were initially wealthy women who found much in its teaching to empower them and offer them a sense of personal spirituality which they could not find in the church at that time. After Blavatsky's death in 1891, her successor in Theosophy's

Esoteric Section was Annie Besant, formerly an atheist and birth control campaigner. Besant would later call on 'Abdu'l-Bahá when He visited London and invite him to speak at the Society's new headquarters in the city.

Following her encounter with Theosophy, Lady Blomfield's familiar society life ceased. She now preferred to associate with people who were involved in philanthropic causes or, at least, shared her more serious interests. Just as Ethel Rosenberg's mother had instructed her daughter to watch for a great teacher who was about to be sent from God, Lady Blomfield told her offspring that a great world teacher was awaited by the enlightened of all religions and she felt that she herself would see him. Whenever a new spiritual teacher came to London she would attend lectures, hoping to find herself one step closer to – if not in the presence of – the Promised One.

The Theosophist Alfred P. Sinnett often visited the Blomfields and delighted in recounting the latest developments in the movement. There was much thrilling talk of astral conflicts between the white and black forces and Lady Blomfield would listen attentively and ask pertinent questions. However, she declined to accept everything she heard as the truth. Instead she demonstrated a wise, inward calm and simply smiled as Sinnett spoke of such wonders, the validity of which he took for granted. Lady Blomfield believed that the way Theosophy compartmentalized other worlds so rationally was somehow disenchanting but she derived pleasure from hearing the history of the lost continent of Atlantis and other stories of mythical lands and events.

Theosophy as a religious experience, however, never really satisfied Lady Blomfield, although she was fascinated by the doctrine of reincarnation until she came to understand the wider interpretation found in the Bahá'í teachings. In later years, one simple remark of 'Abdu'l-Bahá set her mind at rest on this point. He said, 'The Theosophists are mistaken in their concept of reincarnation. Why should the soul return to *this* world, when there are so *many* worlds?'

Lady Blomfield's gradual dissatisfaction with Theosophy grew from the doubt she had about the validity of its spiritualistic sources. She believed that the apparent communications from beyond were so open to fraudulent practice by charlatans that she felt impelled to turn towards the ethical aspects of religion and their practical effect on human behaviour. She began to admire the teachings of R. J. Campbell who had dared to write a book called *The New Theology*, which was considered fearless and radical in its day. But more significantly, she had a great and deep respect for the interpretation of Christianity given by Basil Wilberforce, the then Archdeacon of Westminster. Every Sunday she would take her daughters to St John's, Westminster to hear him preach. That building would later be the scene of one of the most extraordinary events in the history of the Bahá'í Faith in Britain when Wilberforce would welcome 'Abdu'l-Bahá personally to address his congregation.

Basil Wilberforce, who had been made Archdeacon of Westminster in 1900 after 23 years of service at St Mary's in Southampton and then later as Chaplain to the House of Commons, had come to be regarded as a spiritual teacher of the highest order. As the son of the Bishop of Winchester and the grandson of Samuel Wilberforce, the freer of slaves, he was a staunch Liberal, although he had no sympathy with party politics. In his position as Archdeacon, he was regarded as having brought a new light to the church, transforming the old doctrines into living realities, something which must have clearly appealed to Lady Blomfield in her quest for a religion of ethics and action. As a churchman in the post-Darwin age, Wilberforce understood the intellectual difficulties and honest doubts of many of his contemporaries and attempted to demonstrate the spiritual significance of such doctrines as the atonement, the trinity and the resurrection which he believed had been lost in academic interpretations which failed to satisfy the mind or touch the soul. He also decried the materialism that had crept into the life of the church and chose to mix freely with all manner of people from poets to statesmen, from scientists to actors. Mrs Wilberforce too was renowned as a skilled hostess who had mastered the art of blending widely differing personalities into sociable and harmonious company.

Since the 1870s Wilberforce had supported women's suffrage, regarding it as absurd that women could not claim the full rights of citizens. However, he believed the behaviour of the suffragette movement to be deeply damaging, stating that violence in any form was a departure from the kind of sane petitioning by which he believed women could win the vote. It is understandable how Wilberforce could become such a revered and well-loved acquaintance of Lady Blomfield, with whom he shared interests and ideals. They began to meet often, as well as to correspond. Along with Sir Edwin Arnold, the Archdeacon became her most trusted friend – that is, until she heard of the Bahá'í Movement and encountered the truest possible Friend.

So it was that in 1907, eight years after her husband's passing and the beginning of her quest for spiritual truth, Lady Blomfield found herself in Paris, accompanied by her daughter Mary and attending a reception at the home of Madame Lucien Monod. It was there that she and Mary encountered a tall, graceful girl with shining dark eyes by the name of Bertha Herbert, who was also a guest at the reception.[96]

'If I *look* happy, it is because I *am* happy,' were the words that Miss Herbert announced to the room, immediately capturing the attention of the Blomfields.

The young woman continued, 'I have found the desire of my heart!' The statement must have struck an instant chord in Lady Blomfield, whose own search had been going on for so long. Miss Herbert crossed the room and seated herself between Lady Blomfield and her daughter. Recalling that life-changing moment in her book, *The Chosen Highway*, Lady Blomfield explains how Miss Herbert offered to tell them why she was so elated. On expressing their desire to know more, Miss Herbert exclaimed,

It is true! True! We have been taught to believe that a great
Messenger would again be sent to the world: He would set
forth to gather together all the peoples of good will in every
race, nation, and religion on the earth. Now is the appointed
time! He has come! He has come!

Lady Blomfield later wrote,

These amazing words struck a chord to which my inner
consciousness instantly responded, and I felt convinced that
the portentous announcement they conveyed was indeed the
truth. Great awe and intense exaltation possessed me with
an overpowering force as I listened.

Miss Herbert explained to them that Bahá'u'lláh, who she
referred to as 'the Bearer of the Message', had suffered much
persecution and had left the world in 1892 but that His Son
was still a captive in the fortress prison of 'Akká in Palestine.
Lady Blomfield was enthralled. 'The news of the momentous
event,' she recalled, 'long prayed for, steadfastly awaited in
the "Faith, which is the substance of things hoped for", had
come.'

Miss Herbert informed them that there was a lady in Paris
who had 'just returned' from a visit to 'Akká, who had had
the privilege of speaking with 'Abbás Effendi. Sensing her
listeners' great interest, Miss Herbert offered to make an
appointment so that the Blomfields could make the acquaintance of Ethel Jenner Rosenberg. Leaving to go, Bertha
Herbert headed for the door only to realize that, in her
enthusiasm, she had forgotten to note down the Blomfields's
names and address!

The appointment was made. Lady Sara Louisa Blomfield
and her daughter Mary were introduced to Ethel Rosenberg
and Hippolyte Dreyfus who, delighted by the interest shown
by such prominent society women, spent much time explaining to them the Mission of Bahá'u'lláh. Thus, in Paris, a
relationship was born that would sustain and strengthen the
British Bahá'í Movement in its very earliest, formative years.
The Blomfields returned to London having promised that

they would attend the meetings being held at the Higher
Thought Centre by Ethel and Mrs Thornburgh-Cropper.
There, enlightened by the understanding and inspired by the
staunchness of those two devoted souls, they met together
to make plans to spread the glad tidings of the Advent of the
Day of God throughout London and the rest of the British
Isles.

8

The Opening of the Way

Make thou mention of this Day and magnify that which hath appeared therein. It will in truth suffice all mankind . . . It behoveth thee to speak forth in such wise as to set the hearts of true believers ablaze and cause their bodies to soar.[97]

Bahá'u'lláh

Discovering such sincere seekers as Lady Blomfield and her daughters was a tremendous joy for Ethel Rosenberg and Mrs Thornburgh-Cropper. Lady Blomfield's social standing would give the Bahá'í Cause a greater credibility and enable it to be taken to sections of the population where it had barely been noticed. From this time on, what could genuinely be called a 'community' began to emerge in London. Among those souls who would associate themselves with the growing Movement over the next few years were some destined to be key figures in the development of a distinctive Bahá'í community in Britain. One such believer was George Palgrave Simpson, a large, imposing bearded man, who would tirelessly serve the evolving administrative order with great distinction until his death in 1934.

Benefit was also derived from the exemplary character, experience and insights of a young Persian, Luṭfu'lláh Ḥakím, whose grandfather had been the first Jew to become a follower of Bahá'u'lláh. Ḥakím arrived in England in 1910 to study physiotherapy. After a period of service in the Holy Land he would return to England in 1920 with 'Abdu'l-Bahá's eldest grandson, Shoghi Effendi, who was to study at Oxford University. Towards the end of his life in 1963,

Ḥakím would be among the first nine distinguished believers to be elected to the international Bahá'í governing council, the Universal House of Justice.

Another young Persian studying in London, Yu'hanna Dávúd, whose marriage ceremony would be conducted by the Master in London in 1911, also assisted the community to develop a distinctive identity. Among those who embraced the Bahá'í teachings at this time was Eric Hammond. In 1909 he compiled a selection of Bahá'í scriptures entitled *The Splendour of God*, which was published in the popular Wisdom of the East series. The book included an introduction to Bahá'í scriptures, remarks on specific works and an overview of Bahá'í belief.

The satisfaction of witnessing a genuine flourishing of activities in London was offset for Ethel by the death of her mother at the end of 1907. Hannah Rosenberg had spent the last years of her life in the Cornish village of Lelant, close to St Ives, where she lived with Ethel's younger sister, Gertrude – also a painter who regularly exhibited her work in the local area and who had shown two paintings at the Royal Academy. Ethel had unquestioningly taken on board the Bahá'í teachings about life after death and saw her mother's passing as nothing less than a wonderful transition, 'going home', as she put it.[98] Her attitude of thankfulness, faith, hope and confidence was conveyed in letters to friends around the world. One touching response came from Thornton Chase, who assured her of the sympathies of the Chicago believers. 'Surely the fear of death so implanted in the human,' he wrote, 'is only to guard us all from rushing to its embrace under the difficulties of life, rather than remaining in the open field of earthly existence and fighting our battle to its proper end. If we could see the reality within that seeming dissolution, we have been told that we should then so long to fly away that our usefulness here would end.'[99]

Ethel was particularly keen to take advantage of the increasing amount of Bahá'í literature now becoming available in the United States. She ordered new publications from the Chicago Publishing Society and was most pleased with a collection of pilgrims' notes by Julia Grundy entitled *Ten Days in the Light of Acca*. Ethel encouraged Thornton Chase to publish his own recollections of pilgrimage but he was reluctant to do so, believing that the limited financial resources of the community should be reserved for publishing more necessary works of scripture. Such publishing ventures were funded solely by the contributions of believers and not one Bahá'í publication had yet made sufficient money to cover its printing costs. The friends were adamant about giving literature away to seekers free of charge and the prices put on the publications did not allow sufficient margin for this practice nor for the postage costs to other countries. On Ethel's insistence, and assisted by a financial contribution from the London Bahá'ís, Chase's memories were published under the title *In Galilee*. Initially a well-illustrated edition of two thousand copies was printed at the cost of $350.

The American Bahá'ís had been blessed in having amongst them Ali Kuli Khan, sent by the Master to act as a translator for Mírzá Abu'l-Faḍl on his teaching journey to the West. Ethel had previously met the young Khan in 'Akká and had begun to work with him on translations as her command of the Persian language and his English improved. Khan was by now actively involved in translating some of Bahá'u'lláh's most important works, a formidable task for anyone to tackle. Through his efforts however, Bahá'u'lláh's mystical treatise *The Seven Valleys* was made available in English, as were the Tablets of Ishráqát (Splendours) and Ṭarázát (Ornaments). Khan's daughter Marzieh Gail has related the difficulties early Bahá'í translators had in rendering the scriptures from Arabic or Persian into English. For example, in *The Hidden Words*, Bahá'u'lláh's warning to the peoples of the world that 'grievous retribution awaiteth you' was originally circulated to the Western believers as 'a great eagle' awaiteth you. In Persian, the short vowels are not used, so the word *'iqáb* (retribution) is not distinguishable on the page from *'uqáb* (eagle).[100] Accounts of visits to the

Holy Land, such as *The Life and Teachings of Abbas Effendi* by Myron Phelps, which were widely available, also contained a large number of historical and doctrinal inaccuracies. It is no wonder, then, that the early Western Bahá'ís were often not entirely clear about the teachings they had embraced and found themselves clashing with each other over interpretation. The 1908 publication in London by Kegan, Paul, Trench, Trubner and Company of Laura Barney's *Some Answered Questions* did much to clear matters up and was warmly welcomed by the friends. Albert Windust of the Chicago Publishing Society wrote to Ethel praising her for her assistance in putting it together in English for publication. The Society also called upon her to revise its edition of *The Seven Valleys* ready for a second imprint.

The London believers made the effort to host their gatherings on the same days as their counterparts in the United States in order to give themselves the sense of belonging to a worldwide movement. The regular community gathering now known to the Bahá'ís as the Nineteen Day Feast was very much in its infancy and the friends satisfied themselves with gathering together to read the holy scriptures, to listen perhaps to a short talk or presentation and then enjoy refreshments together. There was no formal consultation section to the meeting as there is today, as at that time there were, of course, no formally elected Bahá'í institutions to guide the affairs of the community.

The thoughts of the believers at this time turned often to the Master with whom correspondence had been suddenly cut off. On 3 March 1908 Thornton Chase wrote to Ethel asking whether she had learned anything of the situation in 'Akká. 'We all pray that the times of great trouble will not descend upon the Beloved,' wrote Chase. 'Yet "God doeth what He willeth" and we can only say with firm accord "Thy Will be Done."'[101] The precarious situation in the Ottoman Empire had encouraged the Covenant-breakers to take advantage of the Sultan's fears for his crumbling dominion and to launch a new wave of slanderous rumours against

'Abdu'l-Bahá. A four-member commission from Constantinople arrived in the Holy Land in the winter of 1907 and
immediately dismissed officials in 'Akká who were friendly
to the Master. Spies were again placed around His house and
even the poor who regularly received alms on a Friday ceased
coming. Rumours abounded that 'Abdu'l-Bahá was to be
banished to Tripolitania, a vast expanse of desert where He
would surely die in isolation. 'Abdu'l-Bahá, however, seemingly unperturbed, continued His duties and was seen planting trees and vines and repairing His house.

The Covenant-breakers were ecstatic with the response
of the Ottoman regime and for a whole month were convinced that the demise of the Master was imminent. His
construction work on the Báb's Tomb on Mount Carmel was
under scrutiny and the fabricated stories that it was in fact
a fortress were believed by the Commission. 'Abdu'l-Bahá's
supporters rallied round Him. In one instance an Italian who
acted as Consul for Spain drove to 'Akká and begged the
Master to escape in an Italian cargo boat that had been
commissioned to take Him to any port He chose. 'Abdu'l-
Bahá politely refused to leave His family and responsibilities
behind.

Then one night the boat that had brought the Commission
to Haifa was seen sailing towards 'Akká. At that moment the
whole town believed that 'Abdu'l-Bahá was about to be
arrested and taken from their midst. Yet the Master was seen
to be calmly walking about without fear in the courtyard of
His house. Suddenly, the boat changed direction and made
for the open sea. Shortly afterwards news was received that
the Sultan had narrowly escaped death in a bomb blast. A
revolution was underway in Turkey which greatly occupied
the Sultan's time and the file on 'Abdu'l-Bahá was pushed
aside. On 23 July 1908 the Young Turk Revolution prompted
Sultán 'Abdu'l-Hamíd to set all of his political and religious
prisoners free. Amongst them were 'Abdu'l-Bahá, His family
and His followers. After forty years in the fetid atmosphere
of the penal colony of 'Akká, Abdu'l-Bahá was released from
captivity.

The unexpected release of 'Abdu'l-Bahá appeared to influence the British and American Bahá'í communities, both of which experienced an upsurge in activity. It was at first unclear to the believers whether the freedom granted 'Abdu'l-Bahá by Turkey also signified His freedom from any Persian restriction. Ethel attempted to get news from the Holy Land but it was some time before the full details of the events that had transpired in 'Akká became clear. Nevertheless the Bahá'ís felt that they were on the verge of a larger awakening and dissemination of the Truth. Thornton Chase told Ethel how he had attended six meetings in one week in Seattle, with an average attendance of 25 seekers. In Portland he had given nine meetings in a week with average audiences of 40, and on one night as many as 70 seekers attended. 'The Spirit of God is doing His work in every plane of life,' Chase enthused, 'and all men are becoming His servants altho' in ignorance of the fact. Indeed it behooves us, the banner bearers, to rest not, but to keep at the head of this great procession of discovery and revealing of hidden things, which is marching gloriously in the marvelous Light of His Revelation.'[102]

From 27 July until 1 August 1908 Ethel represented the London Bahá'ís at the Seventeenth Universal Peace Congress held in London at the Caxton Hall. Ethel found the meeting most interesting and wrote to a friend that she had learnt much about the progress of peace in the world. She was also invited to present a paper on 'Bahaism: Its Ethical and Social Teachings' at the Third International Congress for the History of Religions. An account of her address was published in the London *Post* and the paper itself was subsequently published in the Congress's *Transactions*.

Ethel's address clearly demonstrated an evolution in her thinking about the true mission of the Bahá'í Cause. She began her lecture with the words of 'Abdu'l-Bahá that religion 'is the necessary connection which emanates from the reality of things; and as the Universal Manifestations of God are aware of the mysteries of beings, therefore they understand this essential connection, and by their knowledge establish the Law of God'.[103] In her first paragraph she openly and boldly announced Bahá'u'lláh's claim to be the Universal Manifestation of God who had brought Bahaism – a great world religion which had taken rise in their own era. Alluding to the increase and influence of socialist thinking in Britain and elsewhere, Ethel linked the changes in the world with the coming of Bahá'u'lláh, stating:

> ... all Europe is now watching with interest this awakening and reform which was promulgated and foreseen so many years ago by Bahá'u'lláh. He even anticipated and foreshadowed the spiritual and material reforms now taking place among the western nations ... Most thinkers acknowledge this present time in which we are now living to be a period of great spiritual unrest, of deep searching after truth, and of intense desire for a re-statement of the fundamental realities of religion in terms harmonizing with the needs and aspirations of our particular age and that shall satisfy the deepest longings and desires of the hearts and spirits of men. Bahá'u'lláh claims to have answered this need ...[104]

Ethel's address covered the history of the Movement from the Declaration of the Báb through to its spread to the Western world. She spoke of the first Bahá'í House of Worship in the West which was being planned for Chicago and mentioned the near completion of another such building in 'Ishqábád in Russian Turkistán. Ethel also outlined a broad range of Bahá'u'lláh's Teachings designed to meet 'the practical and social needs of our time'[105] and introduced His plan for an administrative order which demonstrated her already deep understanding of principles which many of the believers would take decades to grasp:

> Each body or community of believers is to elect a council called ... House of Justice from among those of its members who are most respected for their upright life, good character and intelligence. There is also to be established a General House of Justice for each nation, and besides this, a Universal House of Justice, consisting of members elected to

represent every nation, which will form a kind of permanent board of arbitration and conciliation to which all international disagreements and difficulties are to be submitted and whose decisions must be accepted by all Bahá'ís as final and authoritative.[106]

Before concluding her presentation with extracts from the holy writings, she emphasized that Bahá'u'lláh taught His followers 'that the first necessity for them is to associate with men of every race and religion in the spirit of true brotherhood, love and sympathy'.[107] Ethel, accompanied by the prominent international Bahá'í travel-teacher Charles Mason Remey, repeated the lecture in Oxford a few weeks later and received a very positive response.

Although she heroically continued to carry out her pioneering activities, Ethel's health once again began to deteriorate, difficulties with her nerves adding to the distress already caused by the ongoing problems with her chest and eyesight. She decided to leave London for the winter to visit Paris and Marseilles, and if she could manage the journey, to continue on to the Holy Land to see her now liberated Master. The journey even to the French capital was an arduous one for Ethel and she fell severely ill in Paris. Nevertheless by January 1909 she had mustered up the energy to face the sea voyage to Egypt and arrived for the third time in the Holy Land.

Since 1907 'Abdu'l-Bahá, despite His confinement, had gradually been transferring His family and their affairs to Haifa, across the bay from 'Akká, at the foot of Mount Carmel. At the time of Ethel's arrival, the Shrine of the Báb was almost completed. It was a simple rectangular building of six rooms, with a vault beneath where on the first day of the Bahá'í New Year (21 March) 1909, 'Abdu'l-Bahá would finally lay to rest the shattered remains of His Father's martyred Prophet-Herald, some 60 years after they had been rescued from the foul moat outside Tabríz where they had been unceremoniously discarded.

For Ethel, this pilgrimage was the first occasion she was

to spend any length of time in Haifa, a town that had been
blessed by the footsteps of Bahá'u'lláh and which was destined to become the international centre of a world-embrac-
ing religious community. Ethel found the Master tired but
in good spirits. The great burden of His incarceration had
been lifted and He was now able to pursue fully the immense
tasks entrusted to Him by Bahá'u'lláh. The following year,
1910, He would transfer His residence to Haifa, marking the
first stage in the establishment the world administrative and
spiritual centre of the Cause in that city.

This short visit was no less valuable than previous pil-
grimages in regenerating Ethel's spirit and reinvigorating
her physical condition. The growth of the Cause was uppermost in her mind and she asked 'Abdu'l-Bahá what could be
done to increase the number of believers and to make the
work more effective. He replied that the only thing to do was
to ensure that the members of the groups loved each other
very much and were devoted friends. The more they loved
each other, the more the meetings would attract and draw
others; and the more they loved, the more their influence
would be felt. He said all people must be considered to be
good – not just the believers – and He hoped everyone would
be good.

He added, 'I say this for you in English. I do not often do
that; but I say also in English, that you may understand how
much I mean it, that love is the foundation of everything and
that all must be good.' While looking from the window
'Abdu'l-Bahá said,

> We hear the murmur of the sea always continuing. It never
> ceases. Were it to cease, the world would be dead, stagnant,
> lifeless. But the waves of the mind of man are far greater
> than those of the sea; they also are ceaseless. They never
> stop for one instant. This movement is good. If these waves
> of the mind are few, the man is dull and quiet. What pearls
> and jewels are contained in the depths of the sea! But the
> pearls and jewels hidden in the mind of man are the knowl-
> edge, virtues, capabilities . . . These pearls can grow and

increase in lustre forever, but the pearls of the sea remain always the same. These waves from our minds go forth and create movement and thought in other minds. From one strong thought of love what great results may be produced![108]

'Abdu'l-Bahá was, as always, full of sympathy for Ethel's testing living conditions and one statement He made to the pilgrims may have been directed specifically towards her:

If any troubles or vicissitudes come into your lives – if your heart is depressed on account of health, livelihood or vocation, let not these things affect you. These things should not cause unhappiness. Heavenly food has he prepared for you; everlasting glory has he bestowed upon you. Therefore these Glad Tidings should cause you to soar in the atmosphere of joy forever and ever. You must render thanks unto God forever so that the confirmations of God may encircle you all.[109]

Refreshed and renewed, Ethel returned from the Holy Land, rededicated to service and ready to begin work on her own introductory booklet on the Bahá'í Movement. Little did she suspect that within just two years the Master would Himself be in her own home in London, bringing His Father's message in person to the peoples of the West.

9

A Brief Account
of the Bahá'í Movement

*Whatever is written should not transgress the bounds
of tact and wisdom, and in the words used there
should lie hid the property of milk, so that the children
of the world may be nurtured therewith, and attain
maturity.*[110]

Bahá'u'lláh

Much of Ethel Rosenberg's time during the year 1910 was
spent working on her own concise exposition of the Bahá'í
teachings which would, in due course, come to be published
and widely used in the teaching work of the British Bahá'ís.
A Brief Account of the Bahai Movement was published 'for
the Bahai Society of London'[111] by the Priory Press in Hampstead in collaboration with J. M. Watkins, 21 Cecil Court,
St Martins Lane in London. The small, green booklet was
sold for just one penny.

The work is as comprehensive an account of the history
and basic teachings of the Movement as could be produced
at that time when there was no authoritatively translated
scripture. Not surprisingly, Ethel drew heavily on her own
pilgrim's notes where published texts were unavailable to
substantiate her arguments. Her deep grasp and commitment to the fundamental Bahá'í teachings is apparent from
the conviction with which she wrote. There are, inevitably,
certain small inaccuracies and the common interpretations
peculiar to the early believers which differ from those later
expounded by Shoghi Effendi, who would be appointed the

authorized interpreter of the Bahá'í scripture in 'Abdu'l-Bahá's will.

Ethel begins her brief account, aimed at a predominately Christian audience, with an overview of the time in which she was writing. She states that many believe that the twentieth century is witnessing the dawn of a new spiritual epoch or era. This renewal of spirit is being felt in churches and in the religious and social life of all lands. This spirit of renewal, she says, is in harmony with the teachings of the Bahá'ís and of their 'Great Leaders, now represented by Abdul Baha the "Servant of God" known to the outside world as Abbas Effendi'.[112] To give the Movement authenticity in the mind of the reader, she immediately links it with the Holy Land saying that 'once again, the Light is shining forth from that land . . . for have not its valleys and hills been trodden from the beginning by the feet of those great Messengers inspired of God – Abraham, Elijah, and last and greatest, Jesus of Nazareth? Is it strange that once more in this century of ours, in this "the cradle of the race", those that were sitting "in darkness have seen a great light", the light of the Sun of Righteousness that rises with healing in his wings?'[113] The Prophet Muḥammad is conspicuous by His exclusion from the entire pamphlet. It is possible that Ethel did not wish to alienate readers by demanding of them the recognition of a religion that was treated with deep mistrust and suspicion by the Christian world.

Not surprisingly, 'Abdu'l-Bahá is given the greatest prominence throughout the work. Immediately Ethel introduces Him as the 'great teacher'.[114] In establishing a context for examining the teachings as they were understood at that time, she embarks upon a generally accurate history of the Faith beginning with the story of the Báb and His teachings as preparing the way for a great religious movement 'destined to quicken the Western World as it is now quickening the east, and to bring the two into unity and harmony'.[115] She pays attention to the 'especially sacred'[116] number 19, explaining that the Báb was the nineteenth member of a hierarchy known as the Letters of the Living and that Bahá'u'lláh declared Himself to be the promised Manifestation 19 years after the Báb had declared His mission. The Báb is presented as the forerunner – an understanding common amongst the Western Bahá'ís of the period – rather than as a Manifestation of God in His own right and co-founder of the Faith. Ethel's historical account ends with her visit in 1901 to the Holy Land where 'Abdu'l-Bahá was superintending the construction of the Tomb of the Báb which, she states, 'is also probably destined to be the resting-place of Baha'u'llah, as well as, eventually that of Abdul Baha. It will also be a House of Praise and meeting place for the Friends from all parts of the world.'[117]

The booklet then goes on to outline the distinct features of the Movement, such as the acceptance of the great world Teachers or Prophets as 'Manifestations' of the one divine Light, the one Holy Spirit of God. They are, Ethel writes, 'one in essence, though their teachings may differ in detail owing to the various conditions and needs of the peoples and nations to whom they are sent'.[118] Bahá'u'lláh fulfils the prophecies of the Báb – in the Book of Isaiah the word 'Bahá' is rendered 'the Glory of the Lord'. The appointment of 'Abdu'l-Bahá 'thus completes this marvellous triad of Prophets'.[119] Four signs demonstrate to the world the authenticity of such Prophets. First, they appear at a time of dire need in the history of the world. Second, they are exemplary in their conduct and service to humanity. Third, their utterance is the 'thought of God',[120] so powerful that its quality is felt at once. Finally, the Prophet is known by His power which can 'transform the minds and souls of those who seek his help, that it is acknowledged without recourse to proof by miracles'.[121]

Ethel's strongest arguments concern the question of whether Christianity, which 'teaches the brotherhood of all mankind, and love and compassion to the highest degree',[122] can realize the establishment of a universal world consciousness. She suggests that:

. . . a practical bond of union is needed between East and West, some common meeting ground for the Christian, the Mohammedan, the Buddhist, etc.: which will *create* the sense of "brotherhood" and make of it a realized experience. To sit at Abdul Baha's table, in his simple home, with Christians, Mohammedans, Jews, and those of other faiths, all of them breathing forth the spirit of living brotherhood, is a privilege not readily forgotten.[123]

Ethel then expounds upon Bahá'u'lláh's teachings on universal education, the equality of men and women, and that every follower should practise some trade, art or profession beneficial to society. 'It takes but little reflection to see what a revolution it would cause in present conditions if this command were followed, and how many present-day difficulties would be solved by these simple regulations.'[124] She goes on to discuss mendicancy, hermitism, marriage – 'the highest estate for man – in contradistinction to other faiths which have taught that the celibate state was the highest'[125] – the prohibition of war and strife, and the administration of 'the faith' (the first time she refers to the Bahá'í Movement in this way) by elected bodies of councils called Houses of Justice.

The book finishes with a compilation of prayers and extracts from Tablets including Bahá'u'lláh's popular prayer for unity in the exact translation that is still used today. Ethel concludes her dissertation with the statement: 'The power of this teaching which is rather a widening of the basis of our faith than a "new religion" is seen by the enormous increase of its adherents year by year, without any organization which can be called a proselytizing body.'[126]

A final interesting feature of the book is an advertisement for the other publications recommended to seekers at that time. Four works of Bahá'u'lláh are listed: the translation of *The Hidden Words* bound together with various 'communes' and prayers sold for sixpence; *The Seven Valleys* was available for one penny, as was 'The Tablet of Ishrakat' (sic) and 'The Tarazat' (sic), which cost tuppence. Of 'Abdu'l-

Bahá's works only *Some Answered Questions* is recommended at a costly four shillings. The rest are largely collections of pilgrims' notes – those by Thornton Chase, Myron Phelps and Julia Grundy – and introductory works by Chase, Sydney Sprague and Eric Hammond. One pamphlet provided a transcript of an address on the Bahá'í Movement by Tammaddun'ul-Mulk – a young Persian student who was visiting London from Paris – given at the City Temple on 16 October 1910. The most expensive of all the books being advertised was a deluxe boxed volume of *God's Heroes*, a poetic drama about the early history of the Movement by Laura Clifford Barney which sold for twelve shillings and sixpence.

At the time of the publication of Ethel's booklet, the Bahá'ís of London were clearly beginning to organize more formally, perhaps inspired by news from Chicago of various administrative institutions that had been established to carry out specific tasks including publishing. Ethel was now the 'Hon. Secretary of the Bahai meetings'[127] and seekers who had been interested by her book were encouraged to write to her for more information at the address of the Higher Thought Centre at 10 Cheniston Gardens, Wrights Lane off High Street, Kensington.

The time was rapidly approaching, however, when the London believers would lose their monopoly on Bahá'í meetings in Britain. A community was about to evolve in another part of the country, a development in which, not surprisingly, Ethel Rosenberg was to play a significant role.

10

A Community Evolves

They who are the beloved of God, in whatever place they gather and whomsoever they may meet, must evince, in their attitude towards God, and in the manner of their celebration of His praise and glory, such humility and submissiveness that every atom of the dust beneath their feet may attest the depth of their devotion.[128]

Bahá'u'lláh

The sense of being part of an increasingly international Bahá'í community was greatly enhanced for the Bahá'ís in London when they began to receive the ground-breaking new publication *Bahai News* – later to become *Star of the West* – which was sent to them from Chicago. First published on the Bahá'í New Year – 21 March – 1910, the magazine was the first publication to make widely available recently revealed Tablets of 'Abdu'l-Bahá as well as reports of Bahá'í activities from around the world. Such reports included the latest developments in the plan to raise the first Bahá'í House of Worship in the West, stories of community life in Persia and accounts of teaching victories for the Cause as far afield as Mandalay and Hawaii.

The steadily growing band of believers in London were swift to make good use of this new organ and began to contribute regular reports giving details of their wide-ranging activities. In issue six, for example, they reported that two of the British believers, Miss Buckton and Miss Schepel, had returned from a few weeks in 'Akká and were inspiring the community with the latest news from the Holy Land. Miss Buckton belonged to many clubs in London and interest in her journey meant that the Bahá'í teachings reached many souls who otherwise would not have heard of them. Other news included the visit to London of Hippolyte Dreyfus, who had addressed a regular gathering of believers held at Ethel's house on a Friday evening. Another, perhaps slightly more exotic, visitor was Khosroe Bohman from Burma, who enchanted the friends with his 'beautiful expositions' of the Cause. One of the believers, a Dr Fisher, had held two afternoon feasts at his attractive studio in Trentishoe Mansions, drawing many friends from as far afield as Eastbourne on the Sussex coast, Hornsey, Surrey and Essex. The report states that Dr Fisher had also been giving a series of lectures on *The Seven Valleys*. The report goes on to note that the British Bahá'ís were regularly receiving letters and literature from prominent American Bahá'ís, including Isabella Brittingham and Roy Wilhelm. The Assembly, the report reads, was 'splendidly harmonious and growing healthily'.[129] For Ethel, who had first encountered the Bahá'í Teachings more than a decade before, such an upturn in the community's fortunes must have been greatly encouraging.

An extremely important figure who gained prominence amongst the circle of Bahá'í sympathizers during this period was Wellesley Tudor Pole. In later years, he would be largely responsible for saving the lives of 'Abdu'l-Bahá and His family at a time of great danger for them.

Tudor Pole was of Welsh ancestry, descended on his mother's side from Squire Tudor of Pembrokeshire, the fierce Welsh patriot who did all in his power to prevent the English from conquering Wales during the reign of Henry II. Wellesley, born in 1884, was the fourth of five children. At an early age he experienced a number of mystical occurrences, such as seeing the 'colour of prayers'[130] rising up in churches. When he was in his late teenage years he suffered from a serious illness – possibly typhoid or diphtheria – and later remembered being outside of his body. At public school Wellesley clashed on a number of occasions with his schoolmasters over their insistence that the King James' Authorized English version of the Bible was the established Word of God.

Wellesley first heard of the Bahá'ís while in Constantinople in 1908 and later discussed the Movement with some of the London believers and with Professor Edward Granville Browne of Cambridge University, who had enjoyed the rare privilege of meeting Bahá'u'lláh Himself. Tudor Pole was fascinated by 'Abdu'l-Bahá's apparent ability to exert a powerful influence from within the walls of a prison and was determined to meet Him. The young Wellesley was also attracted by the notion that the Bahá'í teachings enabled 'every follower of earlier world beliefs to obtain a fuller understanding of the religion with which he already stands identified and to acquire a clear apprehension of its purpose'.[131] In 1910 Tudor Pole realized his ambition when he met the Master – who was accompanied by His thirteen-year-old grandson Shoghi Effendi – in Alexandria where, during a nine-day visit, he was able to present 'Abdu'l-Bahá with gifts from the English believers.

Tudor Pole had travelled from Marseilles on the steamer *The Sphinx* and intended to return overland via Damascus, Smyrna, Constantinople and Vienna. His return ticket and reservations had all been arranged before he left London. Arriving in Egypt, he wasted no time in visiting 'Abdu'l-Bahá. He found Him looking strong and vigorous. Wellesley spoke no Persian and had only rudimentary Arabic so their conversation was carried on through Shoghi Effendi, who acted as an interpreter. At one point, when their young translator was called away, 'Abdu'l-Bahá continued the conversation in His own language yet Tudor Pole miraculously found himself replying. When Shoghi Effendi returned, Tudor Pole's ability to understand the Master ceased. To be certain that he had understood correctly, he asked for a translation of what 'Abdu'l-Bahá had been saying in Shoghi Effendi's absence and this confirmed the fact that he had been able to comprehend and reply accurately in a language of which he was completely ignorant. A few years later while

'Abdu'l-Bahá was visiting Paris, Tudor Pole once again experienced the same phenomenon.

The Master astounded Tudor Pole with His prophetic insights. 'Abdu'l-Bahá anticipated a worldwide upheaval to be preceded by a European war within the ensuing five years. He claimed the seeds for this conflict had already been sown in the Balkans and that this lengthy period of war and revolutions embodied what could be interpreted as becoming the Armageddon prophesied to take place at the end of this present age or dispensation. Without elaborating on the matter, 'Abdu'l-Bahá told Tudor Pole that he was destined to play a particular role in human affairs. He also spoke of His high expectations of the Bahá'í friends in England.

Wellesley asked the Master for a blessing for his return journey. This He gave, adding casually that he should return to Marseilles the following day on the same steamer from which he had disembarked. Wellesley explained that he had made arrangements to go overland but Shoghi Effendi said to him that if the Master said he had to return to Marseilles then that was what would happen. Tudor Pole saw no good reason for changing his plans and suffered a restless night wondering what to do. The next morning, returning to bid farewell to the Master, Tudor Pole surprised even himself by telling 'Abdu'l-Bahá that he would be going back to Marseilles on *The Sphinx*. 'Abdu'l-Bahá asked him to carry out a task for Him in Paris. He said that Wellesley should meet the Persian student Tammaddun'ul-Mulk, who was almost blind, and gave Tudor Pole ten pounds in gold to pay for this young man's fare to Alexandria. He was to tell Mulk to lose no time and to present himself to the Master as soon as he arrived. 'Abdu'l-Bahá had no address for Mulk to give Tudor Pole.

On reaching Paris, Wellesley went to the Persian Consulate but no one had heard about Mulk. Tudor Pole then visited the student quarter on the left bank of the Seine and spent the whole day there searching with no success. He gave up and set out for the Gare du Nord where his luggage was already deposited. Crossing the Seine by the Pont Royale, he looked across the road and saw among a crowd of pedestrians a young man of Eastern appearance using a stick to tap his way along. Tudor Pole dodged his way through the traffic and accosted him, asking whether he was Persian and if he knew a certain Tammaddun'ul-Mulk.

'C'est moi,' replied the young man, adding that he had only arrived in Paris that morning from Vienna where he had undergone three unsuccessful operations on his eyes. He had been told that his sight could not be saved. Tudor Pole passed on 'Abdu'l-Bahá's message and the ten pounds. He later learned that on Mulk's reaching Alexandria, 'Abdu'l-Bahá had poured a few drops of attar of roses into a glass of water and had anointed Mulk's eyes. Immediately his sight was restored. He enjoyed perfect vision for years to come. Tudor Pole arrived back in England to find that he was in time to avert a very serious crisis in his affairs which he would have not been able to deal with had he taken the overland journey.[132]

Towards the end of 1910, Wellesley Tudor Pole recalled his meeting with the Master in an article entitled 'A Wonderful Movement in the East', which was published in the newspaper *The Christian Commonwealth*. This account of his extraordinary experiences with 'Abdu'l-Bahá as well as some basic introductory comments about the Bahá'í Movement was followed by a letter to the newspaper's editor from 'Abdu'l-Bahá Himself, who enclosed some extracts from the sayings of Bahá'u'lláh illustrating the universality of the Bahá'í outlook. These articles were reprinted in *Bahai News* to whose readers Tudor Pole reported that the Bahá'í Movement was 'beginning to take a more serious hold on public attention . . . and that during the next few weeks a number of meetings are to be held in London, Bristol and in the North, which are likely to produce far-reaching results'.[133] A Bahá'í paper was also to be read at the Universal Races Congress due to be held in London the following July.

Tudor Pole's comments were not an exaggeration. There

seemed to be a tangible change in the receptivity of English people towards the Bahá'í teachings. A Bahá'í reading room was opened at 137a Kensington High Street and on 31 December 1910, in the nearby Higher Thought Centre, at the regular meeting organized by Ethel Rosenberg and Mrs Thornburgh-Cropper, Tudor Pole spoke of his visit to 'Abdu'l-Bahá. It was the largest Bahá'í gathering yet held in London. Wellesley told the meeting that he believed 1911 would be a year of very great importance and that London would be the focus point for great events. He hoped that among the congresses, conferences and imperial gatherings to be held, there would be a great Bahá'í congress attended by delegates from all parts of the world. The time had come, Tudor Pole said, for the establishment of an international residential and social club open to all comers without distinction of race, creed or sex. He urged the members of his audience to do all in their power to work together in unity and peace.

In the final few months of 1910, while the activities of the Bahá'í community in London were gaining much more momentum, Ethel Rosenberg once again emerged as a key player in another historic development in the progress of the Bahá'í Cause in the British Isles: the birth of the Bahá'í community of Manchester.

Towards the end of October, Tudor Pole received a letter from a Mr Edward Theodore Hall who was, by his own description, a continual seeker and an omnivorous reader. Hall's abiding interest lay in the ideals of world fellowship and a world religion but he was dissatisfied with the churches in his locality and the various movements he had investigated. He had not heard of the Bahá'í Movement until he had read a letter from Tudor Pole which had also appeared in the *Christian Commonwealth*. Hall wrote to Tudor Pole asking for further information.

The request was passed on to Ethel, who sent Hall a package of Bahá'í literature. After reading the materials, Hall and his wife became very interested in the Bahá'í Movement and immediately passed the literature on to Mr and Mrs John Craven, close relatives of theirs who also turned out to be extremely receptive to the teachings. They asked Ethel if there were any other Bahá'ís in Manchester but Ethel could only inform them of a Miss Ridgeway in Pendleton.

Sarah Ann Ridgeway, born in 1848, was native to Pendleton. She learned silk-weaving and spent most of her life in the United States. In 1899 Miss Ridgeway took Bahá'í lessons in Baltimore and stayed firm in her belief. By 1906 she was again in Britain, living at 16 Smith Street in Pendleton. On 10 November 1906 Mason Remey wrote to her from Washington enclosing a Tablet of 'Abdu'l-Bahá addressed to 'The Beloved of God of the Occident'.[134] Her name appears in the list of those who sent supplications from the West to the Master.

While living at her humble cottage, Miss Ridgeway continued to earn her living by working at the loom in a neighbouring factory, occupying her spare time by attending meetings and religious services. She also corresponded with her various friends, some of whom she wrote to in French. At every opportunity she shared the principles of Bahá'u'lláh through correspondence but never gathered around herself a group of believers, preferring rather to express her belief through the force of personal example in the factory or in conversations after the meetings and services she attended. She was, by Edward Hall's account, gentle and intellectual, solely animated by the Bahá'í Faith, and surrounded by friends who were humble, unassuming and unpretentious. Their reaction to her beliefs indicate that they found her unusual but they trusted and admired her good qualities.

Having received Hall's enquiry, Ethel wrote to Sarah Ridgeway and passed on Hall's address. By 12 November Miss Ridgeway was already in communication with Hall, saying how pleased she was to hear of his interest in the Movement. 'I see the beauties of ceasing wars and the dawn of Universal Peace', she wrote, 'and the unity of Religions.

I hope that you will find that which you need in the teachings; the conditions to live the kingdom upon earth.'[135]

Through Ethel's introduction, the small group began to meet occasionally. Miss Ridgeway lent books to the Halls and, their appetite whetted, they bought what other literature they could find. In January 1911, Ethel arrived in Manchester and stayed for several days, teaching the new believers the principles and history of the Faith. During this visit she also addressed a full meeting of Theosophists. Many people were attracted to the teachings but preferred not to commit themselves to the Movement. Others were even hostile. Despite the disappointing reception, the small community continued to study its scriptures. The Halls became regular visitors to Miss Ridgeway's cottage. Edward Hall commented on the humility of her existence, describing her tiny front room with its 'warm fire burning brightly, a vase of daffodils upon the table and near it several Bahá'í books', including the same American book of coloured views of the Bahá'í Holy Places that Mrs Hearst had presented to Ethel a decade previously. 'Over the fire, upon the front of the light-brown coloured mantelpiece, were several geometrical figures which possessed, to her, mystical meanings – the central figure being a square, painted in neat, black lines.'[136] One day, when Mrs Hall asked her what this figure represented, Miss Ridgeway replied with a smile that she painted it there so that whenever she looked in that direction she would be reminded to meet life 'four square'. 'Her life', wrote Hall, 'was just like that.'[137]

Edward Hall's heart was deeply touched by the Bahá'í message. In a poem addressed to 'Abdu'l-Bahá entitled 'To Him We Love – Late Prisoner in Acca', he wrote:

Teacher benign! The words of purest worth –
That from thy lips passed through the tremulous air
Awakening music in the wistful earth
With sense of love and courage everywhere –
Have reached us here.
Be glad thy generous heart!
For here an echoing love scarce less thine own

Hath moved with fragrance sweet o'er glade and mart
And builds amain her spiritual throne.
Bless'd be the lips that thrilled the passing winds
That moved the palms where Syrian sunshine smiles
And bore the peaceful sweets to waiting minds
'Neath oak and beech in these far-distant isles!

Blessed be the soul that in thy life fulfils
The harmonious truth for happiest guidance given;
The Truth, which from the human blood distils
Such sweetness, and this glorious love of heaven.

The rugged hills, the intervening flood,
Opinions and delusions difficult to trace,
Have sever'd peoples-stirred the feverish blood,
But ONE remained the spirit of the RACE.

And now the words divine with power resound
And reach abroad where many faiths have flamed
And the thought leaps with one triumphant bound
Right unto Thee, Who hath this thing proclaimed!

Honoured be thou, whose very presence calms
The impulsive fret of jaded brain and nerve;
And blessed be they who fear not earth's alarms,
But love Thy Cause, and seek to rightly serve![138]

Edward Hall's address at 1 North Street, Higher Broughton became acknowledged as the Manchester Bahá'í Centre. Writing of the way the Teachings had touched his family's hearts, he proclaimed that the 'flame burns undimmed on these little Manchester altars.'[139]

Just as Tudor Pole had predicted, activities continued to flourish in London throughout 1911 with the believers guided and inspired by their ongoing correspondence with the Master, who had left the Holy Land to reside in Egypt. In one Tablet, addressed in May 1911, Abdu'l-Bahá wrote:

O ye sons and daughters of the Kingdom!
Your letter which was written by heavenly inspiration, whose contents and meanings are full of interest, and whose discrimination springs from hearts that shine, has been

received. Of a truth, the believers of London, being steadfast servants, stand firm. They shall not slacken, nor, in the lapse of time, shall their light grow dim. For they are Bahais, children of Heaven and of the light of the Godhead. Surely, without doubt they shall be the cause of spreading God's Word, and the channel for spreading the Divine Teachings and bringing about the unity and equality of mankind.

It is easy to accept the Kingdom, but it is difficult to endure therein for the tests are hard and heavy. On all occasions the English are firm and are not turned aside, being neither prone to begin a matter for a little while nor ready to abandon it for a little reason through failing in zeal. Verily in every undertaking they show firmness.

Though you dwell in the West, praise be to God, you have heard the Divine Call from the East, and like unto Moses you have become warmed by the fire of the Tree that has been lighted in Asia, and you have found the true Path, becoming kindled like lamps, having entered into the Kingdom of God. Now in thanksgiving for this bounty you pray for blessing upon the people of the world, till by light of the Kingdom of Splendour their eyes become illuminated and their hearts become even as mirrors attaining the rays of the Sun of Truth.

My hope is this: – that the outbreathing of the Holy Spirit be inspired into your hearts, that your tongues begin to reveal the mysteries and to expound the meaning and the truth of the Holy Books. May the friends become physicians to cure by the Divine Teachings the deep-rooted diseases of the body of the world, to give sight to the blind, hearing to the deaf, life to the dead and awakening to the sleepers. Be sure that the blessing of the Holy Spirit will descend upon you, and that the Hosts of the Kingdom will come to your aid.

Upon you be the Glory of God![140]

On 25 February Tudor Pole met with the London Bahá'ís and spoke to them once again of his visit to 'Abdu'l-Bahá. Tudor Pole believed strongly that the friends should remain in existing organizations and churches as far as possible,

endeavouring to spiritualize them and to communicate the
Bahá'í spirit to others within those movements and groups,
rather than by 'coming out and forming new assemblies,
which might only result in a new sect'.[141] Tudor Pole read
to the meeting a translation of 'Abdu'l-Bahá's address to the
First Races Congress to be held at the University of London
in July.

The Congress was an initiative of the Union of Ethical
Societies of America and England, given support from more
than 50 countries by, among others, some 30 presidents of
parliaments and 40 colonial bishops. The purpose of the
Congress was to cultivate mutual knowledge and respect
between occidental and oriental peoples. Tudor Pole believed
it the duty of the Bahá'ís to do all in their power to help the
Congress to be a success. Indeed it was hoped that 'Abdu'l-
Bahá Himself might make the journey from Egypt to address
the gathering.

The forthcoming Congress was not the only public platform where the tenets of the Bahá'í Movement were about
to get a wide airing. On Sunday 1 March, Lady Blomfield's
old friend and mentor Archdeacon Wilberforce spoke in his
church – St John's, Westminster – about the teachings and
the following week answered many questions which he had
received by post. Within ten days, Sidney Sprague's *Story of
the Bahai Movement* sold more than two hundred copies,
clearing out the last of the second edition and forcing the
publication into its third print run. Following on from
Wilberforce's presentation, a Unitarian minister from High-
gate asked for a Bahá'í to speak from his pulpit on the Faith.

In addition to these remarkable developments, Marion
Jack, one of the Movement's most distinguished teachers and
an English teacher to the Master's daughters, arrived in
London. She took a studio flat at Hanover Street in West
London where she held Sunday afternoon meetings for
inquirers. The London friends were also very excited to be
able to greet Louis G. Gregory, who stayed in the capital for
four days on his way home to Washington DC after visiting

'Abdu'l-Bahá in Egypt.

Gregory, the son of a freed slave, was born in 1874 in Charleston, South Carolina. He studied law and practised until 1906, when he took a position in the United States Treasury Department. 'To meet such a great soul,' the English believer Arthur Cuthbert wrote to *Star of the West*, 'so filled with true Bahai spirit in any man is an inspiration; but when this man is a negro, and wise enough to be proud of his colour, then it is a revelation impressive with great significance as one contemplates the difficult problems existing between the white and black populations. How these problems can be changed by a few such men aflame with God's Word!'[142] The London Bahá'ís formally requested that all those travelling to or returning from a pilgrimage give the longest notice possible of the time of their arrival so that the English friends could benefit by their visit.

Hopes that 'Abdu'l-Bahá might come to London to address the Universal Races Congress were dashed when the believers learned that He did not intend to leave Egypt for an extended tour of the West until August. It has been suggested that He may not have attended the Congress owing to the appearance there of Mírzá Yaḥyáy-i-Dawlatábádí, a follower of Bahá'u'lláh's treacherous half-brother Subḥ-i-Azal. In later years, 'Abdu'l-Bahá would write that a 'Persian took the substance of the Epistles of His Holiness Bahá'u'lláh, entered that Congress, gave them forth in his own name and published them, whereas the wording was exactly that of His Holiness Bahá'u'lláh'.[143]

Despite the presence of this Covenant-breaker, the Congress was deemed by the Bahá'ís to have been a great success. Tudor Pole wrote:

Ten years ago the holding of such a gathering would have been impracticable, and it has created a foundation from which to work for future congresses. The immediate tangible results of the discussions may not be very evident; the press reports have been inadequate; and many of the speakers could not be heard beyond the platform. Also it must be admitted that the stifling heat of the hall did not conduce toward clear thinking or debate. Nevertheless, this congress has triumphantly demonstrated the possibility of bringing together in friendly intercourse representatives of nearly every race and religion under the sun, and the spiritual and moral effects of this fact alone can never be undone.[144]

'Abdu'l-Bahá addressed a letter to the president of the Congress in which He stated that He hoped the Congress would be 'successful in founding a noble institution which shall be permanent and everlasting; that it may ignite a candle from which a heavenly light shall beam, and plant a tree whose fruit may be friendship, love and unity between all the children of men, so that conflict and warfare may be abolished, and patriotic, racial, religious and political prejudices become unknown.'[145]

In the letter itself, 'Abdu'l-Bahá wrote:

The call to arbitration, to peace, to love, and to loyalty is the call of Baha'u'llah. His standard floats since fifty years, summoning all of whatever race and creed . . . Where love dwells, there is light! Where animosity dwells, there is darkness! . . . This Congress is one of the greatest of events. It will be forever to the glory of England that it was established at her capital. It is easy to accept a truth; but it is difficult to be steadfast in it; for the tests are many and heavy. It is well seen that the British are firm, and are not lightly turned aside, being neither ready to begin a matter for a little while nor prone to abandon it for a little reason. Verily, in every undertaking they show firmness.

O ye people! cause this thing to be not a thing of words, but of deeds. Some congresses are held only to increase differences. Let it not be so with you. Let your effort be to find harmony. Let brotherhood be felt and seen among you; and carry ye its quickening power throughout the world. It is my prayer that the work of the Congress will bear great fruit.[146]

Tudor Pole's desire to see a great Bahá'í Congress was partly fulfilled by the arrival of a large number of believers from around the world, particularly the United States, who arrived in London for the gathering. Julia Culver and Sidney Sprague were just two of the many distinguished American friends who ventured to London and contributed towards an ambitious programme of evening fringe meetings staged by the Bahá'ís.

The interest generated by the Congress continued undiminished after it had ended. Tudor Pole was invited to address the International Theosophical Summer School in Derbyshire. Through him the participants sent fraternal greetings to 'Abdu'l-Bahá and expressed their desire to unite with Him in His work towards universal racial understanding, peace and fellowship. Tudor Pole reported that he had never before seen such enthusiasm and interest aroused.

The stage was truly set for the arrival of 'Abdu'l-Bahá Himself to British shores.

11

'Abdu'l-Bahá in the West

O that I could travel, even though on foot and in the
utmost poverty, to these regions, and, raising the call
of 'Yá Bahá'u'l-Abhá' in cities, villages, mountains,
deserts and oceans, promote the Divine teachings![147]

'Abdu'l-Bahá

The English supporters of the Bahá'í Movement must have
been fascinated to witness the social and political upheavals
that rocked the British establishment as the second decade
of the twentieth century opened. While the Empire reached
its apex, the Liberal government began to address many of
the critical issues arising from a greater consciousness of the
extremes of poverty and wealth in Britain. The influence on
mainstream thinking of left-wing ideologies and the rise of
trade unionism resulted in the introduction of old-age pen-
sions and free school meals and the establishment of labour
exchanges and sickness and unemployment benefits. Most
vocal in the call for change was the movement for women's
suffrage. Women's exclusion from voting in elections was
seen as a denial of a basic human right, and in its desire to
bring about reforms to the law, the Pankhurst's Women's
Social and Political Union increasingly advocated violence
against property and individual politicians. Such was the
condition of Britain when 'Abdu'l-Bahá arrived to proclaim
His Father's own message of social and spiritual reform.

On 11 August 1911 the Master stepped on board the S.
S. *Corsica* bound for Marseilles in France. 'He arose', Shoghi
Effendi would recall a full century after his grandfather's
birth, 'with sublime courage, confidence and resolution to

consecrate what little strength remained to Him, in the evening of His life, to a service of such heroic proportions that no parallel to it is to be found in the annals of the first Bahá'í century . . .'

> He, who in His own words, had entered prison as a youth and left it an old man, Who never in His life had faced a public audience, had attended no school, had never moved in Western circles, and was unfamiliar with Western customs and language, had arisen not only to proclaim from pulpit and platform, in some of the chief capitals of Europe and in the leading cities of the North American continent, the distinctive verities enshrined in His Father's Faith, but to demonstrate as well the Divine origin of the Prophets gone before Him, and to disclose the nature of the tie binding them to that Faith.[148]

What joy must have been experienced by 'Abdu'l-Bahá's expectant British followers as He arrived in London on Monday, 4 September, having spent a few days resting at the Swiss resort of Thonon-les-Bains. 'A silence as of love and awe overcame us, as we looked at Him,' wrote Lady Blomfield,

> the gracious figure, clothed in a simple white garment, over which was a light coloured Persian 'abá; on His head He wore a low-crowned táj, round which was folded a small, fine-linen turban of purest white; His hair and short beard were of that snowy whiteness which had once been black; His eyes were large, blue-grey with long, black lashes and well-marked eyebrows; His face was a beautiful oval with warm, ivory-coloured skin, a straight, finely-modelled nose, and firm, kind mouth. These are merely outside details by which an attempt is made to convey an idea of His arresting personality.
>
> His figure was of such perfect symmetry, and so full of dignity and grace, that the first impression was that of considerable height. He seemed an incarnation of loving understanding, of compassion and power, of wisdom and authority, of strength, and of buoyant youthfulness, which

somehow defied the burden of His years; and such years! One saw, as in a clear vision, that He had so wrought all good and mercy that the inner grace of Him had grown greater than all outer sign, and the radiance of this inner glory shone in every glance, and word, and movement as He came with hands outstretched.[149]

Ethel Rosenberg was foremost among the many Bahá'í friends and sympathizers who assembled to greet their Master. Having encountered Him on three previous occasions in the land of His incarceration, to welcome Him to her own city must have been overwhelming. 'Heaven has blessed this day,' 'Abdu'l-Bahá told the gathering of friends on the evening of His arrival. 'It was said that London should be a place for a great proclamation of the Faith. I was tired when I went on board the steamer, but when I reached London and beheld the faces of the friends my fatigue left me. Your great love refreshes me. I am very pleased with the English friends.'[150]

Lady Blomfield and her daughters gave over their home at 97 Cadogan Gardens for the use of 'Abdu'l-Bahá and His personal attendants. It fell upon Lady Blomfield's shoulders to guarantee that while people of prominence and importance were granted the honour of meeting the Master, the humble and diffident were also admitted to His presence. In fact, it transpired that it was often the humbler ones who remained faithful to the Cause, while, with a few exceptions, the great – perhaps so impressed by their own importance that they came solely to air their own views – went away having ignored the majesty of the Master.

Ethel Rosenberg's task was to deal with the endless succession of visitors who thronged to Cadogan Gardens to meet 'Abdu'l-Bahá, making certain all were given an opportunity and an appointment. 'I can see Miss Ethel Rosenberg, that devoted follower, ever practical and busy with an interview book in her hand, taking down names and times for appointments,' reminisced Lady Blomfield's daughter, Mary Basil Hall, many years later.

I can see my beloved mother, eager, vital, full of sublime
enthusiasm, never losing a word or a movement of the
Master's, fully realizing that this visit was an event which
belonged to the world . . . At this time she had the beauty
of a mature soul. The moulding of her face was lovely and
she remained beautiful to the last. Her facial expressions,
ever changing, reflected the spiritual harmony within. Her
dress, not fashionable in the ordinary sense, was distinctive
and individual, without being strange. She wore garments
with long flowing lines which made her seem taller than her
natural height, and she was as upright always in her outward stature as she was in her soul . . . I can see her, her
eyes shining, welcoming the pilgrim guests to the presence
of the Master.

'Isn't it wonderful,' she would exclaim. 'Isn't it wonderful?' and her hands would emphasise her words in an em-
phatic movement, difficult to describe because it was never
the same.

Then I can see another ardent friend of the Cause . . .
Mrs Thornburgh Cropper . . . She put her car at the Master's disposal during His visit to London. I can see her tall,
graceful figure with her serene angel face shining beneath
a crown of silver hair, her blue eyes and the soft blend of
blues and purples in her dress, gracious to all, and ready to
be of constant service to our exalted guest . . .'[151]

'It was especially touching to see Mrs Thornburgh Cropper
and Miss Ethel Rosenberg,' wrote Lady Blomfield, 'who had
visited Him in the prison fortress of 'Akká, and who had been
the first to bring the Message to London, coming day after
day, as though transported with gratitude that He was now
free to give His Message to those who were hungering and
thirsting after righteousness . . .'[152]

Apart from Ethel and Mrs Thornburgh-Cropper, scores
of Bahá'í friends arrived every day during the Master's stay
at Cadogan Gardens: Hippolyte and Laura Dreyfus Barney,
now married, had travelled from Paris to assist the Master
with translations; the elderly English believer Annie Gamble;
the Liverpudlian Elizabeth Herrick; Mrs Scaramucci; distin-

guished American Bahá'ís – the artist Juliet Thompson, Mountfort Mills, Mason Remey, Claudia Coles, Julia Culver, Louise Waite and countless others. From the northwest of England, Sarah Ridgeway – who had just two years left to live – journeyed from Pendleton to meet her Master for the first time. While in London, she encountered a very spiritual young man from St Ives in Cornwall, Daniel Jenkyn. Thinking that he would make an appropriate supporter to the new believers in Manchester, she informed them that Jenkyn had promised to write to them. E. T. Hall, keen to develop the friendship, wrote to Jenkyn saying that he trusted the believers in Manchester would soon hear from him. A first, inspiring letter arrived on 1 October 1911. Thereafter a powerful spiritual correspondence ensued throughout 1912.

A number of extremely reverent believers from Persia also arrived in London, many of them never having been in the Master's presence before. Some were the relatives and descendants of heroic Bábí martyrs, some had themselves suffered long years of confinement, danger and persecution. 'Abdu'l-Bahá showered these friends with a special measure of love and affection.

'Oh, these pilgrims, these guests, these visitors,' Lady Blomfield recalled.

Remembering those days, our ears are filled with the sound of their footsteps – as they came from every country in the world! . . . Ministers and missionaries, Oriental scholars and occult students, practical men of affairs and mystics, Anglican-Catholics and Nonconformists, Theosophists and Hindus, Christian Scientists and doctors of medicine, Muslims, Buddhists and Zoroastrians. There also called: politicians, Salvation Army soldiers, and other workers for human good, women suffragists, journalists, writers, poets, and healers, dressmakers and great ladies, artists and artisans, poor workless people and prosperous merchants, members of the dramatic and musical world, these all came; and none were too lowly, nor too great, to receive the sympathetic consideration of this holy Messenger, who was ever giving His life for others' good.[153]

Some of Lady Blomfield's own friends and long-standing associates were counted among the visitors who came to greet the Master: the Reverend R. J. Campbell extended an invitation to 'Abdu'l-Bahá to speak to his congregation at the City Temple; Annie Besant and A. P. Sinnett of the Theosophical Society called upon Him to address meetings of their movement; Mrs Pankhurst, the suffragette, arrived to be encouraged by Him to continue her work steadfastly, for women would, He said, very shortly take their rightful place in the world; the writer Constance Elizabeth Maude, who was extremely moved by her encounter with 'Abdu'l-Bahá and who included a sympathetic pen-portrait of Him in her book *Sparks Among the Stubble*; and Mrs Alexander Whyte, the wife of one of Scotland's leading churchmen and a friend of Mrs Thornburgh Cropper, who had made the journey to 'Akká in 1906, renewed her acquaintance with and allegiance to 'Abdu'l-Bahá. It was she who would subsequently play an important role in 'Abdu'l-Bahá's visit to Scotland in 1913 on his return to Britain from the United States.

Ethel enthused to Albert Windust, editor of *Star of the West*:

> Those who have sought interviews with him have been of all ranks and classes, amongst them many clergy of the Anglican church and other denominations. It is indeed a most marvellous privilege to have him in our midst and I hope that blessing may be yours next year. He has said many kind things about the firmness and steadfastness of the English believers. Many have brought their young children to him to be blessed and it is very beautiful to see him with the little ones, folding them in his arms, kissing and blessing them.[154]

Lady Blomfield was delighted to see how Archdeacon Wilberforce was particularly taken with their Oriental visitor.

> Our dear friend, the Archdeacon, sat on a low chair by the Master. 'Abdu'l-Bahá spoke to him in His beautiful Persian.

He placed His hand on the head of the Archdeacon, talked long to him, and answered many questions. Evidently His words penetrated further than the outer ears, for both were deeply moved. On this occasion the invitation was given for 'Abdu'l-Bahá to speak to the congregation of St. John the Divine, at Westminster, on the following Sunday.[155]

The Master's days in London took on a regular pattern. Waking at around five o'clock in the morning, He worked for several hours on correspondence before breakfast and then met His visitors between nine o'clock and midday. After taking lunch He rested and then usually was driven, courtesy of Mrs Thornburgh-Cropper, to the London parks or to visit individuals and groups who were interested in His ideas. Gatherings with the friends filled most of His evenings. One significant development of His visit to London was His agreeing, with very great reluctance and as the result of insistent pressure, to be photographed. The believers were thrilled at the prospect of finally being able to possess and cherish pictures of their perfect exemplar.

On 8 September Ethel hosted a Unity Meeting in her home at which 'Abdu'l-Bahá spoke. He enthralled His audience with an overview of the purpose of the Messengers of God:

> Praise be to God, that such a meeting of purity and stead-fastness is being held in London. The hearts of those present are pure, and are turned towards the Kingdom of God. I hope that all that is contained and established in the Holy books of God may be realized in you. The Messengers of God are the principal and the first teachers. Whenever this world becomes dark, and divided in its opinions and indifferent, God will send one of His Holy Messengers.
>
> Moses came during a time of darkness, when ignorance and childishness prevailed amongst the people, and they were waverers. Moses was the teacher of God; he gave the teachings of holiness and educated the Israelites. He raised up the people from their degradation and caused them to be highly honoured. He taught them Sciences and Arts, trained

them in civilization and increased their human virtues. After a while, that which they had thus received from God was lost; the way was prepared for the return of evil qualities, and the world was oppressed by tyranny.

Then again the rumour of the Light of Reality and the breathing of the Holy Spirit became known. The cloud of Bounty showered, the Light of Guidance shone upon the earth. The world put on a new garment, the people became a new people, the oneness of humanity was proclaimed. The great unity of thought transformed humanity and created a new world. Again, after a time, all this was forgotten by the people. The teachings of God no longer influenced their lives. His prophecies and commandments became fainter and were finally obliterated from their hearts, and tyranny and thoughtlessness once more prevailed.

Bahá'u'lláh then came and once more renewed the foundation of Faith. He brought back the teachings of God, and the humane practices of the time of Christ. He quenched the thirst of the thirsty, He awakened the careless and called the attention of the heedless to the Divine secrets. He declared the unity of humanity, and spread abroad the teaching of the equality of all men.

Therefore, all of you ought with your hearts and minds to endeavour to win the people with kindness, so that this great Unity may be established, that childish superstitions may pass away, and all may become one.[156]

Ethel told Albert Windust on 20 September:

It is a truly wonderful experience we are passing through, but I am sure that you will understand . . . the pressure on the time of the Bahais that it is really quite impossible to send you all the details you need until the visit is over . . . It is a matter of extreme difficulty for us to find time for the interviews of the many hundreds of people who desire to see Him. There have been notices of his visit in nearly all the daily papers, most of them extremely sympathetic, notably so the interviews in the Daily News of Sept. 14th, of which I will enclose a cutting; also that of the Daily Mail. However Abdul-Baha has warned us that after he leaves this country,

many attacks will be made upon him and upon the Bahai
Cause. He said it was the same after the departure of Jesus
Christ from this world. Many things were written against
Jesus, but now, as the Master says, the very names of those
authors and of their writings is forgotten, whereas the
Words of the Christ are eternal and remain forever. Abdul-
Baha also says that a book will be written against him
anonymously by a very influential person.[157]

'Abdu'l-Bahá made a particular point of reiterating His
station as the 'servant' and dissuading His followers from
attributing divinity to Him personally. While generally
accurate, most of the press coverage of the time referred to
Him as a great Persian Prophet, but *The Observer* of 10
September quoted 'Abdu'l-Bahá's description of Himself as
the Son of a Prophet and referred all inquirers to the teachings and inspired life of Bahá'u'lláh.

Wellesley Tudor Pole noticed during the Master's visit to
Bristol that He was quite keen to transform the emphasis
that the believers placed on Him personally into a deeper
understanding of the station of Bahá'u'lláh. 'To idolise
Abdul-Baha in exaggerated terms or forms is to delay the
spread of the Bahai spirit of *Unity*,' warned Tudor Pole. 'We
are wonderfully blessed to have him among us, but imagination, exaggerated emphasis must not be laid upon his personality or the whole movement will suffer. This is a matter of
supreme import.'[158]

Ethel also played an extremely important role in helping
the believers to understand the Master's station. One early
British believer commented how 'Ethel Rosenberg was able
to give the English accurate teaching. She had a very clear
brain and the English Bahá'ís owe a great deal to her as she
kept to the words of 'Abdu'l-Bahá and did not fall back into
the error of thinking Him the Divine Manifestation as some
did in those days.'[159]

Two of 'Abdu'l-Bahá's most significant public addresses
in London were widely reported, partly because He addressed
congregations in prominent venues and partly because the

editor of *The Christian Commonwealth*, Albert Dawson,
personally covered the Master's visit for his newspaper,
which described itself as 'The Organ of the Progressive
Movement in Religion and Social Ethics'. On the newspaper's
editorial board were a number of individuals who played key
roles in the success of 'Abdu'l-Bahá's tour, including the
Reverend R. J. Campbell, Professor T. K. Cheyne and Sir
Richard Stapley.[160]

The first of these outstanding events took place at the City
Temple in Holborn where, for the first time in His life,
'Abdu'l-Bahá addressed a public audience. Reverend Campbell told his congregation that the Bahá'í movement stood
for the unity of mankind and universal peace among the
nations. 'These are good things,' he said, 'and the man who
teaches them to three millions of followers must be a good
man as well as a great.'[161] 'Abdu'l-Bahá spoke for some eight
minutes in Persian 'with considerable animation, his voice
rising and falling as in a rhythmic chant.'[162] A translation
of the address was then read aloud by Tudor Pole. In this
talk 'Abdu'l-Bahá clearly spelt out the basic tenets of His
Father's Cause:

> There is one God; mankind is one; the foundations of reli-
> gion are one. Let us worship Him, and give praise for all His
> great Prophets and Messengers who have manifested His
> brightness and glory.[163]

Charles Mason Remey reported to *Star of the West* that there
'must have been 3,000 persons present . . . When the people
dispersed a crowd gathered about the door, remaining there
until Abdul-Baha left the building. As he crossed the pave-
ment, many hands were extended toward him, some to clasp
his hands others to touch his robe as he passed. Later on in
the evening Abdul-Baha said that Baha'o'llah had told him
many years before that he would proclaim the coming of the
Kingdom in those parts.[164]

Archdeacon Wilberforce was just as welcoming when he
introduced the Master to an enormous congregation at St

John's Westminster on the following Sunday. He spoke of the Master's 'sufferings and bravery, of his self-sacrifice, of his clear and shining faith.'[165] Wilberforce voiced his own conviction that religion was one, just as God was love. 'Abdu'l-Bahá, as He would do so many times during His Western visits, once again chose to emphasize the essential unity of religion:

> ... men have always been taught and led by the Prophets of God. The Prophets of God are the Mediators of God. All the Prophets and Messengers have come from one Holy Spirit and bear the Message of God, fitted to the age in which they appear. The One Light is in them and they are One with each other.[166]

As the congregation sang a rousing hymn, the believers were touched to see their Master join hands with the Archdeacon as they processed down the aisle together.

Towards the end of 'Abdu'l-Bahá 's visit a young Persian couple expressed their wish to be married in His presence. The bride had journeyed from Baghdad accompanied by her uncle in order to meet her fiancé in London and be married before 'Abdu'l-Bahá's departure. Her father and grandfather had been followers of Bahá'u'lláh during the time of His banishment to Iraq. This may well have been the first Bahá'í marriage ceremony ever to be celebrated in the British Isles. On the morning of Sunday, 1 October, Regina Núr Maḥal Khánum and Mírzá Yu'hanna Dávúd attained the Master's presence. 'Abdu'l-Bahá told the young man, who had been studying in London for a number of years, 'Never have I united anyone in marriage before, except my own daughters, but as I love you much, and you have rendered a great service to the Kingdom of Abhá, both in this country and in other lands, I will perform your marriage ceremony today. It is my hope that you may both continue in the blessed path of service.'[167] In a private room 'Abdu'l-Bahá formally joined the couple in marriage and afterwards, the assembled friends from both Persia and Britain congratulated them on their

great honour. At the wedding feast which followed, one of the
believers asked 'Abdu'l-Bahá how He had enjoyed his stay
in London. He replied:

> I have enjoyed London very much and the bright faces of the
> friends have delighted my heart. I was drawn here by their
> unity and love. In the world of existence there is no more
> powerful magnet than the magnet of love. These few days
> will pass away, but their import shall be remembered by
> God's friends in all ages and in all lands.
>   . . . The English nation is a living one, and when in this
> spiritual springtime the divine truth comes forth with
> renewed vitality, the English will be like fruitful trees and
> the Holy Spirit will enable them to flourish in abundance.
> Then will they gain not only materially, but in that which
> is far more important, spiritual progress, which will enable
> them to render a greater service to the world of humanity.[168]

Just two days before His departure from London for France,
the Master accepted an invitation to visit the Higher
Thought Centre in Kensington where Ethel had been organizing weekly Bahá'í meetings for many years. The Centre
would later publish favourable comments about the visit in
its *Quarterly Record of Higher Thought Work*. The Master
in His unique manner gave a kind greeting to the assembled
friends followed by a short, impressive speech dwelling on
the blessedness of such an assembly gathered in a spirit of
unity. He concluded with a 'lowly uttered fervent prayer in
his own tongue, and a benediction which all present felt to
be very real'.[169] The next day 'Abdu'l-Bahá sent a written
message to the Centre expressing His appreciation for the
kindness shown to the Bahá'ís and concluding, 'it matters
not what name each calls himself – The Great Work is
One'.[170]

The sadness of the Master's departure from London was
lessened somewhat for Ethel and a few of the English friends
by the fact that they planned to accompany Him and His
entourage to Paris, the next port of call on His tour of the
West. To bid Him farewell, Mrs Thornburgh Cropper orga-

nized a huge gathering for more than four hundred people at the Passmore Edwards' Settlement in Tavistock Place on the eve of His departure. The meeting was enriched by the 'lofty spiritual tone of the proceedings' and the speeches were felt to be 'so well-conceived, so sincere, so exquisitely phrased'.[171] The feelings of all those assembled were summarized by the chair of the meeting, Professor Michael Sadler, who addressed the meeting after recitations of the Lord's Prayer and prayers of Bahá'u'lláh:

> We have met together to bid farewell to 'Abdu'l-Bahá, and to thank God for his example and teaching, and for the power of his prayers to bring Light into confused thought, Hope into the place of dread, Faith where doubt was, and into troubled hearts, the Love which overmasters self-seeking and fear.
>
> Though we all, among ourselves, in our devotional allegiance, have our own individual loyalties, to all of us 'Abdul'-Bahá brings, and has brought, a message of Unity, of sympathy and of peace. He bids us all be real and true in what we profess to believe; and to treasure above everything the Spirit behind the form. With him we bow before the Hidden Name, before that which is of every life the Inner Life! He bids us worship in fearless loyalty to our own faith, but with ever stronger yearning after Union, Brotherhood, and Love; so turning ourselves in Spirit, and with our whole heart that we may enter more into the mind of God, which is above class, above race, and beyond time.[172]

The Master's farewell words to His friends and followers in England were at once a vision of the future of the planet and a call to unity:

> As the East and the West are illumined by one sun, so all races, nations, and creeds shall be seen as the servants of One God. The whole earth is one home, and all people, did they but know it, are bathed in the oneness of God's mercy. God created all. He gives sustenance to all. He guides and trains all under the shadow of his bounty. We must follow the example God Himself gives us, and do away with all

disputations and quarrels.

Praise be to God! the signs of friendship are appearing, and as a proof of this I, today, coming from the East, have met in this London of the West with extreme kindness, regard and love, and I am deeply thankful and happy. I shall never forget this time I am spending with you.

. . . I leave you with prayer that all the beauty of the Kingdom may be yours. In deep regret at our separation, I bid you good-bye.[173]

'Abdu'l-Bahá, accompanied by a group of His followers from England and America as well as His own entourage, left London on 3 October for a nine-week stay in Paris. He took up residence at a charmingly furnished, sunny and spacious apartment at 4 Avenue de Camoens in the area of Quai de Passy. Hippolyte and Laura Dreyfus Barney were on hand to serve and translate for Him, as were Lady Blomfield, her daughters and Ethel, armed once again with their notebooks to capture accurately His every word and exhortation. It was through their combined efforts that His addresses in Paris were noted and published in England shortly afterwards under the title *Talks by Abdul Baha Given In Paris*, later known as *Paris Talks*.

The Master's stay in the French capital saw Him once again expounding the fundamental verities of His father's Cause to a spiritually hungry Western audience. Whether He was addressing the friends in His private rooms, meeting with large groups of seekers or simply promenading in the Trocadéro Gardens, 'Abdu'l-Bahá entranced everyone who came into contact with Him. In the words of Shoghi Effendi:

Persian princes, noblemen and ex-ministers, among them the Zillu's-Sultán, the Persian Minister, the Turkish Ambassador in Paris, Rashíd Páshá, an ex-válí of Beirut, Turkish páshás and ex-ministers, and Viscount Arawaka, Japanese Ambassador to the Court of Spain, were among those who had the privilege of attaining His presence. Gatherings of Esperantists and Theosophists, students of the Faculty of Theology and large audiences at l'Alliance Spiritualiste were

addressed by Him; at a Mission Hall, in a very poor quarter
of the city, He addressed a congregation at the invitation of
the Pastor, whilst in numerous meetings of His followers
those already familiar with His teachings were privileged
to hear from His lips detailed and frequent expositions of
certain aspects of His Father's Faith.[174]

'Abdu'l-Bahá's sadness at the condition of humanity was
becoming more apparent in the words of warning He addressed to His audiences. Many of the events taking place in
the world caused Him great distress. He was disturbed by
news of battles and calamities and wondered at the human
savagery that still existed. He charged his listeners to concentrate all their thoughts on love and unity: 'When a
thought of war comes, oppose it by a stronger thought of
peace.'[175]

Even though the influence of the Covenant-breakers had
diminished somewhat and 'Abdu'l-Bahá had clearly established His ascendancy over His faithless family members,
certain individuals emerged during His Western visits who
tried to cause trouble and undermine His authority. It was
largely thanks to the indefatigable efforts of Lady Blomfield
that these people were prevented from causing too much of
a disturbance. One person in particular began to whisper
slanderous lies about the Master and came daily to distort
the teachings amongst the pilgrims. Lady Blomfield told her
daughters that one morning she withdrew into a quiet room
and repeated the prayer of the Báb known as the Remover
of Difficulties: the individual did not appear that day nor did
she ever come again. Lady Blomfield spoke to the Master
about those, even among his own entourage, who tried to
damage His reputation. 'Abdu'l-Bahá took her aside and said,
'. . . you must realize that never for one moment is my life
out of danger. So has it been ever since I can remember. But
fear not. I shall live till the appointed time.'[176]

One day 'Abdu'l-Bahá took Ethel aside and told her that
He found Lady Blomfield entirely sincere, pure-hearted and
of a single intention and mind, that in her there was no

diversion of any kind. He instructed Ethel to value Lady Blomfield's friendship.

One of the most significant things for the future development of the Bahá'í community in Britain that 'Abdu'l-Bahá did while in Paris was to call into being an embryonic component of the administrative order of Bahá'u'lláh. On 19 November, in a special meeting with Ethel, 'Abdu'l-Bahá discussed the formation of a committee in London which would have 'absolute power to decide what is to be done'.[177] Initially this committee was given the task of deciding what to do about the collection of funds and the production of Bahá'í publications, in the first instance the proposed book of the notes of 'Abdu'l-Bahá's talks and addresses in London. The Master expressed His desire for this duty to be undertaken by a committee formed of Ethel, Mrs Thornburgh-Cropper, Mrs Alexander Whyte, Alice Buckton, Lady Blomfield, Tudor Pole and Mrs Gabrielle Enthoven, who lived in the same block of flats as Lady Blomfield and who 'Abdu'l-Bahá had named Hamsáyih, meaning 'neighbour'. He spoke with Ethel at considerable length about the procedure He wished the committee to follow in regard to general expenses, funds and collections. He said, first of all, that they had to make it very clearly understood that all offerings were to be entirely voluntary. There was to be no obligation in this matter and if a believer felt unable to afford to contribute then giving nothing was acceptable. Those who wished to give, however, should choose a sum within their means and contribute this regularly. He told Ethel that it would be a good plan to have the amount decided upon paid into the fund each month and entered into a book so at the end of a year the amounts could be balanced. Thus the committee would know how much it had at its disposal after general expenditure. Out of this fund the committee could pay the expenses of hiring meeting rooms and of issuing publications. Ethel asked the Master if He wished them to have two separate funds, one for publications and one for hiring meeting rooms. He very decisively said no, it should all go

into the one fund or treasury. He also instructed Ethel that
these funds were not to be sent abroad or used for other
purposes but if, at the end of the year, the committee had
more money than was needed for their working expenses,
that money was to be used to help the poorer Bahá'í friends.
As the community's numbers increased and when the committee wished to do so, money could be sent abroad to help
others.

Ethel noted that 'Abdu'l-Bahá was very interested in all
the details of the fund and spoke very fully and enthusiastically about it. He told Ethel that the meetings in London
would grow in numbers and would improve in every way. He
particularly wished that the Bahá'ís whom He had named
should consult together and arrange matters as they thought
wisest and best on the general basis He had suggested.

The following day 'Abdu'l-Bahá again received Ethel,
along with Edith Sanderson and some other believers, in His
private rooms. He welcomed them all in His usual kind and
loving way and commented how the weather was cold that
morning but that the cold could be very healthy. In some
parts of Persia, He laughed, where it was extremely cold, the
people sometimes lived to be a hundred years old while in
warmer climates people did not live so long. But for the
Bahá'ís, He remarked, there was no end to life.

'Abdu'l-Bahá's first visit to Europe was nearing its end
and He was preparing to return to Egypt for the winter
before embarking on His magnificent tour of the United
States the following year. He told Ethel that the preparations
and the thought of leaving would make Him very sad were
it not for the fact that every day he saw her and the other
friends constantly so that He had no time to think of leave-
taking or of sad thoughts. Ethel assured Him that for her it
was a great joy and happiness to see Him. Abdu'l-Bahá
replied it was also a great happiness for Him.

The Master frequently sent messages to His English
friends while in Paris. On the eve of His departure for Alexandria, He urged His English and French followers to work
unceasingly

... for the day of Universal Peace. Strive always that you may be united. Kindness and love in the path of service must be your means.

I bid a loving farewell to the people of France and England. I am very much pleased with them. I counsel them that they may day by day strengthen the bond of love and amity to this end, – that they may become the sympathetic embodiment of one nation. – That they may extend themselves to a Universal Brotherhood to guard and protect the interests and rights of all the nations of the East, – that they may unfurl the Divine Banner of justice ...'[178]

Lady Blomfield and her daughters, exhausted yet exhilarated by the many weeks spent in the presence of their Master, left Paris for Switzerland where they edited the rough notes of the talks He had given in Paris. These, when completed, were sent to 'Abdu'l-Bahá, who had them read to Him and made corrections. Returning to London from France, Ethel set about the task of ensuring the careful and economical publication of both *'Abdu'l-Bahá in London* and *Talks by Abdul Baha Given In Paris.* On 16 March 1912 she wrote to the United States informing the friends that she had received a letter from Lady Blomfield in Switzerland. They were, she wrote, extremely sorry about the delay in getting the book out but it had been unavoidable owing to one disappointment after another in collecting funds. Lady Blomfield believed that the book would be ready within a week. Ethel feared that it could not be ready for at least another three but stated that they were doing their best to hurry matters forward. 'Abdu'l-Bahá had expressed His wish for the book to be available in the United States before His arrival there. Despite the delays, the publication *'Abdu'l-Bahá in London* was shortly afterwards available at the cost of one shilling a copy and Ethel saw to it that appropriate numbers were shipped to the United States to coincide with the Master's tour there.

'Abdu'l-Bahá set sail for the United States on 25 March 1912 to begin an extended journey lasting thirteen months and taking in seven countries in North America and Europe. The British Bahá'ís were elated at the news they gleaned from correspondence and *Star of the West* of the extraordinary acclaim and press coverage He received and the powerful, penetrating insights He conveyed in His many talks and lectures. While delighting in the reports of His great mission to America, the London believers noted that the Master's visit to them had had a spiritual effect on the many different groups He had encountered. Arthur Cuthbert reported:

> The difference that his visit seems to have made is the increased freedom that one feels for mixing with the people and co-operating with them in whatever efforts one finds them making, for any good purpose – not to trouble them about a new name nor disturb them in the position where they are, but rather to encourage and inspire them to greater humanitarian efforts; not to make a new sect and add to sectarian strife, but to leven [sic] and raise the spirituality of all religious bodies and assisting all whom we find to be doing this.[179]

The emphasis on not compelling believers of other faiths to leave their traditions and practices, while entirely appropriate for the time, led to great tests for many Bahá'ís when in later years Shoghi Effendi called upon them to leave their churches and to form themselves into distinctive Bahá'í communities with formal registration and administrative procedures.

As 'Abdu'l-Bahá carried out His exacting task across the Atlantic, the momentum He had generated in London continued. Some of the believers started a movement, in co-operation with East Indians living in London, to establish greater social understanding between East and West. There were some two thousand Indian students in the city and the group worked to improve their social position and to create bonds of knowledge and friendship.

Returning from Switzerland, Lady Blomfield took on the role of hosting the regular weekly meetings while the Higher

Thought Centre was temporarily closed. Marion Jack continued her Sunday afternoon studio meetings as did Annie
Gamble – who lived to be a hundred years old – at her home
in Putney. There was hope also to initiate gatherings in East
Sheen at the home of the Jenner family. Ethel supported
these gatherings as best as she could but preferred not to
aggravate her chest complaint by going out when it was too
cold or dark in the late afternoons or evening. Her tireless
services to the community continued through the publishing
work she was pioneering and through her ongoing correspondence with friends around the world.

One significant development in England during 1912 was
the publication by Longmans of *Bahaism, The Religion of
Brotherhood*. Its author was Francis Henry Skrine, a retired
member of the Indian Civil Service who had met 'Abdu'l-
Bahá during His visit to London. His conclusion about the
ideals which the Master had preached was that 'Bahaism
may come with a rush that nothing can resist.'[180]

In October 1912 Ethel was saddened to learn of the death
of Thornton Chase who had passed away on 30 September.
He was one of her most regular and faithful correspondents
and his great loving character was deeply missed by the
American friends. 'Abdu'l-Bahá paid tribute to Chase's life
of dedication when He visited his grave in Inglewood, Los
Angeles on 19 October:

> The purpose of life is to get certain results; that is, the life
> of man must bring forth certain fruitage. It does not depend
> upon the length of life. As soon as the life is crowned with
> fruition then it is completed, although that person may have
> had a short life . . . Praise be to God! the tree of Mr. Chase's
> life brought forth fruit. It gave complete fruit, therefore he
> is free. He attained to eternal rest. He is now in the pres-
> ence of Baha'o'llah.[181]

'Abdu'l-Bahá arrived in England, triumphant from the
United States, at the end of 1912, docking in Liverpool on
13 December. Elizabeth Herrick joined Hippolyte Dreyfus-

Barney and a group of a dozen or so believers from Manchester, Liverpool and Leeds to greet Him on His return to British shores. After staying two days in Liverpool at the Adelphi Hotel and having given two public talks, He departed for London. In the early afternoon of 16 December His train reached Euston station where Ethel and some 50 other believers were present to welcome Him. Lady Blomfield had brought a car to the station and drove Him back to Cadogan Gardens. She and her daughters were amazed to hear the Master conversing freely with them in English without an interpreter being present.

'Abdu'l-Bahá's second visit to British shores followed a similar pattern to His first. Once again, followers and friends, dignitaries and diplomats, the poverty stricken and the press all turned out in force to meet this wise man from the East, now anxious to hear news of His visit to America. A believer arrived from Belfast in Northern Ireland having travelled all day and night to see the Master. He informed her that she must become the cause of the illumination of her country. A large meeting was also held in the Caxton Hall where the Master paid tribute to the Americans and emphasized the love and unity that existed between Britain and the United States. The Master expressed His delight that notes of His addresses in Paris and London had been published so quickly and efficiently and He hoped that His talks in America would also be published promptly.

On 18 December, among the guests to hear the Master speak was Professor Edward Granville Browne who arrived from Cambridge. 'The last time I met you', said the Master, 'was twenty-two years ago in Acca under different environment, but now I have the pleasure of seeing you in London.' The two men spoke together in Persian.[182]

A remarkable, cosmopolitan gathering was held at the Westminster Palace Hotel on the evening of Friday, 20 December where the Master addressed scientists and diplomats, Oriental visitors and leading thinkers of the day. He bewailed the plight of the Balkans where blood was 'being freely and copiously shed, lives are being destroyed, houses are pillaged, cities are razed to the ground, and all this through religious prejudice; while in reality the foundation of the religion of God is love.'[183] The Master's speech was followed by addresses by Alice Buckton and the suffragette Mrs Despard, President of the Women's Freedom League. Closing remarks were made by Hippolyte Dreyfus-Barney, who emphasized how the Cause of Bahá'u'lláh appealed to humanity's sense of reason.

On 21 December, for the first time in His life, 'Abdu'l-Bahá went to see a theatrical performance – a nativity play entitled *The Eager Heart* by Alice Buckton, in which Lady Blomfield's daughter Mary was playing. 'Abdu'l-Baha wept when the actors playing Mary and Joseph appeared on stage with the baby Jesus in their arms. After the performance, the Master went backstage and spoke with the cast and musicians, telling them about the prophecies of the Old Testament regarding the coming of the Messiah. Meeting the performers who had played angels He recommended they all be angels as long as they lived.

Having 'Abdu'l-Bahá amongst them during the Christmas period gave the believers a wonderful example of how the true spirit of the season of good will should be celebrated. On Christmas night, the Master visited the poor of the Salvation Army Shelter in Westminster where around one thousand souls had gathered for their annual Christmas dinner. 'Abdu'l-Bahá identified strongly with the downtrodden and the dispossessed, telling them that His lot had 'ever been with those who have not the goods of this world . . . Sorrow not, grieve not. Be not unhappy because you are not wealthy. You are the brothers of Jesus Christ. Christ was poor; Baha'o'llah was poor. For forty years he was imprisoned in poverty. The great ones of the world have come from a lowly station. Be ever happy; be not sad! Trust in God and if in this world you undergo dire vicissitudes I hope that in the Kingdom of God you will have the utmost happiness.'[184] The Master left 20 gold sovereign coins with the Salvation Army's

Colonel so that the assembled gathering might enjoy a similar dinner on New Year's night. The men, with one accord, jumped up and, waving their knives and forks, gave a rousing farewell cheer to the Master. On the 2 January 'Abdu'l-Bahá once again spent the afternoon with the poor, this time gathered at the Cedar Club House in Battersea, run by the Women's Service League and devoted to providing food to toiling mothers.

This visit to London was not without its humorous moments. When 'Abdu'l-Bahá joined His followers for dinner on Christmas Eve, He told them He was not hungry but He had to come to the table because Lady Blomfield was very insistent. Two despotic monarchs of the East had not been able to command Him and bend His will, He laughed, but the ladies of America and Europe, because they were free, gave Him orders!

'Abdu'l-Bahá ventured away from London to Oxford on New Year's eve to pay His respects to Thomas Kelly Cheyne, the distinguished professor, historian and critic. Their meeting, Lady Blomfield said, was almost too intimate to describe. The early days of the new year were spent in Edinburgh where 'Abdu'l-Bahá and his entourage including Lady Blomfield, Alice Buckton and Dr Hakím were the guests of Mrs Whyte. While in Scotland, the Master gave several public talks and His visit was widely reported in the Scottish press. For the first time in the British Isles, opposition was vigorously expressed against the Master. Once He had left Edinburgh a correspondence ensued in the Scottish press denouncing His teachings as damaging to the missionary achievements and unique message of Christianity.[185]

On His return to London and shortly before His final departure from England, 'Abdu'l-Bahá called upon His followers to teach the Cause in an unprecedented way. Speaking at Cadogan Gardens on 16 January, the Master animatedly rallied His troops into a new arena of service and action:

The Cause has become very great. Many souls are entering it – souls with different mentalities and range of understanding. Complex difficulties constantly rise before us. The administration of the Cause has become most difficult. Conflicting thoughts and theories attack the Cause from every side. Now consider to what extent the believers in God must become firm and soul-sacrificing. Every one of the friends must become the essence of essences; each one must become a brilliant lamp. People all around the world are entering the Cause, people of various tribes and nations and religions and sects. It is most difficult to administer to such heterogeneous elements. Wisdom and Divine insight are necessary. Firmness and steadfastness are needed at such a crucial period of the Cause.

All the meetings must be for teaching the Cause and spreading the Message, and suffering the souls to enter into the Kingdom of Bahá'u'lláh. Look at me. All my thoughts are centred around the proclamation of the Kingdom. I have a lamp in my hand searching through the lands and seas to find souls who can become heralds of the Cause. Day and night I am engaged in this work. Any other deliberations in the meetings are futile and fruitless. Convey the Message! Attract the hearts! Sow the seeds! Teach the Cause to those who do not know . . .

If the meeting or Spiritual Assembly has any other occupations the time is spent in futility. All the deliberations, all consultations, all the talks and addresses must revolve around one focal centre and that is: Teach the Cause. Teach. Teach. Convey the Message. Awaken the souls. Now is the time of laying the foundation. Now we must gather brick, stone, wood, iron, and other building materials. Now is not the time of decoration. We must strive day and night and think and work; what can I say that may become effective? What can I do that may bring results? What can I write that may bring forth fruits? Nothing else will be useful to-day. The interests of such a Glorious Cause will not advance without such undivided attention. While we are carrying this load we cannot carry any other load![186]

During the Master's remaining few days in Britain, He

declined Lady Blomfield's offer to try to arrange an audience with King George V, as He felt this might be misconstrued. One final meeting was held at the Higher Thought Centre before His departure on 21 January for the remaining stages on His tour of the West. 'Abdu'l-Bahá would return to Egypt via France, Germany, Austria and Hungary. Shoghi Effendi reflected:

> A most significant scene in a century-old drama had been enacted. A glorious chapter in the history of the first Bahá'í century had been written. Seeds of undreamt-of potentialities had, with the hand of the Centre of the Covenant Himself, been sown in some of the fertile fields of the Western world. Never in the entire range of religious history had any Figure of comparable stature arisen to perform a labour of such magnitude and imperishable worth.[187]

There can be no doubt that the visit of the Master made a profound impact on Ethel Rosenberg, who had laboured so conscientiously to establish the Cause of Bahá'u'lláh in England. Whereas once she and Mrs Thornburgh-Cropper had been the only two souls in the entire country attempting to spread the message, there were now literally thousands of people who had been touched by the light of 'Abdu'l-Bahá. As new friends arose to carry out the duties which for several years Ethel had shouldered alone with a small handful of fellow believers, Ethel's main duty was to share her expert knowledge of the teachings and assist in developing the embryonic stages of Bahá'u'lláh's administrative order in the British Isles.

It was to be an extremely testing and difficult process. While the Master's visit must have exhilarated the British Bahá'ís to the point of feeling that their Cause was unstoppable, the forces of history were about to deal them a painful blow. The Great War was looming on the horizon and with it would come a sharp decline in interest in the movement of peace which 'Abdu'l-Bahá had worked so long and hard to proclaim on His historic travels to the West.

12

Years of Darkness

*O God, my God! Thou seest how black darkness is
enshrouding all regions, how all countries are burning
with the flame of dissension, and the fire of war and
carnage is blazing throughout the East and the West.
Blood is flowing, corpses bestrew the ground, and
severed heads are fallen on the dust of the battlefield.*[188]

'Abdu'l-Bahá

On 26 October 1912 'Abdu'l-Bahá, addressing a gathering
in Sacramento, California, called upon His audience to
become advocates of peace. 'The European continent', He
warned, 'is like an arsenal, a storehouse of explosives ready
for ignition, and one spark will set the whole of Europe
aflame, particularly at this time when the Balkan question
is before the world.'[189] Just two years later, His premonition
became reality. On 14 August 1914, following Germany's
invasion of Belgium, Britain declared war – a conflict, as the
then Chancellor of the Exchequer David Lloyd George put
it, 'on behalf of liberal principles, a crusade on behalf of the
"little five-foot-five nations" like Belgium, flagrantly invaded
by the Germans, or Serbia and Montenegro, now threatened
by Austria-Hungary.'[190] Throughout Britain there was a
broad consensus about the justice and rightness of the war.
This opinion also won the backing of church leaders and it
was widely anticipated that the fighting would be 'over by
Christmas'.[191] This, of course, was not to be the case. Yet
despite the devastation and the enormous loss of lives,
including the slaughter of 750,000 British men and 200,000
Empire troops, throughout its four year duration the major-

*17. Lady Sara Louisa Blomfield
whom Ethel met in Paris on her return from
pilgrimage in 1901.
Lady Blomfield soon afterwards became a leading
figure in the
British Bahá'í community.*

1. Miss McArthur
2. Miss Goodall
3. Miss Mazzron Park (George)
4. Miss Sophullah Hakim
5. Miss Martin
6. Miss Stielof Broadway
7. Mrs Crosby
8. Mrs Anderson
9. Mr Willard

10. A. Ruwian
11. Mrs John Marshall
12. Mrs E. W. Child
13. Mrs Arthur Cuthbert
14. Mrs Courney Amandel
15. Mrs Eric Hammond
16. Mrs Farnhill
17. Mrs Rochforn
18. Miss Y. Jameih Daniel

17. Mrs George
20. Mrs Young
21. Mrs Erittenson
22. Miss Kerr
23. Miss Campbell
24. Mr Porter
25. Mrs Omos
26. Miss Gottschaulk
27. Miss Bruaré

28. Mrs Willard
29. Miss Cross
30. Mrs Norlodge
31. Mrs Honeywood
32. Cyril Willard
33. Leo Benjamin
34. Miss Hewish
35. Mrs Richard Whitwell
36. Mrs Porter

37. Miss Gamble
38. Master Porter
39. Mrs Caunter
40. Frank Willard
41. Eric Willard
42. Miss Vera Lyle
43. Miss Barnfather
44. Miss Olive Lyle
45. Arthur Caunter

18. Bahá'ís in London, circa 1913

19. Luṭfulláh Ḥakím and Daniel Jenkyn in London
Dr Ḥakím, who served on the first Universal House of Justice, was
Jenkyn's closest friend. Ethel said of Jenkyn that 'He was a most
spiritually minded young man, a very sincere, ardent Bahai and a
most hard worker for the blessed Cause'.

20. Wellesley Tudor Pole,
shown here in military uniform circa 1914-18. His letter to The
Christian Commonwealth *was instrumental in attracting the Halls*
and Cravens in Manchester to the Bahá'í Faith.

Mrs. E. T. Hall & family
Manchester
July 1918

21. *Edward Theodore Hall and family, shown here in July 1918. The Hall's home in Manchester was acknowledged as the Bahá'í Centre.*

22. *Manchester Bahá'ís John Craven and Edward Hall on the ferry at Liverpool, travelling to meet 'Abdu'l-Bahá 13 December 1912.*

23. *Shoghi Effendi with Manchester Bahá'ís, October 1921*
Left to right, from the back: *Albert Joseph, John Craven, Jim Birch, Sam Joseph, H. Jarvis,
Rebecca Hall, Lucy Hall, Mrs Heald, Mrs Chessell, Jeff Joseph, Olive Jarvis, Mrs Hoferer, Mrs Birch,
Nora Crossley, Jas Chessell holding Helen, Shoghi Effendi, Edward T. Hall, Díá'u'lláh
Asgharzádih, Mr Heald, Norman Craven, Mrs Craven, Harold Taylor, Edward R. Hall,
Ronald Craven, Mabel Chessell*

ity of the population maintained that the conflict was just and necessary. In addition to the loss of life, the violent events of those years turned out to be spiritually destructive, negating much of the goodwill and sympathy towards the cause of universal peace that 'Abdu'l-Bahá had tirelessly promoted on His travels through the West. The Master entertained no such thoughts about the war being constructive and necessary. In a Tablet to one of the English believers, Beatrice Irwin, He stated that:

> No sane person can at this time deny the fact that war is the most dreadful calamity in the world of humanity, that war destroys the divine foundation, that war is the cause of eternal death, that war is conducive to the destruction of populous, progressive cities, that war is the world-consuming fire, and that war is the most ruinous catastrophe and the most deplorable adversity.
>
> The cries and lamentations are raised from every part to the Supreme Apex; the moanings and shriekings have thrown a mighty reverberation through the columns of the world; the civilized countries are being overthrown; eyes are shedding tears, hearing the weeping of the fatherless children; the hearts are burning and being consumed by uncontrollable sobbings and piercing wailings of helpless, wandering women; the spirits of hopeless mothers are torn by rayless grief and endless sorrows and the nerve-racking sighs and the just complaints of fathers ascend to the Throne of the Almighty . . .
>
> The results of this crime committed against humanity are worse than whatever I may say and can never be adequately described by pen or by tongue.[192]

Just four months before the war had broken out, Ethel Rosenberg – now in her mid-fifties – had written once again to 'Abdu'l-Bahá complaining of her health. She wrote about the upset caused by the astigmatism of her eyes and also mentioned a severe illness brought on by the eye-straining work of painting copies of miniatures. 'Abdu'l-Bahá was, as always, full of encouragement for His faithful follower. In one letter addressed to the Bahá'ís of London, He thanked God that in the English capital 'which is often dark because of cloud, mist, and smoke, such bright candles (as you) are glowing, whose emanating light is God's guidance, and whose influencing warmth is as the burning Fire of the Love of God.'[193]

One woman who lent great support to Ethel during these taxing times was Florence George, known to the community by the title bestowed upon her by the Master, 'Mother George'. Outwardly, she was a formidable person – 'tall, erect, dark, direct and rather brusque in speech,'[194] but beneath an imposing surface, those who came to know her well found a warm, sympathetic and understanding character. Mother George had lived in Paris since the turn of the century and learned of the Bahá'í Movement around 1910 from Hippolyte Dreyfus and Edith Sanderson. She attended a very strenuous Bahá'í study class where the students were frequently asked to write out all they remembered from the previous lesson to test their understanding. She joined the London Bahá'ís in 1913 and soon was of great assistance to Ethel, whose keen desire to carry on the work of the Cause was frustrated by her personal health complaints and the marked lack of interest in the teachings resulting from the prevailing war mentality.

Mother George helped Ethel by preparing the room at the Higher Thought Centre for their regular meetings. The believers held a total of five 'fireside' meetings a week before the Germans began the Zeppelin airship bombing raids on London and evening meetings were made impossible. Up to that time, however, Ethel continued to teach classes designed for the intensive study of the Bahá'í writings. Mother George reported that Ethel was very thorough in instruction. After it became too dangerous to host the meetings at the Higher Thought Centre, classes continued at Ethel's home. Mother George also started her own fireside meetings on a Saturday afternoon and the well-attended children's classes she later held must rank among the first attempts in Britain at the

Bahá'í education of children. One Bahá'í still surviving from those early days – Rose Jones, now in Devon – remembers attending the classes with a Bahá'í friend. Rose's family were not believers, nevertheless she went regularly to Mother George's house in the Kings Road, Chelsea on a Wednesday afternoon. Many speakers came to address the children, among them Ethel and Dr Ḥakím. To the young Rose, Ethel had the appearance of a headmistress, often apparently very stern but at other times quiet with a kind expression. Rose recalls that Ethel appeared to subscribe to the school of thought that says children should be seen and not heard. Ethel told the children stories about her experiences in the Holy Land but, as far as Rose remembers, she never had them undertake any artistic activities.

At the outbreak of war, Britain was in a critical condition. The so-called triple alliance of railwaymen, transport workers and miners threatened a mass united strike to back the railway workers' claim for union recognition and a 48-hour week. There were nationalist rumblings in Ireland, India and Egypt. Britain was thus torn by tensions with which its existing political and social institutions were unable to cope. At the same time, however, a new institution was being born in England that would signal the birth of a constituent element of a new world order: an early attempt at administering community affairs based on the principles annunciated by Bahá'u'lláh. While the London believers had very little guidance to direct their deliberations, they attempted for a brief period to organize themselves formally into an administrative committee.

On 16 November 1914 the new Bahá'í 'Consultation Committee' met at Ethel's home in Sinclair Road. Present were Eric Hammond (who was elected chairman), Ethel (unanimously elected secretary), Mrs Thornburgh-Cropper, Annie Gamble, Mother George, Elizabeth Herrick, Dr Ḥakím and a Mrs Crosby. The membership was noticeably different from that initially chosen by 'Abdu'l-Bahá and it can only be assumed that the members recommended by the Master were unable either to be present or to serve. In any event, it seems that the membership of this institution was quite flexible in that different people were asked to serve on it and for varying lengths of time. On several occasions other individuals who may have been visiting London were asked to come and join the consultation.[195]

At its first ever meeting, the committee, after deciding upon its membership and officers, discussed community issues including whether it should take responsibility for the organization and programme of the regular public meetings being held by Marion Jack in Hammersmith. The Bahá'í library and bookcase which was then located at Kings Weigh Church House was also a topic of discussion. Ethel was extremely concerned about the continuation of Unity Feasts during the winter months when there was a reduction in street lighting and she suggested that they be held just once a month on either a Saturday or a Sunday. This was agreed. The committee resolved to hold its own meetings six times a year on the last Saturday of every other month. The public meetings were later postponed for the winter because of this same problem of the street lighting. At its second meeting, the Committee decided to call itself the Bahai Council.

The early months of 1915 saw a serious threat to continued communication with the Master in Haifa. Jamal Pasha, Commander of the 4th Army Corps, took up his mission to overrun the Suez Canal and drive the British out of Egypt. A reign of terror came to Syria and the Covenant-breakers discovered fresh opportunities to plot against the Master with the new regime. In the event of guidance from the Holy Land being completely cut off, the Bahai Council decided that those believers specifically named by 'Abdu'l-Bahá to serve on the committee would be authorized to resolve any difficult questions which might arise.

One of the greatest worries for the Council was the shortage of funds. Ethel said that she hoped public meetings might be held during the following summer months, beginning in April, but the community's funds were so low that something had to be done to increase them otherwise there would be no money available for the hire of a room for meetings. Ethel shared with her colleagues the Master's clear instructions to her in Paris about the organization of the funds. The promotion of these public meetings once summer had come was also a matter for concern. At the Council's request, Ethel agreed to place advertisements in *The Christian Commonwealth.*

One of the tasks given to the original committee by 'Abdu'l-Bahá was to oversee the publication of literature. Mother George wanted to see a new edition or a portion of the *Hidden Words* printed and it was finally decided that it would be best to print a one shilling edition of the Arabic *Hidden Words* alone. Ethel was authorized by the Council to obtain an estimate for the cost of printing an edition of either five hundred or a thousand copies. The total bill eventually came to three pounds, ten shillings for one thousand copies. In the meantime, Lady Blomfield had offered personally to subsidize a second edition of *Paris Talks.*

Lady Blomfield witnessed first hand the disastrous, initial stages of the war. When fighting broke out, she and her daughters were staying in Switzerland, but shortly afterwards they moved to Paris to assist the French Red Cross in the Haden Guest Unit at the Hospital Hotel Majestic. For Lady Blomfield, the experience was heart rending. 'Any kind of suffering touched my mother profoundly,' recalled Mary Basil Hall, 'but the sight of young men maimed for life, and the new and horrible experiences she had to endure during the dressing of wounds, her mental agony reflecting their pain, tortured her beyond words. After that first heart-rending morning in the wards, we were silent as we walked back to the Hotel d'Jena for luncheon. We imagined ourselves unable to touch any food. But my mother's courage and strength of mind prevailed. She said quietly: "We must eat, or we shall be ill ourselves. Then we shall not be able to help."'[196]

In March 1915 the hospital unit moved away from Paris

and in April the Blomfields returned to London. For the rest of the war, Lady Blomfield offered her services at several hospitals. She served on a number of committees and kept open house for the convalescing soldiers from Australia and New Zealand, the Anzacs. Despite the demands of these humanitarian duties, she never neglected the sparsely attended Bahá'í meetings which were held when and where circumstances permitted and kept in touch with the Master and friends overseas whenever correspondence was possible.

Lady Blomfield watched with great interest the unrest developing in her homeland of Ireland as well as the activities of the militant Women's Suffrage Movement. Two hundred thousand men were under arms in protestant Ulster and the catholic South and civil war seemed imminent. Lady Blomfield sympathized with home rule for Ireland but deplored the violence and would not speak much about it. When it came to the behaviour of the suffragettes, she initially admired their militancy and self-sacrifice but later came to disapprove of their activities of burning houses, pouring corrosive acid into post boxes and destroying works of art. However she helped the suffragettes in many ways and was appalled by the way the government treated them. She gave a cottage on her small estate over to the suffragettes and put them up under assumed names and disguises. The village policeman prowled around the house suspecting their presence but never reported them to the authorities.

Early in 1915 the Bahai Council was distressed to hear about the murder of Shaykh 'Alí-Akbar-i-Quchání, one of the most distinguished Bahá'ís of Khurásán, Persia. He had been shot dead on 14 March in the bazaar in Mashhad where he had gone to teach the Bahá'í message. The Bahá'ís of Khurásán were under constant threat in the weeks that followed. News reached London via a telegram to Lady Blomfield. The telegram, dated 15 April, read: 'Venerable Behai martyred Meshed. Preparing uprising against Behais. Help us, ask justice from Persian Government, parliament. Telegraph your Legation here. Advertise Paris others.'[197]

The Council meeting at Ethel's home on 24 April discussed the situation at length. It was decided that Sir Richard Stapley, who had been such a strong supporter of the Cause when the Master had been in Britain, would be approached with a view to a question on the subject being put in the Houses of Parliament. However, at its next meeting the Council heard that Sir Richard advised against this, saying that in the war climate it would not be wise to table such a question. Lady Blomfield also corresponded with Lord Lamington, who dealt often with Middle Eastern matters, as well as with Lady Mary, Countess of Wemyss, who consequently enquired about the situation from her sister's brother-in-law, Jack Tennant, the Under Secretary for War. From his sources he was able to inform her that there was not a general uprising against the Bahá'ís and that the powers in the Foreign Office felt it unwise for the British government to champion 'an heretical sect in Persia'.[198] Ethel and the other Council members wrote letters to prominent personalities including Lord Lamington, Lady Morell – the wife of an MP who had interested himself in the matter – and to the British Admiral in the Persian Gulf. The expected massacre of Bahá'ís in Persia did not occur, but the high level of activity generated by the British believers in order to respond to the request of their brethren served to remind the prominent people of British society of the existence of the Bahá'ís, who had received little attention since the departure of 'Abdu'l-Bahá from their shores.

Perhaps the most significant development for the British Bahá'ís during the years of the Great War was the beginning of the third major community of believers, in Bournemouth. The origins of that community are inseparably linked with Dr John Ebenezer Esslemont, a Scotsman by birth. He first heard of the Movement during a conversation in December 1914 with the wife of a colleague, Katherine Parker, who had met 'Abdu'l-Bahá when He was in London. Dr Esslemont was immediately interested and asked to be lent pamphlets. The following March, having read a number of Bahá'í books,

Esslemont enthusiastically fasted for the nineteen days of the Bahá'í fast and addressed the Bournemouth Lodge of the Theosophical Society on the Bahá'í teachings. Others, too, were attracted to the Bahá'í Movement, including a Miss Martyn who was a resident patient at the Home Sanatorium run by Dr Esslemont.

Esslemont was delighted to have discovered the Faith, saying in a letter to Luṭfu'lláh Ḥakím that 'in this time of strife and bloodshed it is a great comfort to have Baha'u'llah's promise of the Most Great Peace and to feel that a spiritual power is at work which by-and-by will turn the swords into plough shares and the spears into pruning hooks.'[199] Dr Esslemont was a keen Esperantist and was thus able to communicate with Bahá'ís all over the world. Together with Ḥakím he translated the *Hidden Words* into Esperanto in 1916.

One of the first Bahá'ís to offer assistance to the new Bournemouth community was Mother George, who spent a holiday amongst them and addressed small gatherings where a certain amount of interest was aroused. Tudor Pole's family lived at nearby Southbourne and he also called to meet Esslemont, afterwards broadcasting widely this new believer's devotion and enthusiasm for the Cause.

The suffering caused by the War was very severely felt by the Bahá'ís in Manchester. A few days after fighting broke out, John Craven received a Tablet from the Master which praised the activities of the friends in the city:

> Praise be to God that in Manchester, the fire of the Love of God is ignited, the Sun of Reality has cast a penetrating splendour, the Breeze of Divine Providence wafted, and the Call of the Kingdom reached your ears . . . I hope that you may become baptized with the Fire of the love of God and the Water of the Holy Spirit, and that each one of you may become a divine farmer and sow in the farm of the world of humanity the seeds of reality, irrigating them with the water of the teachings of Bahá'u'lláh, so that the Light of Truth may illumine that country.[200]

Sadly, the group soon found that the destructive effect of the war not only harmed their countrymen overseas but seriously jeopardized the close links which they had struggled so hard to achieve among themselves. The group was split up, with a family of German Bahá'ís, the Treubers, being sent back to Germany as aliens and the Chessel family removed to work on munitions in Kent. Amidst all the turmoil, at the end of December 1914, Daniel Jenkyn, the spiritually illumined young Cornishman who had built up a warm friendship with the Manchester community, died suddenly at his home in St Ives.

Ethel Rosenberg had also enjoyed the friendship of Jenkyn. In April 1913, he and Edward Hall had made a special visit to her mother's grave at Lelant in Cornwall and said prayers there for the progress of her soul in the next world. When Ethel was in Cornwall in November 1914, possibly to visit her younger sister, she called to see Jenkyn in St Ives where she found him regaining his strength after a serious illness. However, he failed to recover and on the last day of 1914 he passed away. Ethel conveyed the news to the Bahá'í world via a letter in *Star of the West*:

> It is with sincere grief I have to tell you of the 'passing on' of our dear brother, Mr. Daniel Jenkyn, of St. Ives, in Cornwall. He died from the effects of a prolonged and serious attack of influenza. I had occasion to visit St. Ives during the month of November and I saw him during the latter part of the month. He was then better and we all hoped for a speedy restoration to health; but a short while afterwards he had a serious relapse from which he never recovered, and he passed away on December 31st.
>
> He was a most spiritually minded young man, a very sincere, ardent Bahai and a most hard worker for the blessed Cause. Not long since he visited Holland for the purpose of meeting some of those attracted to the Movement and confirming their faith. He joined the Christian Commonwealth Fellowship and found that association brought him into contact with numbers of earnest seekers for the

truth and reality of the Bahai teachings. He undertook a
vast correspondence in connection with the Faith and by
this means did a great amount of teaching.

We all most deeply deplore his loss which will be much
felt in all the English groups.[201]

Ethel invited Jenkyn's closest friend, Dr Ḥakím, to send on
to *Star of the West* a copy of the last letter he had received
from Jenkyn, dated 22 November 1914. The letter conveyed
the spirit and steadfastness that Jenkyn demonstrated
during his illness.

My dear Lotfullah:
  I feel sure you have excused me for delay in answering
your letter of the 10th. I have had an attack of influenza
from which I am quickly getting better and looking forward
soon to be in much better working order than I have been
of late.
  Thanks for news of Remey and Latimer and am delighted
to hear of their mission in America. How one longs to have
been in Acca during the two weeks they were there. Would
it not build one up to be strong against the war forces that
impregnate the atmosphere of Europe! 'The wrong side of
human character is up.' 'The world is topsy turvy!' as Abdul-
Baha says.
  It is cheering to know that the friends in Persia are
progressing well and that they are thinking and praying for
us here in Europe. Oh! if the Bahais were more in number
and more powerful in spirit so that they could have prevented this carnage! We are not yet a great influence in the
world, as the beloved Abdul-Baha wants to see, and yet he
says: 'A weak man can, through assistance, become a strong
man, a drop can become a sea . . . through the assistance of
God any one of us can perform wonders . . .'[202]

The passing of Daniel Jenkyn was a great blow to the British
Bahá'ís. While sorrow overwhelmed the friends in Manchester, they called to mind his devotion and faithfulness to
'Abdu'l-Bahá and shared with their brethren throughout the
world some of the powerful Tablets which the Master had

addressed to this true believer:

> O thou who art confirmed by the Divine Spirit!
> A thousand times bravo because thou didst forego the physical comfort and rest in order to proclaim the glad-tidings of the heavenly illumination. Thou didst gird up the loins of service and traveled to Holland to diffuse the Fragrances of God. Shouldst thou realize how blessed is this trip, unquestionably thou wouldst not rest for one moment, and uninterruptedly thou wouldst engage in the promotion of the Cause of the Almighty. Thou didst well to hasten from London to Holland.[203]

Among the other tributes paid to Jenkyn was a poignant message from Dr Esslemont, who wrote from Bournemouth to John Craven on 25 February 1916, saying that Jenkyn 'seems to have been a wonderful source of inspiration and help for the Bahai Movement. I wish I had known him, but we can each become like him, if we make the "great surrender" of self and selfishness and become "willing channels" for the Divine Spirit. There is no limit to what the human spirit can achieve in the strength of Divine Inspiration.'[204]

In 1916 Dr Esslemont visited the struggling Manchester community but no measure of inspiration or encouragement seemed able to revive interest there. While the friends continued to study to understand more of the Cause and endeavoured to prepare themselves to answer questions of all kinds, they felt that the war had finally overwhelmed them and obliterated the group. Added to the pain caused by the war, Edward Hall also suffered grievous personal losses. In June 1916 his brother Leonard was killed in an accident in Birmingham; the following December his mother passed away. Hall was filled with uncertainty about his future. 'I know not where I shall be sent after New Year's day (January 1st),' he wrote, 'for I am a conscript and under military law, and the war is, perhaps, not nearly over. But I am a follower of Abdul-Baha and a true believer in God, and meet the future with resignation and peace of heart, for with all

my faults and mistakes, I have come nearer and nearer the
love of God and the radiance of Abdul-Baha. God be praised!
I shall hope to be able to do good wherever I get to.'[205]

In February 1917 Hall joined a Labour Company at
Oswestry Camp. Just a few days later his brother John died
on board the ship *Valdez*, which had been torpedoed. Hall
was so distraught to hear of this third death in his family
that he almost felt relieved when he was transferred into
another Labour Company bound for France.

While working in the Forest of Blavincourt with the 25th
Canadian Forestry corps, Edward told his comrades about
the Cause and managed to interest nearly twenty of them.
When in November 1917 the company moved on to a forward
area where they were attacked by German troops, Edward
was still able to continue teaching, inspiring his fellow
soldiers with 'wholesome spiritual conversation' before they
slept. For one who struggled to convey the teachings of
Bahá'u'lláh to the unreceptive citizens of Manchester, life
in the tents provided the kind of 'good fellowship' that he
had been unable to find at home.[206]

By the end of February 1918 the war was taking its toll
on Edward's health and he came down with an inflammation
of the kidneys. He was returned to Scotland to convalesce in
the War Hospital in Cambuslang near Glasgow. By May he
was well enough to take short walks in the park and make
occasional trips into Glasgow. He wrote to Ethel Rosenberg
in London requesting the latest news of the progress of the
Cause, which she happily supplied. During this period he
wrote the poem *The Woods of Blavincourt*, which records his
spiritual experiences there. Here is an extract:

> Yet never could I link those glorious woods
> With dreadful war! Nay rather, there I found release
> From sordid human strife and troubled moods;
> Discerning in their midst, sweet beauty linked with peace.
>
> Deep in the heart thereof, a peerless beech
> Of mighty strength and height and regal sheltering head,

Reminded me of him who lives to teach
With love and wond'rous power the Word that God hath said!

Praise be to God! Can we be silent, when,
In this our day, from Carmel's height the Holy Voice
Proclaims the Promises fulfilled to men,
And waiting Sinai and Bethlehem rejoice!

So was I moved that many times I told
The comrades near, of all the ills and trials sore
Abdul Baha o'ercame; that so they might behold
The love of God, so bright on far off Syria's shore![207]

The poem was sent to the Master who praised Hall, describing its verses as 'eloquent and consummate'. 'Abdu'l-Bahá said that His perusal of it 'stirred the heart' as it 'set forth the evils of war and conflict in the world of existence.[208]

On 30 May 1918 Hall left the hospital and returned to Manchester to try to pick up the threads of his life and begin teaching the Bahá'í Cause once again.

One of the dangers for the promoters of the Bahá'í Movement during the war was being considered political agitators. There was a great deal of persecution of radical or anti-war critics. This would change around 1917 when war-weariness set in and groups calling for a negotiated peace began to make an impact on public opinion. In the meantime, however, the Bahai Council in London struggled to decide how best to continue its meetings and to deal with the conflict occupying everyone's minds.

On 19 February 1916 the Council met and individual members expressed their concerns about the advisability of continuing public meetings. Mother George said she believed that it was a time of great spiritual awakening and that many people who would not listen before were now beginning to do so. The main problem seems to have been the difficulty of actually getting people to attend gatherings and it was felt that a public meeting with very few in attendance conveyed the wrong impression.

Ethel's minutes of this meeting give a fascinating insight

into how the early believers attempted to consult. There seems to have been no attempt made to shape or control the consultation so that a group consensus might emerge. Rather, everyone spoke their mind and if a point was lost amidst other suggestions, the individual who originally raised it would reiterate it more forcefully. The minutes document every contribution and ideas were usually proposed, seconded and then agreed in a very traditional business-like manner – a far cry from ideal Bahá'í consultation as it is now understood. In between the lines of such minutes, one can detect the strength of the personalities of the believers and sense the tension which arose.

As far as the public meetings were concerned, a conclusion was eventually reached that all energy should be expended on private, daytime meetings. Mother George strongly felt that the war should only be discussed from a spiritual point of view and that 'Germans should not be mentioned'. Elizabeth Herrick, who believed free expression and freedom of speech was more desirable than any restrictions, requested to know what exactly the spiritual standpoint was. 'Exactly', interjected Eric Hammond, 'that is the question.' Eventually the Council resolved that the war should not be discussed during any Bahá'í meetings.[209]

The next set of minutes in Ethel's book were taken more than four years later, so it appears that, for whatever reason, the Bahai Council ceased meeting for the duration of the war and a good two years beyond. It has been suggested[210] that one reason for this might be the continual clash of the strong personalities who constituted the membership of the Council. Letters of Dr Esslemont to Dr Ḥakím support this, for Esslemont notes that tensions had arisen among the members of the London community as well as between believers in London and Manchester. It seems that in this era, to survive as a Bahá'í – which was, after all, a very odd and non-conformist thing to be – one had to have a strong character and independent spirit. These characteristics, however, are not necessarily conducive to the harmonious running of an administrative structure.

During those dark and difficult years, Ethel was grateful that she was able to keep her correspondence going with Bahá'í friends around the world. On 23 November 1917, she wrote to Helen Goodall in California:

> How fearful is this terrible Armageddon war – yet one sees strong gleams of light and hope for it looks as if this grand League of Nations really will be formed does it not. And we all look to your splendid country to further that in every possible way. The air raids have been of course very terrible and trying. The noise of the firing is tremendous. Our chief danger in these parts is from unexploded shells – some of which have fallen very near. What anxiety we feel about our dear friends in Palestine – God keep them safe and protected.[211]

With the air raids on the capital, the believers in London suddenly felt very much a part of the war. Despite the obvious danger in which they found themselves and poor attendances, their meetings continued. Ethel addressed a Unity Meeting at Lady Blomfield's apartment in November 1917. Annie Gamble continued to hold regular meetings on Sunday afternoons which Ethel attended as often as possible. Mother George also held her meetings every Saturday but Ethel found it rather too late an hour for her to attend, as her chest problems were aggravated by being out after dark. By this time Mrs Cropper had left London completely to live in the country. Amidst all the danger, there was a notion current among the believers that the war was in effect the final calamity that Bahá'u'lláh had prophesied would occur before the nations of the world united. It is easy to see how the Bahá'ís interpreted the establishment of the League of Nations as a major step towards the Lesser Peace, anticipated to follow catastrophic events.

Great strength and encouragement was derived from news about, or Tablets received from, 'Abdu'l-Bahá. In August 1917 He addressed a Tablet to a Bahá'í in Persia which Ethel received, translated and circulated among the friends in London and those with whom she corresponded. In this Tablet 'Abdu'l-Bahá called upon the Bahá'ís to be steadfast and firm and to act in such a way that all human beings would be astonished by their firmness, uprightness, strength and courage. How shocked the London believers were, then, to learn that 'Abdu'l-Bahá's life was once again in danger. It was apparently through the magnificent efforts of Tudor Pole that the Master survived the turbulent final months of World War I.

At the beginning of the war, Tudor Pole was managing director of a private company, Messrs. Chamberlain Pole and Co., Flour, Grain and Cereal Merchants, of Bristol. The company also owned a biscuit factory. As the company was engaged in government work, Tudor Pole was exempt from military service. However, feeling that he was failing in service to his country, he joined up as a Royal Marine in November 1916.

After a year of training, Tudor Pole sailed from Plymouth on the troopship *Bellerophon*. He arrived in Egypt on 23 November 1917 and was immediately sent up to the Palestine Front. Wounded on 3 December, he was taken to the Nasrieh Military Hospital in Cairo. By the end of January 1918 he was posted as an intelligence officer to the general headquarters of General Allenby in the Second Echelon of the Occupied Enemy Territory Administration. By March he was the director of administration, by April a staff captain and by November a major.

Sometime near the end of December 1917 information reached him from British espionage services that the Turkish commander-in-chief, whose headquarters were then between Haifa and Beirut, 'had stated his definite intention to take the lives of Abdu'l Baha and those around him should the Turkish Army be compelled to evacuate Haifa and retreat north'.[212] The British were preparing to move towards Haifa but for several reasons the advance had to be delayed until the summer. Tudor Pole tried without success to arouse

interest in 'Abdu'l-Bahá's plight among those who were
responsible for intelligence activities, including General
Gilbert Clayton, Sir Wyndham Deedes, Sir Ronald Storrs,
the recently-appointed Governor of Jerusalem, and Major-
General Sir Arthur Money, the Chief Administrator of Occupied Enemy Territory, Tudor Pole's own chief.

Tudor Pole then set out on an extremely dangerous course
of action. Risking a court martial, he decided to evade the
very strict censorship, bypass his military superiors and the
War Office in London and find a way to approach directly the
British Cabinet. Major David Ormsby Gore was in Egypt as
an attaché for the Foreign Office to the Zionist Commmission
then visiting Egypt and Jerusalem. Tudor Pole met Gore at
the Sporting Club in Alexandria and enlisted his services. As
a serving officer he too was subject to King's Regulations and
Censorship Control, but he agreed to carry an uncensored
letter from Tudor Pole to London addressed to Walburga
Lady Paget. She passed the letter to her son-in-law, Lord
Plymouth, who took it directly to Balfour. Balfour arranged
for its contents to be placed on the agenda of a Cabinet
meeting at which he, Lloyd George and Lord Curzon were
present.

At the same time, Lady Blomfield and the London believers were also actively pleading for 'Abdu'l-Bahá's protection.
Lady Blomfield, herself apparently alerted by Tudor Pole,
went to see Lord Lamington, who had 'considerable influence
in government circles'.[213] He wrote to Balfour himself in
January 1924, asking that the protection of the British
authorities in Palestine be extended to 'Abdu'l-Bahá and His
family.

Mrs Whyte, who had invited 'Abdu'l-Bahá to Edinburgh,
also learned of the dangerous situation and wrote to her son
Frederick, who was Member of Parliament. He too wrote to
the Foreign Office about 'Abdu'l-Bahá, his letter arriving on
the same day as Lamington's.

All this sudden activity on behalf of 'Abdu'l-Bahá alerted
the British authorities to His presence in Palestine. A cable

was sent to the British High Commissioner in Egypt asking that he 'warn the General Officer Commanding that he and his family should be treated with special consideration in the event of our occupying Haiffa [sic]'.[214] When the British did take Haifa in September 1918, information about 'Abdu'l-Bahá's safety was quickly transmitted to London, to the great relief of the British believers.

From that time until His passing 'Abdu'l-Bahá became a popular and widely-respected figure among the British officers in Palestine. General Allenby and his wife were regular social callers as was Colonel Edward Staunton, the military Governor of Haifa who became a firm friend. By early 1919, 'Abdu'l-Bahá had been visited by all of the important military personnel in Palestine. The following year, on General Sir Arthur Money's recommendation, the British king agreed to bestow a knighthood upon 'Abdu'l-Bahá for His humanitarian activities, storing grain and averting a famine in Palestine during the war years.

Tudor Pole called on the English friends to send a Memorandum to both General Allenby and Sir Arthur Money expressing their gratitude for the consideration shown to the Master since the British occupation. At the same time, he also suggested a letter be sent to Balfour at the Foreign Office thanking him for giving 'Abdu'l-Bahá the British government's full protection. On 28 March 1919 Ethel wrote to a number of believers around the world, including Roy Wilhelm in New York and Helen Goodall in California, telling them that the Bahá'ís in London were 'preparing and signing these letters . . . We have thought it best to have these Memoranda or letters signed by four or five of the leading friends of Abdul Baha on behalf of the rest of the friends . . . From all that Major W. T. P. has told us we feel that we can hardly be sufficiently grateful to the personages named in His Memorandum for all they have done for our beloved Abdul Baha, his friends and his family.'[215] Ethel invited her co-workers around the world to send similar messages to the same people.

Despite being unable to communicate freely with His followers in the West during much of the war, 'Abdu'l-Bahá sensed that all was not well as far as their unity was concerned. Meeting Tudor Pole in Haifa in February 1919, the Master expressed his anxiety that any friction which might have arisen between individual believers in England or America should be entirely alleviated so that a thoroughly united front could be shown to the world, proving that the Bahá'í Movement was one of a spiritual nature which unites rather than creates discord. Such a concerted display of unity was essential as the war came to an end and the expectant eyes of humanity were fixed on the League of Nations and whatever solutions were available to make sure such a terrible conflict did not happen again. Dr Esslemont felt convinced that the Bahá'í Cause would make great strides in England if the friends 'were . . . really united and were we real Bahais, even with our present numbers the country would soon be transformed. O that we may be all freed from the least trace of selfishness, and give ourselves wholly to God and the service of his Cause . . .'[216] With Ethel's encouragement, on 12 November, the 101st anniversary of the Birthday of Bahá'u'lláh, Dr Esslemont penned a letter expressing devotion to 'Abdu'l-Bahá which he sent to Ethel so that as many as possible of the English Bahá'ís could sign it.

The necessity of having a comprehensive and thorough introductory text book on the Bahá'í Movement impelled Dr Esslemont to begin work on just such a publication. As early as 1916 he had begun contemplating the book but progress was slow owing to his professional commitments. Word reached the Holy Land once the war was over that Esslemont's book, entitled *Bahá'u'lláh and the New Era*, was in progress and 'Abdu'l-Bahá requested to see a copy. Dr Esslemont forwarded the first nine chapters for 'Abdu'l-Bahá's comments and approval.

In July 1918 Ethel travelled down to Bournemouth for a visit, staying with Tudor Pole's family in Southbourne.

Ethel enjoyed reading the draft chapters of Esslemont's book and thought one of them in particular should be printed as a separate pamphlet before the book's publication. The pamphlet carried an announcement that it was a chapter of a forthcoming publication on the Bahá'í religion. Ethel's suggestion was taken up and the 31-page booklet entitled 'What is a Bahá'í' was published by the Malvina Press in West Kensington in 1919.

Dr Esslemont's work was by all accounts timely if not ground-breaking. Writing of *Bahá'u'lláh and the New Era*, Shoghi Effendi described it as 'that splendid, authoritative and comprehensive introduction to Bahá'í history and teachings, penned by that pure-hearted and immortal promoter of the Faith, J. E. Esslemont'.[217] Queen Marie of Rumania, who openly allied herself with the Cause of Bahá'u'lláh, described it as 'a glorious book of love and goodness, strength and beauty', affirming that 'no man could fail to be better because of this Book'.[218] Just as with *Some Answered Questions* and *Paris Talks*, Ethel's wealth of experience and depth of knowledge had a part to play in the writing of this classic text.

Ethel spent two weeks with the Tudor Poles and spoke at two 'delightful meetings'.[219] During her stay in Bournemouth, Ethel and Dr Esslemont travelled to the cathedral city of Winchester to pay a visit to a Mrs Drower who, under the name E. S. Stevens, had written a romantic novel for Mills and Boon in 1911 entitled *The Mountain of God* which used the Bahá'í community in the Holy Land as its setting. Dr Esslemont described it as a most interesting visit, saying he was charmed with Mrs Drower.

Returning to London, Ethel was faced with another challenge, this time at home. Her brother George, with whom she shared a house and whose health, like hers, was always 'delicate',[220] frequently became ill in the winter. In September 1918 George underwent surgery from which it took him some time to recover. Despite her own health problems and financial difficulties as well as all of her Bahá'í commitments,

Ethel nursed George back to health.

'Abdu'l-Bahá was very concerned about Ethel's health and financial situation. On the day of Dr Esslemont's departure from Haifa following his first pilgrimage in 1919, the Master spoke to him about Ethel, saying that the Bahá'ís should try to take care of her. He gave Esslemont £50 in Turkish gold to pass on to her.[221]

With the war now over, Mother George begged Ethel to begin meetings once again. Ethel asked her friend to go to various addresses and find a room to rent, as she herself was not well enough to do it. They settled on the Lindsay Hall at Notting Hill Gate where regular meetings were initiated on Wednesday nights.

A most exciting development for the British Bahá'ís was the arrival in England of 'Abdu'l-Bahá's eldest grandson, Shoghi Effendi, who took up his studies at Balliol College, Oxford during July 1920. Shoghi Effendi was already well-known to Ethel, Dr Esslemont and Tudor Pole and had become an increasingly prominent figure on the international Bahá'í scene through his letters to *Star of the West* and excellent translations of 'Abdu'l-Bahá's Tablets. His reason for studying in England was to perfect his English to such an extent that he could act as the Master's secretary and adequately translate the scriptures of the Faith. Shoghi Effendi became intimate friends with the English Bahá'ís and was perhaps, after Ethel, the first person successfully to bridge the gap between the London friends and the Manchester and Bournemouth believers, becoming a uniting factor in all their lives.

Dr Esslemont was most surprised one Wednesday night in late July to arrive at the Lindsay Hall and find Shoghi Effendi in the doorway.

> I was delighted to see him and we embraced in true oriental fashion. Then shortly Mr and Mrs Ober turned up too, so we had a real Bahai meeting with both East and West well represented. I spoke shortly, then both of the Obers, and then Shoghi spoke and chanted. Miss Rosenberg was in the

chair and seemed very happy. The hall was full and all seemed to enjoy the meeting greatly.[222]

Shoghi Effendi spent the following Friday at Ethel's home, where Dr Esslemont joined them in the afternoon. In the evening all three went to Helen Grand's house for a drawing room meeting at which seventeen seekers were present. One of the believers, Elizabeth Herrick, felt disappointed that it had not been possible to arrange a Unity Meeting for all the friends while the Obers, Shoghi Effendi and Dr Esslemont were in London. She had tried hard with no success to establish such a meeting and wept as she told Dr Esslemont how she felt the need for some form of organization and cooperation amongst the believers so that such opportunities were not missed.

Shoghi Effendi did much to cheer the hearts of the British Bahá'ís during his brief stay amongst them and Ethel proved to be a kind and supportive friend to him. His experience, studying at Oxford, according to his widow Rúḥíyyih Rabbaní, 'shaped and sharpened his already clear and logical mind, heightened his critical faculties, reinforced his strong sense of justice and reasoning powers, and added to the oriental nobility which characterized Bahá'u'lláh's family those touches of the culture we associate with the finest type of English gentleman'.[223]

Elizabeth Herrick's frustration at the lack of cooperation and organization amongst the believers was to be short-lived. 'Abdu'l-Bahá had told Dr Esslemont while he was on pilgrimage that the London Bahá'ís should re-form their Council. A preliminary meeting was held on 22 October 1920 to discuss what to do with the Bahá'í library. Present at this meeting were, from the original Council, Ethel Rosenberg, Annie Gamble, Mother George, Elizabeth Herrick and Eric Hammond, plus Dr Esslemont, Miss Musgrave and George Simpson, who was destined to become a dominant figure in the early years of the Bahá'í administrative order in Britain. Eric Hammond began the meeting with a prayer and then

spoke about the necessity for unity and harmony, saying that
unity was the one essential foundation of the Bahá'í brotherhood and that it should be remembered that everyone in the
Movement were brothers and sisters. Regarding the library,
Ethel suggested that Ronald Jones, the secretary of the
Lindsay Hall, be asked to spare a shelf in one of the cup-
boards in the small hall where the Wednesday night meetings
were being held. This was unanimously accepted and subsequently acted upon.[224]

On 7 December 1920 the Bahai Council formally met for
the first time in almost five years. As well as those who had
met two months earlier, this consultation was joined by
Helen Grand, Mrs Crosby and Mrs Thornburgh-Cropper. The
meeting was held at Miss Grand's house in Eccleston Place.
Dr Esslemont described the meeting as 'very harmonious'.
'I think,' he wrote to Dr Ḥakím in Haifa, 'we all felt that it
marked the beginning of a new era in the history of the
Cause in this country. The meeting was arranged in accordance with the advice given by Abdul Baha through me that
the old members of the council who were still able to act
should add to their number a few new ones whom the friends
approved and they should then work together.'[225] The Council agreed to meet three times a year, but should occasion
arise for discussion of an important point, an emergency
meeting could be called at any time by communicating with
the secretary. The quorum was fixed at five members although it was resolved that all members should be given
notice of such meetings.

Dr Esslemont and Claudia Coles, who had recently arrived
from the United States, spoke to the Council about the
Bahá'í House of Worship being planned for Chicago. 'Abdu'l-
Bahá had indicated that this was now the most important
work for the Cause and that when the building was erected,
great results would come to pass for the Bahá'í Movement.
Esslemont was appointed by the Council to collect and
forward gifts for the Temple. Ethel then read to the Council
'Abdu'l-Bahá's directions for the establishment of a Bahá'í

fund. Mrs George was also keen to share news of a proposed school for girls in Haifa which she had heard about in a letter from 'Abdu'l-Bahá's wife. Mother George had undertaken to collect funds for the school from the English believers. By the Council's next meeting, Esslemont had collected eleven pounds and one shilling for the Temple while the Girls School fund had reached four pounds and ten shillings.

The Council discussed the question of publicizing meetings once again and the general opinion was that the high cost of advertising made it almost prohibitive. Elizabeth Herrick was asked to investigate suitable publications where advertisements could be placed at a reasonable cost. She suggested *The Inquirer* and a Unitarian organ. *The Inquirer* was subsequently chosen but the Council was later disappointed that only two people responded to the advertisements.

At its next meeting on 22 March 1921, which was also attended by Major Tudor Pole, the Council bade farewell to Mrs Crosby, who was going to live in the United States, and to Helen Grand, who was leaving for Canada. The members resolved to invite Yu'hanna Dávúd to serve on the Council as well as a new believer, Miss Fry. Much of the consultation centred on the establishment of a formal Bahá'í Publishing Society in England. Dr Esslemont had expressed his desire to have his book published first in America where he believed interest would be greater. It was proposed that the Society could be established on the basis that each author of a book or pamphlet should pay for the cost of producing the work. Elizabeth Herrick offered storage space in her home. She had met with the largest distribution agency in London and it was quite willing to undertake distribution of any Bahá'í publication on the basis of taking seven pennies for every shilling of the published price of the books. The general conclusion reached was that all of the members longed to have a Publishing Society on account of the great delay and expense of getting publications from America but that they could not see how to provide the guaranteed funds necessary.

Shoghi Effendi had also expressed a desire to publish a
pamphlet and there was a possibility of a new translation of
the *Hidden Words*, as well as the need for a reprint of
'Abdu'l-Bahá in London, but no money was available. It was
finally agreed that the Council should come to no definite
decision with regard to a Publishing Society or Publishing
Office. Ethel proposed at the next meeting that a small
advisory sub-committee be established for publications. The
idea was unanimously approved.

Thus the Bahá'ís in London began to put behind them the
long, dark years of disappointment and disunity. Their
efforts in this were greatly bolstered by the arrival from the
United States of Claudia Stuart Coles who would become a
close friend and great help to Ethel Rosenberg. Orphaned at
five years old and widowed at the age of twenty-nine, Claudia
Coles learned of the Bahá'í message from Mariam Haney in
Washington around 1905. By 1910 she was one of twelve
women who formed a Unity Band, writing monthly to one
of the twelve Bahá'í assemblies in the East which were
composed of women. From that time on she emerged as a
compelling speaker at the annual Bahai Temple Unity Conventions in Chicago. Her first encounter with the London
believers was during 'Abdu'l-Bahá's visit in 1911. However
it was not until 1920 that she transferred her residence to
London where her daughter Lelia Skipworth Aldridge and
her granddaughter – also named Claudia – lived. She would
go on to render invaluable services to the British community,
particularly assisting Dr Esslemont with research for his
book and typing the entire manuscript.[226]

The London Bahá'ís were also told by Dr Ḥakím of the
devotion to their Cause of George Townshend, a distinguished scholar and clergyman from Ireland who had recognized Bahá'u'lláh yet retained his position in the church. At
the very end of her life, Ethel worked with Townshend in the
final major achievement of her distinguished life of service
to the Bahá'í Cause – assisting Shoghi Effendi in the translation of the *Hidden Words* of Bahá'u'lláh into matchless and

majestic English.[227]

Throughout this entire period Ethel Rosenberg had struggled on heroically. If there were moments of disunity and conflict among the London believers, she never once mentioned them in her letters to her co-workers around the world. If there were difficulties in arranging public meetings, she never failed to share her vast knowledge and experience with those who sought enlightenment. If there were moments when it seemed that all of the back-breaking work of the past two decades would come to nothing and that her own fragile health would prevent her from carrying on, she never lost sight of the deep, spiritual connection with her Master. At the end of November 1921, Ethel Rosenberg set off once again to the Holy Land to rejuvenate her soul in the incomparable presence of 'Abdu'l-Bahá. She would, alas, be terribly disappointed.

13

The Heroic Age Ends

*Friends, the time is coming when I shall be no longer
with you. I have done all that could be done. I have
served the Cause of Bahá'u'lláh to the utmost of My
ability. I have laboured night and day all the years of
My life. O how I long to see the believers shouldering
the responsibilities of the Cause! ... My days are numbered, and save this there remains none other joy for
Me.*[228]

'Abdu'l-Bahá

In the early hours of the morning of Monday, 28 November
1921 the Master passed away. He was 77 years old. His
'great work', Shoghi Effendi would later observe, 'was now
ended'.[229] His spirit had 'winged its flight to its eternal abode,
to be gathered, at long last, to the glory of His beloved Father, and taste the joy of everlasting reunion with Him.'[230]
The passing of 'Abdu'l-Bahá marked the end of the Heroic
Age of the development of the Bahá'í Faith and the commencement of its Formative Age.

Unaware of the momentous events transpiring in the Holy
Land, Ethel Rosenberg set sail for Egypt, fully intending to
visit 'Abdu'l-Bahá again. Yet strangely, as the long voyage
got underway, she had the curious feeling that for some
unknown reason she would not be able to see Him. Later,
when trying to come to terms with the news of His passing,
she recollected that during the journey she could never quite
convince herself that she was going to have the joy of meeting Him once more. She was puzzled by this sensation and
began to wonder if some accident would happen to her that

would prevent their reunion. Her premonition would sadly
come true but in a manner that would take her completely
by surprise.

The voyage ended at Port Said on Thursday, 1 December.
Ethel was met on board the ship at around seven o'clock in
the morning by the prominent Egyptian believer Mírzá
Maḥmúd, who arranged for her luggage to be collected and
placed in his boat from which the two of them landed ashore.
Mírzá Maḥmúd accompanied Ethel to the passport office
where she left her documents to receive the visa by which she
could enter the Holy Land. They then moved on to the
Customs House where her luggage was examined and they
breakfasted together in the small restaurant.

While Mírzá Maḥmúd arranged for Ethel's bags to be
taken to his own house, she went alone to explore the bazaar
and look for some Christmas presents for her family back in
England. Her initial worries during the sea journey must
have been dispelled as she joined other Bahá'í friends to eat
ices at a hotel where Mírzá Maḥmúd insisted on paying the
bill. Ethel then visited a post office to send a cablegram to
Haifa saying that she would arrive there by train at noon on
the next day. She ate lunch at Mírzá Maḥmúd's house where
she had the joy of meeting his wife and daughters. Ethel
greatly appreciated the kind hospitality of her hosts.

After a short rest, they departed for the railway station
so that Ethel could catch the train for Haifa. The train
arrived at half past ten and she boarded to take her seat
although it was not due to leave until half past one in the
morning. She bought herself an ordinary first class ticket as
she wished to avoid the extra expense of taking a sleeping
berth. Ethel found the wait 'somewhat disagreeable' as the
farrásh brought on board a large party of 'third-class immi-
grant Jewesses'.[231] Zionist immigration into Palestine had
been stepped up since the Balfour Declaration some four
years earlier had called for the establishment of a Jewish
homeland in Palestine, providing it did not prejudice the
religious and civil rights of other nationalities residing there.

One elderly woman climbing onto the train suffered from very bad asthma and appeared to Ethel to be dying. Another passenger, who was able to communicate in French, told Ethel that the travellers had come from Berlin, Vienna and Poland. Ethel asked her if she knew it was a first class carriage. The woman called the *farrásh* and the party, burdened with innumerable packages, all trooped out again. Finally, the *farrásh* brought in another passenger to share Ethel's compartment, a quiet young woman who was going to Haifa to be married. Ethel was glad of her company as it prevented the 'half-tipsy English soldiers'[232] from sitting with her.

Around midnight the women were paid a visit by the young Englishman whose job it was to examine and stamp passports. Examining her papers and discovering that Ethel intended to stay in Haifa, he asked her where she planned to reside while in the town.

'With Sir 'Abdu'l-Bahá,' she replied, courteously.

Clearly surprised, the young inspector exclaimed. 'Oh! The one who has just died!'

Ethel's alarm at this shocking announcement swiftly turned to puzzlement. 'I don't think this news can be true,' she replied, 'as I heard nothing of it in Port Said this morning.'

The officer could clearly see that his statement had come as a mighty blow to his passenger and attempted to play down the news in case a mistake had been made. 'It may be a false rumour, but I was told he had died on Monday. I hope, Madam, this has not been a great shock to you?'

'Of course,' said Ethel, 'it is a tremendous shock.' She could scarcely believe it. The young man left the carriage but Ethel looked out into the corridor and asked him to return. She explained how impossible it seemed that the news could be true. She then asked him whether he had known Sir 'Abdu'l-Bahá Abbás.

The young man replied, 'He was one of my greatest friends.' He bowed and went away.[233]

When all the commotion had died down and she felt able
to sit quietly and collect her thoughts, Ethel began to wonder
whether this heart-rending news might after all be the truth.
As the train started on its long night journey, Ethel instinc-
tively felt that it was. With her travelling companion now
sleeping, Ethel allowed herself to shed a tear. This release
of emotion, she later recalled, was followed by the sensation
that somehow 'Abdu'l-Bahá Himself had come and put His
arm around her. She remembered feeling the most wonderful, spiritual comfort. Unable to sleep, she sat quietly, her
mind filled with thoughts and memories, until around seven
o'clock in the morning when she was able to go and eat some
breakfast in the train's restaurant car.

It later emerged that the friends who had shown Ethel so
much love and hospitality in Port Said had decided not to
inform her of 'Abdu'l-Bahá's passing as they feared it would
cause her too great a sadness and would spoil her journey to
Haifa. They subsequently telegraphed Dr Luṭfu'lláh Ḥakím
in Haifa informing him that Miss Rosenberg was unaware
that the Master had ascended. On receiving the cable, Ḥakím
remarked, 'She will learn of it during the journey here.' [234]

During that seemingly endless night, Ethel concluded that
she would be sure of the truth as soon as she saw the face of
Ḥakím, whom she was expecting to meet her from the train.
At noon on Friday, 2 December Ethel arrived for the fourth
time in Haifa, almost thirteen years since her previous visit
and a full decade after having had the priceless opportunity
of receiving the Master in her own home. As the train pulled
into Haifa, she caught a glimpse of Ḥakím's expression and
knew instantly that the news was indeed true, that her
beloved Master was no longer there to welcome her.

What thoughts must have passed through Ethel's mind
as she caught that first precious glimpse of the Shrine of the
Báb, 'nestling in the heart of Carmel'? What emotions might
have stirred in her heart as she gazed out on that building
'at once, massive, simple and imposing', [235] every stone of
which was 'raised and placed in position' with 'infinite tears

and at tremendous cost'[236] by 'Abdu'l-Bahá? At the time of
her third visit to Haifa the mausoleum had yet to receive the
mortal remains of the Báb. Now it also housed all that was
left of the physical temple of 'Abdu'l-Bahá, united in death
with His Father's Prophet-Herald who had unveiled His
mission on the same night that the Master was born. For
more than a decade Ethel must have longed to feel the
exquisite love and fellowship of 'Abdu'l-Bahá's devoted
family once more. How disappointing, then, must it have
been for her to discover them wrapped in grief, mourning the
loss of their Lord and Master, desperately wondering how
they and the Cause of Bahá'u'lláh could ever continue without His peerless example and guidance.

'. . . Tooba Khanum, I grieve, is ill with the heart,' Ethel
wrote to Mother George of one of 'Abdu'l-Bahá's daughters.
'She poured out all her strength and energy in sustaining
others . . . and finally collapsed from overstrain. She has been
in bed for some days and is now better, I am told.'[237]

The days immediately after Ethel's arrival were filled with
moments of calm, personal reflection. Writing to Julia
Culver, she mourned being unable to 'hear his dear, dear
voice once more', yet on Saturday, 3 December, whilst making her first visit to the Shrine of 'Abdu'l-Bahá, she 'felt a
deep and abiding joy'. 'When we think of his great happiness
and freedom,' she wrote, 'we cannot help but be happy can
we?'[238] Ethel found 'Abdu'l-Bahá's Shrine 'most bright and
beautiful. There are wonderful carpets spread upon the floor
and a ten-branched candlestick on either side, besides all the
other lights . . . it is all so bright and joyous.'[239] Praying for
so many dear friends in His Shrine removed all the poi-
gnancy from Ethel's grief, its atmosphere inspiring her to
think of nothing but 'Abdu'l-Bahá's supreme joy.

Ethel was also grateful that she was able to spend precious
hours with 'Abdu'l-Bahá's beloved sister, Bahíyyih Khánum,
the Greatest Holy Leaf. Ethel had taken to Haifa a miniature
she had painted of the Master which she presented to
Khánum. It was placed alongside miniatures which Khánum

kept of Bahá'u'lláh and the Báb. Khánum expressed her
desire to get an Indian silver frame for it, similar to the one
that enclosed Bahá'u'lláh's portrait. Ethel felt 'greatly
honoured at this privilege'.[240] Each day, she accompanied the
women of the household to the Shrine for prayers. 'Khanum
is wonderful,' she wrote to Mrs George, 'so are all the ladies
... Monever Khanum sends her love and says will you please
pray for them *all*. They all need your prayers *so much* . . .'[241]

The days of mourning, however, spent with the women
of 'Abdu'l-Bahá's household tested Ethel's very English
sensibilities. 'Of course,' she explained, 'the ladies are overwhelmed with visits of condolence from guests who sit all day
long and every day according to the custom of the East – a
most truly trying custom I call it!'[242]

Ethel was grateful not to be entirely alone in the little
cottage room at the guest house where she had been given
accommodation. Mrs Stannard was also there, having has-
tened to Haifa as soon as she heard of 'Abdu'l-Bahá's passing. Also present were the formidable Dr Florian Krug and
his second wife, Grace, from New York; Mr John and Mrs
Louise Bosch from California; Miss Johanna Hauff from
Stuttgart and the young American Curtis Kelsey, who had
come to Haifa at the Master's request to install electric light
at the Shrine of the Báb and at Bahjí. Despite there being
such a distinguished group of early Western Bahá'ís to
console one another, Ethel nevertheless longed for the
company of some of her closer friends. On receiving a cable
from Claudia Stuart Coles, Ethel advised her and two other
English believers, Miss Fry and Miss Bevan, to come immediately on pilgrimage.

The grief of losing their Master must have done much to
cement the hearts of His saddened followers. Indeed prior
to this event stories existed that suggested Ethel and Dr
Krug, for example, did not always see eye to eye. One story
that survives tells of a talk given by 'Abdu'l-Bahá in the Holy
Land some years previously on the subject of love and unity.
As the Master stressed that the true believer must love

everybody, Dr Krug is reported to have asked, '*Everybody*,
'Abdu'l-Bahá?'

'Yes, Dr Krug, *everybody*,' replied the Master. Then
pointing His finger, He added, 'But you stay away from Miss
Rosenberg!'[243]

Ethel heard much during those days of 'Abdu'l-Bahá's
extraordinary funeral, 'a funeral the like of which Palestine
had never seen',[244] with its long procession made up of some
ten thousand mourners, including dignitaries, clergy and
notables of many creeds and races who delivered funeral
orations and paid tribute to the Master's life and work.

Ethel spoke with Mrs Krug about the circumstances
surrounding the Master's passing and then conveyed the
story to the friends in England in a letter dated 8 December
1921. While there are small discrepancies between Ethel's
version of the story and the version later prepared by Shoghi
Effendi with the assistance of Lady Blomfield, it is interesting to see in what detail Ethel wished to share the news of
the Master's passing with the friends at home:

> Dr. and Mrs. Krug arrived only nine days before his depar-
> ture. She tells me they were both much struck by his ex-
> treme fatigue and weariness, and they entreated him not
> to visit the Guest House, but to allow them to visit him.
> However, he continued to come over to see the friends here
> and to take a meal with them, right up to the Friday. On
> that day they were particularly impressed by his very loving
> and impressive farewell, 'Good night! Good night!' he re-
> peated several times, stretching out his hands towards
> them. On Saturday he was taken ill with fever, and his
> temperature rose to 104. On Sunday, the 27th, he seemed
> much better and he had no fever. At 5 p.m. that day he
> received the Quazi (the Mohammedan judge). This gentle-
> man said to him, 'I think it would be much better for your
> health if you would build a small house entirely of wood
> instead of living in a stone house.' Abdul-Baha replied, 'I
> have no time left now to build houses.' Then he also re-
> ceived the two principal Police Authorities – after that he
> retired to rest at about 8:30. At midnight or so, he arose

from his bed and took his temperature and showed his daughter Rouha Khanum that he had no fever. He refused milk and lay down again. Later on she once more entreated him to drink a little milk. He looked at her and said, 'You would give me milk when I am going!' – and with that he was gone.

I have told you these details that you may know how easy and rapid was the passing and that practically he had no illness – at any rate, no serious illness.

During the previous week he had given his family many hints of his approaching end, if they had but understood them.

To Rouhi Effendi he said, 'I have decided to go far away, where no one can reach me.' Rouhi Effendi and another young man who was present, thought he was joking and Rouhi Effendi said, 'You know, Master, that is impossible; they will always find you.'

About ten days before the end, he left his little bedroom in the garden and came into the house. He told his family that he had dreamed in the night that Baha 'Ullah had come to him and had said, 'Destroy this room immediately,' and therefore he did not like to sleep outside any more, but would come into the house. The family were thankful, as they felt he would be nearer to them if he needed any service during the night. They now understand the spiritual symbolism of the saying – the 'room' being the Beloved One's body.

So you see, he did what he could to make them ready that the blow might not be too unexpected and sudden. During all those days he was extraordinarily loving and tender to every one with whom he came in contact – they all say, so much so, that they remarked upon it.[245]

Losing the Master, Ethel felt impelled to meditate upon her responsibilities as a believer. 'Now is the time of crises and now is our heavenly opportunity!' she wrote to Julia Culver. 'How greatly privileged are we who have known the Beloved and have been so long in His presence. A great responsibility is ours to convey a faint reflection of the wonderful charm of his personality to others as well as to spread his teaching.'[246] In her letter to the friends in England, she added,

> I know so well how heartbroken you have all been at this (for *us*) sad, sad news and how you must all be longing for a word directly from this sacred spot – made doubly sacred for all of us now as it is the resting-place of our Beloved Abdul-Baha.
> I cannot sufficiently thank God for allowing me to be here at this solemn time. You are, I know, all feeling with me that *now* is the 'accepted time'; *now* is the moment when we must all dedicate our lives afresh to the service of our beloved Abdul-Baha, the Perfect Servant of God – and of us all.
> . . . I am sure we all feel that now is the time for us all to be united with the utmost love and firmness – to increase our activities tenfold in teaching and spreading the good news of the Kingdom.[247]

Each day after the passing of 'Abdu'l-Bahá, between 50 and a hundred of Haifa's poor and down-trodden citizens gathered around His home to be fed. On the seventh day, Sunday 4 December, more than a thousand people, of all creeds and races received corn, distributed in 'Abdu'l-Bahá's memory. Observing from the front steps of the Master's house, Ethel found the sight wonderful and picturesque. Around 40 pounds of corn – nearly enough to fill a petroleum tin – was given to every person who asked. From early dawn they waited around the gateway of the Master's house. Ethel noted that 'many of them were decent poor people and many were professional beggars in rags and tatters'.[248] Young and old, men and women, mothers with babes in arms, small boys and girls gathered in crowds. Some of the children were so small that they could barely stagger along under the weight of the bags of corn and the Bahá'í friends lent assistance and in some cases even carried the corn for them.

They entered by the main gate, and as each one received his portion, they left by the steps into the garden and went out through the lower entrance. On the steps of the house, Ethel and Mrs Stannard agreed that 'Abdu'l-Bahá would have loved the occasion. The sight conjured up memories for Ethel of watching the Master in 'Akká on a Friday giving money to the assembled poor. She was told that even on the Friday before His passing He had gone to the Mosque and distributed his usual alms.

On the ninth day after 'Abdu'l-Bahá's ascension, which was the final official day of mourning, Ethel joined almost 140 pilgrims who went to pay their respects at the Shrine of Bahá'u'lláh. They took the morning train to 'Akká and walked in procession to Bahjí while Dr Krug, Curtis Kelsey and Dr Ḥakím took photographs of the impressive sight. Concerned that she would be unable to walk the entire way to the Shrine, Ethel rode in a carriage that had been especially sent over from Haifa. After a prayer chanted at the Shrine, the Western friends all lunched together in the room that the Master had used.

For Ethel, it was a wonderful moment to see so many friends gathered there. At the end of the visit the whole group was once again photographed by Curtis Kelsey before returning to Haifa by train, the friends completely filling two railway carriages. They were disappointed, however, that it had not been possible for them to visit the prison cell in 'Akká where Bahá'u'lláh had been held for more than two years. The Covenant-breakers in 'Akká had given 'Abdu'l-Bahá a great deal of trouble during the last few months of his life and it was considered unwise for the pilgrims to go to the prison.

Not all of the people who arrived to pay their respects to the grieving family were welcomed through the door of the Master's home. His shameless half-brother Muḥammad-'Alí was turned away. On his arrival at the house, the Greatest Holy Leaf sent a message to him saying, 'Our Beloved does not allow and does not like you to come in, and if you come in you will add to our sorrows.'[249] Muḥammad-'Alí wrote an article in the newspapers calling the Bahá'ís to turn to him

and filed a claim based on Islamic law for a portion of
'Abdu'l-Bahá's estate. He also called for his son, who had
been stirring up trouble in the United States, to join him in
a renewed series of attacks on the Master's family.

Ethel's thoughts during those difficult moments must
have turned often to Shoghi Effendi, the Master's eldest
grandson whom she had made feel so welcome in England.
The young Oxford scholar first learned the news of his
grandfather's passing while unintentionally glancing at a
cablegram lying on the desk of Major Tudor Pole in London.
At around half past nine in the morning on Tuesday, 29
November, Tudor Pole had received the cablegram addressed
'Cyclometry London' at his office in St James's Street. It had
been dispatched from Haifa at three o'clock the previous day
and read: 'His Holiness Abdul Baha ascended to the Kingdom of Abha. Please inform friends. (Signed) Greatest Holy
Leaf.'[250]

Tudor Pole immediately notified the Bahá'ís in London
by wire, telephone and letter and called for Shoghi Effendi
to come from Oxford without revealing the reason for his
call. Another cable was sent to the Holy Family in Haifa
expressing sorrow and loving sympathy from all the British
Bahá'ís. Shoghi Effendi arrived at Tudor Pole's office at
around noon. Returning to the room to meet his young
visitor, Tudor Pole found Shoghi Effendi collapsed, deeply
disturbed by the news that he had accidentally read. The
distraught youth was taken to the home of Helen Grand
where he remained bedridden for a number of days and was
tended by his hostess as well as Lady Blomfield and his own
sister, Rúhangíz, who was in London studying at the time.

Wellesley Tudor Pole had established his own firm, W.
Tudor Pole & Co., at 61 St. James's Street in December
1919. The office specialized in negotiating direct trade,
particularly in tea, to Russia and Eastern Europe. Difficulties
in trading direct with the new Russian regime involved
Tudor Pole in the formation of an Anglo-Dutch Trading
Group which facilitated trade through Holland and removed

the problems of dealing direct from Great Britain. The company was represented in New York, Paris, Amsterdam, Constantinople, Alexandria and Haifa, resulting in many activities including selling clothes and paper to Holland, as well as publishing and publicity agencies.

Tudor Pole conveyed the news of 'Abdu'l-Bahá's passing internationally through his network of highly-placed acquaintances. Cables were sent to the High Commissioner and Sir Wyndham Deedes at Jerusalem and consequently, the British Authorities in Palestine promised to show respect for the memory of the Master and to render any services required by the Holy Family and the Bahá'í community in Haifa and 'Akká. Lord Lamington, wiring his condolences, informed Tudor Pole that he had asked for the British government to be represented at the Master's funeral. General Sir Arthur Money, formerly Chief Administrator of Palestine, also wrote, expressing his grief on learning of the death of 'Abdu'l-Bahá. 'I had a strong regard and admiration for him,' he wrote, 'and I always valued his advice. He exercised all his influence in Palestine for good, and was always ready to assist the Administration toward the establishment of Law and Order.'[251]

At the suggestion of Ḍiá'u'lláh Aṣgharzádih, a cable was dispatched to the Bahá'ís in 'Iṣhqábád notifying the community there of the Master's ascension and conveying the love and sympathy of the friends from every part of the world. In order to ensure delivery of this message, arrangements were made with the American Red Cross Authorities and the British Trade Mission at Moscow to persuade the Soviet Foreign Minister to allow the important news to be telegraphed to 'Iṣhqábád.

Nor did 'Abdu'l-Bahá's passing go unnoticed by the British Press. On 30 November, *The Times* printed an appreciation of some seven column inches under the heading 'DEATH OF THE BAHAI – CHIEF OF THE BABIST CULT'. In a generally accurate obituary, the *Times* reported that 'Abdu'l-Bahá 'was a man of great spiritual power and commanding

presence, and his name was held in reverence throughout the
Middle East . . . The British Authorities recognized his
position of influence, and it was at Lord Allenby's suggestion
that he was knighted last year.'[252]

On the following day, the *Morning Post* reported that the
Master's passing would 'give cause for sorrow wherever his
name is known. At his table Buddhist and Mohammedan,
Hindoo and Zoroastrian, Jew and Christian sat in amity
. . .'[253] The *Daily Mirror* too published a photograph of
'Abdu'l-Bahá with a short notice and the *Daily Mail* reported
that the 'journeying forth of one of the very few missionaries
of an Asiatic faith is recalled by news of the death of Sir
Abdul Baha Abbas al Bahai . . . The Bahai claimed that his
faith expressed the essential truth of all the Religions of the
World.'[254] Even *The Children's Newspaper* published an
article entitled 'WHO WAS ABDUL BAHA? INTERESTING MAN
PASSES'.[255]

The day after Shoghi Effendi's collapse in Tudor Pole's
office, the Major wired Shoghi Effendi's devoted friend Dr
Esslemont, inviting him to London. In a letter of 8 December, Esslemont described those days to Dr Luṭfu'lláh Ḥakím:

> It was a most unexpected shock when we heard of the
> passing of our Beloved Master. On the Sat. night before He
> passed on we celebrated His Fete day (the Day of the Covenant) in Bournemouth, at Mr. King's house, and on the
> Sunday night at our usual weekly meeting I spoke for an
> hour about the Beloved, but even then the shadow of his
> approaching departure seemed to have cast a gloom over us.
> Mr. King was troubled and could not sleep, these two nights.
> Mrs. Dunsby felt depressed and, when I asked her to read
> these Benedictions of the Beloved that you copied out for
> me, she broke down in the middle, and handed me the
> paper. On the Saturday night, Nurse Challis had a vivid
> dream about the Master – dreamt that He was in great
> trouble, and she and I were trying to help Him. On the
> Sunday, she felt very depressed and wondered whether
> Abdul Baha was all right. She told me about her dream and

her feeling troubled about the Master.

On the Monday night, Mrs. Dunsby had a dream about the Master but a happy one, in which He comforted and reassured her. On the Tuesday night, Nurse Challis also had a vision of Him in which He looked very happy and told her: 'Let not your heart be troubled, neither let it be afraid!' These visions of Him after His Ascension have greatly comforted them both.

We got the news from Major Tudor Pole on Tues. morning and on Wed. he sent a wire to me saying that Shoghi was in London, at Miss Grand's, and asking me to come up if possible. I went up on Thurs. morning and found poor Shoghi in bed, absolutely prostrate with grief. At first he seemed absolutely overwhelmed by the loss, unable to eat, to sleep, to think. During the day, however, he recovered, and after tea he got up and came through to the drawing room, where we had a little meeting – Miss Grand, Lady Blomfield, Mirza Dawud, Ziaoullah and myself. Shoghi read and translated to us the last tablet he had received from the Master, and chanted for us. These four friends I have just mentioned and Mr. Tudor Pole have all been exceedingly kind, and were of the greatest help to Shoghi in his hour of need. I spent the night with Mirza Dawud, and the following day we all gathered at Miss Grand's again. We decided that Lady Blomfield would go with Shoghi and Ruhangiz Khanom to Haifa, as soon as the journey could be arranged. Ziaoullah also offered to go, and to bear all expenses of the journey, so far as necessary.[256]

At the same time that Ethel Rosenberg arrived in Haifa, Shoghi Effendi was preparing to leave London to spend a few days convalescing in Bournemouth in the company of Dr Esslemont before making the return journey to Haifa . At times he was, according to Dr Esslemont, 'very sad and overcome with grief, but on the whole he kept up very bravely, and gradually, the conviction that although the bodily presence was removed, the Spirit of the Beloved was as near, as powerful and as accessible to us as ever, seemed to revive his strength and hope.'[257]

Shoghi Effendi managed to muster up the strength to attend two small meetings with the Bournemouth friends the following weekend at which he spoke 'with real power'.[258] On 7 December a cable arrived from the Greatest Holy Leaf urging him to return early to the Holy Land, as great work awaited him. He left Bournemouth for London immediately to prepare for his journey home with Rúḥangíz and Lady Blomfield. Word reached the Bahá'ís in the Holy Land that the three would leave on 16 December.

They set sail for Port Said on the *Kaiser-i-Hind* and arrived in Haifa thirteen days later on the train from Egypt. A number of friends met the train as it rolled into Haifa's station at twenty past five in the evening of 29 December. The trauma of 'Abdu'l-Bahá's passing was still apparent in the appearance of His beloved grandson who, overcome with grief, had to be physically helped up the steps of the Master's house.

A few days after his arrival, Shoghi Effendi received yet another shock. The Greatest Holy Leaf and other members of the family shared with him the contents of 'Abdu'l-Bahá's last Will and Testament. The Will was addressed to Shoghi Effendi but had already been scanned by the Greatest Holy Leaf, and probably other members of the family, following the Master's Ascension to see if He had left any instructions as to where His mortal remains should be laid to rest. What they discovered was the announcement of the appointment of Shoghi Effendi as Guardian of the Bahá'í Faith, a sacred institution of which neither he nor the Bahá'ís had any previous knowledge.

Shoghi Effendi now discovered that he was 'the youthful branch branched from the two hallowed and sacred Lote-Trees', 'the sign of God, the chosen branch, the Guardian of the Cause of God'[259] to whom the descendants of the Báb and Bahá'u'lláh, the Hands of the Cause of God and the believers were to turn for guidance, advice and authorized interpretation of the sacred writings. He learned that he was to be the permanent head of the Universal House of Justice and that both it and the guardianship were 'under the care and protection of the Abhá beauty, under the shelter and unerring guidance of His Holiness, the Exalted One'.[260]

The new Guardian also learned that a few weeks before 'Abdu'l-Bahá had passed away, He had instructed Shoghi Effendi's father to cable his son to return to Haifa immediately. His mother and grandmother had decided that such a message might shock Shoghi Effendi unnecessarily so a letter had been posted instead. It arrived after the Master's passing. How Shoghi Effendi must have wished that this reunion had taken place, hoped that His grandfather might have had some words of advice to offer him before he took on his monumental duties. Alas, destiny or simply the interference of his family did not allow them that final meeting.

On 3 January 1922, after Shoghi Effendi visited the Shrine of the Báb and the tomb of his grandfather, the Will and Testament of 'Abdu'l-Bahá was read aloud for the first time to a group of nine men, predominately members of the Master's family, gathered in the house of Shoghi Effendi's aunt where he was living. That the Will was in the Master's own handwriting and contained a number of His seals and signatures was clearly demonstrated to the gathering. Shoghi Effendi was not present at the reading.

Two days prior to the reading of the Master's Will and Testament, Ethel Rosenberg was sitting in the little cottage room where she had been staying when she received a visit from a Bahá'í carpenter by the name of Ahmed. Lady Blomfield had just returned from visiting Saint Luke's Mission Church and a garden with some of the American and German friends when Ahmed arrived to repair the lock and window of the room. Ahmed spoke little English but was able to convey to Ethel how the Master had, in the days prior to His passing, given an intimation of the events that were about to transpire. Ahmed related how 'Abdu'l-Bahá had been heard by one of the gardeners at the Shrine of Bahá'u'lláh to say, 'Oh Bahá'u'lláh! You are very strong. Will you not pick me up and carry me away and hide me in some corner where the friends cannot find me, and where I cannot see the friends – for I am very tired.' Ahmed also related how a few days before His ascension, the Master called him and said, 'Go into the bazaar and buy me some gum.' So Ahmed went and purchased european liquid gum as well as dry gum arabic. He gave them to the Master and wondered a little why He needed the gum, as He had never been known to use it previously. Then he saw the Master take a number of papers and documents, fold them in paper and with His own hands gum up the package.[261]

Forty days after 'Abdu'l-Bahá's passing, at one o'clock in the afternoon of 6 January, Ethel and Lady Blomfield arrived at a large gathering of some six hundred believers and dignitaries from Haifa, 'Akká and the surrounding parts of Palestine and Syria who had been invited for a Memorial Feast at the home of Rúḥá Khánum. Among them was the Governor of Phoenicia. A beautifully arranged dinner was served, arranged entirely by the members of 'Abdu'l-Bahá's household, who had worked for the entire week from morning until evening on the preparations.

Ethel and Lady Blomfield had been given a quick glimpse of the table arrangements by Rúḥá the night before the banquet. Lady Blomfield wrote,

> The long tables were decorated with trailing branches of bougainvillaea. Its lovely purple blooms mingled with the white narcissus, and with the large dishes of golden oranges out of the beloved Master's garden, made a picture of loveliness in those spacious lofty rooms, whose only other decoration was the gorgeous yet subdued colouring of rare Persian rugs. No useless trivial ornaments marred the extreme dignity of simplicity.[262]

The places were set out either side of the table while every plate had a linen table napkin in its centre arranged in mitre form. Down the centre of the tables were alternatively placed dishes of olives and cut radishes.

In addition to these arrangements within the house, about

150 of Haifa's less privileged residents were gathered in a place prepared especially for them where they were also fed and entertained. As was always the custom when the Master was alive, every single guest, regardless of creed, class or rank, received the same loving welcome.

Ethel remarked how the serving of the food went perfectly, like clockwork. So impressed was the English governor that he enquired who had organized and arranged everything so well. When he was informed that it had all been prepared by the women of the household without outside assistance, he was greatly astonished as to how it could have been done with nothing more than the primitive resources at their command.

Having eaten well, the guests then transferred into the large central hall of the Master's house, also sparsely decorated except for a portrait of the Master and some antique Persian tapestries hanging on one wall. A platform had been set out from which speeches were to be made in honour of 'Abdu'l-Bahá. The name of each speaker was announced as he mounted the rostrum.

Abdullah Effendi Mukhlis, the Secretary of the National Mohammedan Society, opened the service, no doubt moving many who heard him to tears with his words of grief:

> Many a time have we assembled in this home, which was the place of pilgrimage for scholars and the fountainhead of virtues. Then we used to find it budding and blossoming, the fragrance of its flowers pervading everywhere, the birds singing on its tall trees, the Water of Life overflowing and beauty of happiness on the faces of those who lived herein.
>
> But today, why do we see its pillars fallen in ruins, everything sad and sorrowful, its face beclouded, its flowers wilted, its leaves fallen and scattered, its birds silent, everything completely submerged with grief and anxiety – the mineral, vegetable and human sharing alike in this desolation?
>
> We have more than once partaken of the food from this Hatimic table. (Hatim Tai was known to be the most gener-

ous man according to Arabian history.) We used to partake
of its food with the utmost ease and drink its water copiously; today – why are we so choked with every mouthful
and strangle with every drop?

This roof has covered us at many scientific and educa-
tional meetings – gatherings that were full of happiness and
joy, wherein voices sounded, and argument and discussion
continued – today, why do we not utter even a word? It is
as if birds were perched upon our heads (so silent are we).
That happiness has changed to sorrow, that joy into grief,
and those discussions to quietness and silence. Is it because
this home was confronted by circumstances and overpow-
ered by the hosts of torture, or surrounded by calamities
from all sides? No. It is neither this or that; nay rather, it
is because the Lord of this home, its departed mystery, its
spirit and its joy, Abdul-Baha Abbas, has ascended from this
mortal world.[263]

Mukhlis closed by drawing attention to the wide range of
peoples in the room, a living testament to all for which
'Abdu'l-Bahá had worked.

Today, the Arab, the Persian, the Oriental, the Occidental,
the Mohammedan, the Christian, and the Jew have equal
share in this memorial service. Since his departure is a
calamity for the whole world, therefore the people of the
East and the West weep for him. Even though our calamity
be most great, yet, praise be to God, his family has been
spared for us. This is our great recompense. [264]

True, the family had been spared but its grief was unspeakable. Away from the gathering, Shoghi Effendi and the
Greatest Holy Leaf sat together in her room, the young
Guardian unable to join the assembly, 'too distressed and
overcome'[265] to meet the assembled guests.

As the speeches continued, the Governor of Phoenicia took
the platform, fondly recalling 'Abdu'l-Bahá's humility. 'Most
of us here have, I think, a clear picture of Sir Abdul-Baha
Abbas,' he told the gathering,

of his dignified figure, walking thoughtfully in our streets, of his courteous and gracious manner, of his kindness, of his love for little children and for the flowers, of his generosity and care for the poor and suffering. So gentle was he, and so simple that, in his presence, one almost forgot that he was also a great teacher and that his writings and his conversations have been a solace and an inspiration to hundreds and thousands of people in the East and in the West.

It is possible to regard his teaching in many lights. Some may say that it did merely reassert truths which form the basis of all religious teachings. Some may declare that it was premature and impractical, but everybody can appreciate the beauty of his ideals and agree that if the doctrine of universal brotherhood was carried out this world would be a better and a happier place.

To us who have just passed through the throes of one of the fiercest wars in the history of mankind, and whose minds and lives are still disturbed – words of peace and goodwill sound almost strange upon our ears. We find it difficult to credit them, but everywhere men of many nations and of diverse creeds proclaim the imperative needs of peace. The conscience and imagination of mankind have been stirred and there is a widespread hope that one by one the conflicting interests and misunderstandings that promote strife and hatred will be removed, and that better and more friendly relations will prevail between the nations, between communities and between individuals. Whenever these better times come we may be sure that the name of Abdul-Baha who lived among us here in Haifa, will be remembered with gratitude and affectionate esteem.[266]

Speaker followed speaker to the platform. The poet Wadie Effendi Bestani pleaded,

Oh, Abdul-Baha!
Who will guide the astray who are groping in the dark?
Oh, ye who are commemorating Abdul-Baha,
Mention ye His words!
Oh, ye who are commemorating Abdul-Baha,
Comprehend ye His ideals![267]

Another speaker, Youssif Effendi El-Kahtib, said he firmly believed 'that Abdul-Baha, after remaining four scores of years in this world, teaching with his thought, guiding with his pen, giving the best example in his glorious deeds, at last has chosen to teach and guide by his silence.[268]

Ahmad Effendi El-Imam concluded,

> When we mention Abdul-Baha, we recall sublimity of character and firmness of determination; we recall purity of the heart and the nobility of personality; we recall unexcelled intelligence and Oriental genius. Yea, when we mention Abdul-Baha, we recall the excellence of morals, the exalted principles, and the noble susceptibilities. We mention him, because he loved the poor equally with the prince; we mention him because he used to entertain both adults and children; we mention him because he was merciful to the orphans and gave freely to the helpless and the stranger.[269]

The hushed and solemn gathering was also told the provisions of the Master's Will. They were anxious to have the new Guardian address a few words to them, but as Shoghi Effendi was unable to attend he quickly composed a short message to be read to the guests. 'The shock has been too sudden and grievous for my youthful age to enable me to be present at this gathering of the loved ones of beloved 'Abdu'l-Bahá'. He thanked the Governor and the guests for their tributes to the Master, saying they had 'revived His sacred memory in our hearts . . . I venture to hope that we his kindred and his family may by our deeds and words, prove worthy of the glorious example he has set before us and thereby earn your esteem and your affection. May His everlasting spirit be with us all and knit us together for evermore!'[270]

The next day, 7 January 1922, 'Abdu'l-Bahá's Will and Testament was once again read in its entirety, on this occasion to an assembled gathering attended by Bahá'ís from Persia, India, Egypt, England, Italy, Germany, America and Japan. Ethel recorded in her diary that the entire Will was

chanted in its original language by two believers, taking a
full hour and a half. Whenever Shoghi Effendi's name was
mentioned during the reading, the entire gathering rose to
its feet as a mark of its respect for the new Guardian, chosen
and appointed by 'Abdu'l-Bahá.[271]

The Guardian however was once again absent. His emotional state was still extremely delicate. It was 'Abdu'l-Bahá's
sister, the Greatest Holy Leaf, who on that same day sent
two cables to Persia. One informed the believers that in His
Will and Testament, the Master had left instructions on how
the Bahá'í world should continue to function. The other
announced 'Will and Testament forwarded Shoghi Effendi
Centre Cause'.[272] In the following months, Shoghi Effendi
came to rely heavily on the experience, wisdom and strength
of his great aunt.

As far as Ethel was concerned, there was absolutely no
question of her doubting the provisions of the Master's Will
nor of the ability of the young Guardian to rise to his sacred
tasks. She immediately pledged her unquestioned allegiance
to Shoghi Effendi and wrote to the friends in England urging
them to do the same:

> As you have no doubt heard, by the last will and testament
> of our beloved Master Abdul Baha, Shoghi Effendi has been
> appointed permanent chief (or president) of the Universal
> House of Justice and in his hands is left the guardianship
> of the Cause. All the believers are commanded to obey him,
> and it is said that those who do so will be blessed and those
> who refuse to do so will be blamed and condemned . . . His
> weight of responsibility is very great and he feels it most
> deeply, but he is being sustained and guided by the Holy
> Spirit in a wonderful way and is showing great wisdom in
> all those matters which he is called upon to decide.[273]

With the days of formal mourning now over, the visitors were
able to enjoy greater freedom to speak with 'Abdu'l-Bahá's
family in a more relaxed and intimate way. Memories of the
Master were still however uppermost in their thoughts.

On 8 January Ethel had the pleasure of spending some

time with 'Abdu'l-Bahá's widow, Munírih Khánum – known
as the Holy Mother – and her daughter, Munavvar. The Holy
Mother told Ethel about a dream that the Master had had
about two months before His ascension. 'Abdu'l-Bahá said
He dreamt that He was inside a very large mosque, facing
the qiblih standing in the place of the imám. He realized
without looking round that a great number of people were
entering the mosque and arranging themselves in the customary rows for prayer. Then, when the whole building was
quite full, 'Abdu'l-Bahá thought, 'As I am standing in the
place of the imám, they will expect me to lead the prayer.'
So He began to chant the call to prayer as is done from the
minaret. When He had finished this He felt the desire to
leave so instead of leading the prayer He put His hand into
His pockets to find His gloves and then left the mosque,
passing out behind the crowd. When he got outside He
thought, 'Why, this is very strange. I have given the call to
prayer but I have not said the prayer. However, now that I
have come out, it is all right. As I have given the call to
prayer they will now surely pray themselves.' And with that
He awoke. The Holy Mother had exclaimed to the Master
that it was surely a wonderful dream. 'Abdu'l-Bahá had
replied, 'Yes. It was a wonderful dream but I did not lead
the prayer.' This, the Holy Mother said to Ethel, was one
of the first indications He had given of His approaching
departure.[274]

Munavvar told Ethel how she wished that the Bahá'ís in
the West could read Bahá'u'lláh's writings in the original
language: 'All that Bahá'u'lláh wrote satisfies the mind and
goes straight to the heart,' she enthused. 'It makes you so
content. He desired very much that we should enjoy everything in the world. That all our senses should be fed and
satisfied. If your ear does not enjoy beautiful melodies, this
means that your ear is imperfect. His Writings make everything easy to you. If you are sad they console you. If you are
happy they give you more joy.

'Bahá'u'lláh wished all young people to be dressed beautifully,' she added. 'If He saw on the Feast days any young person clad in their ordinary dress, He would say to them, "Why did you not change ? Go and put on your most beautiful dress, your newest dress!"'

The Holy Mother agreed. 'Everything most beautiful and precious should be used for the friends – for the best servants of God. The Báb said, "Everything must reach its highest perfection – its paradise." You must make everything most beautiful so that it may attain its paradise and so find its reward. For everything this must be so.'[275]

The hospitality and wisdom of the Holy Family continued to sustain and inspire the pilgrims from the West for the ensuing weeks. Yet there were also revealing insights into the pain and suffering which they had been subjected to over the years. On 9 January, Munavvar told Ethel and Louise Bosch what an immense difference it would have made had it been possible to get away alone for a time and concentrate very deeply on prayer so that God would help one to have no thought save for the Cause and the spreading of the teachings. She spoke of their life in Haifa saying it was always such a turmoil of duties and constant demands upon their time and attention for outward things. She was frustrated that it was hard to get even a few moments for quiet thought and reflection. She said that in all her lifetime and the whole time she had been with the Master she had never once heard Him use the word 'I', so completely was He devoid of self, from personality and from the world.[276]

From the evidence of Ethel's diaries, it seems that the attention she had formerly paid to the insights offered by the Master was now transferred, for the moment, to His sister, the Greatest Holy Leaf. On 17 January Lady Blomfield and Ethel enjoyed the company of Bahíyyih Khánum, who spoke to them of miracles. She told them that despite the fact that the Báb, Bahá'u'lláh and 'Abdu'l-Bahá had carried out many miracles, particularly of healing, these were of no importance except to those who witnessed them.

'If a good carpenter were to make for you a beautiful dress

and coat,' she said, 'you could not use this fact as a proof that he was a good carpenter! In the same way the fact that the prophets can produce miracles is no argument or proof of the validity of their spiritual message.'

She went on to relate a wonderful story about someone who had dared to test 'Abdu'l-Bahá's abilities. There was a woman who lived in Persia, she told them, who was a very devoted Bahá'í but her husband was not a believer. He was a Muslim who opposed his wife and made difficulties for her in every possible way. She was very keen to have Bahá'í meetings in her house but her husband would not permit this and did his utmost to discourage and oppose her beliefs. At last in desperation she said to him one day, 'What should I do to make you believe in the truth of the Bahá'í teachings? Do you want a miracle? Shall I ask 'Abdu'l-Bahá to perform one for you?'

The husband replied, 'I will tell you what will convince me – if the Master will write me an answer to all my questions and difficulties without my telling Him what they are!'

The wife at once accepted this challenge, saying, 'I am sure he will do this.'

'Very well,' replied the husband. 'I will write my questions down without telling you what they are.' So he secretly proceeded to write down all his questions, took the paper and locked it up in a box which he sealed so that no one could open it without his knowledge.

The wife then wrote to the Master relating the whole incident, saying how she was tormented and opposed by her husband to the point where she could hardly endure it. She enclosed a blank sheet of paper entreating the Master to write upon it the answers to her husband's questions. When 'Abdu'l-Bahá received the letter containing this request and the blank paper, he took it laughingly to His family saying, 'See! Here is a man who would test me!'

'Abdu'l-Bahá sat down and wrote a long letter to the woman, sending her the answers to the questions He had not received! In Persia then, two people were most eagerly awaiting the Master's reply: the woman, quite convinced and certain that He would answer the questions, and her husband, equally sure that the Master could not do so. At last, the man who received all the letters for that city brought them the reply from the Master.

The woman approached her husband, saying, 'Let us not open this letter immediately, but you invite some of your friends for this evening, explain the circumstances to them and in their presence you must open the box containing your questions.' Then she prepared quite a feast for the husband's friends. After they had eaten, both the box and the letter from 'Abdu'l-Bahá were opened. To the husband's dismay, he found that not only had the Master replied to every one of his questions but He had written down the questions in the exact order in which they had originally been written and He had then given categorized replies to them!

When the man saw the Master's answers, he was so overcome that he fainted and remained unconscious for about two hours. After that he became a most convinced and firm believer and later he and his wife visited 'Abdu'l-Bahá. The man in fact became a great teacher and expounder of the Bahá'í Cause instead of being an opponent and enemy of it.[277]

Despite suffering the overwhelming pain and anguish of bereavement and the feeling of helplessness in the face of the enormous task that had been given to him, Shoghi Effendi was quick to realize the importance of promptly circulating translated extracts from the Master's Will to the believers around the world so that they might familiarize themselves with the document, obedience to which would ensure their continuing unity and prevent schism. By 28 February, Ethel wrote to Julia Culver that Shoghi Effendi had 'mailed one copy to each country as soon as he had finished [the translations] and could get them typed . . . Everyone is quite satisfied about the Will of the Beloved Master.'[278]

Not so some of the members of His own family, however. The perfidious Covenant-breakers continued to take every opportunity to bring more heartache to the new Guardian.

The sudden passing of 'Abdu'l-Bahá was their springboard into a new and relentless wave of scheming and disruptive activity. Muḥammad-'Alí called on the civil authorities to grant him the custodianship of the Shrine of Bahá'u'lláh, claiming that he was 'Abdu'l-Bahá's rightful successor. On being refused by the British authorities and subsequently by the Muslim religious head, Muḥammad-'Alí arranged for his younger brother, Badí'u'lláh, and a group of supporters forcibly to seize the keys of the Shrine. The Governor of 'Akká ordered the keys to be handed over and put guards at the Shrine but refused to return the keys to either Shoghi Effendi or his thwarted enemies. Thus the Guardian was unable even to enter the sacred shrine of his great-grandfather and his plans to complete its illumination were severely restricted. 'You will be interested to hear that the electric light is now installed in the Tomb and here on Mount Carmel,' wrote Ethel to Julia Culver. 'They have a powerful light on the top of the Tomb which shines like a star at night!'[279]

Ethel was extremely concerned for the health and well-being of Shoghi Effendi during this distressing time. 'Poor dear Shoghi Effendi is nearly overwhelmed by the immense amount of work that now rests on his shoulders,' she wrote. 'There is so much to be done and arranged for! And in addition he has much translation to do!'[280] But there were already encouraging signs that the new Guardian was more than capable of discharging the heavy responsibilities laid upon him. Ethel called upon Julia Culver to lend her spiritual support: 'Please pray constantly for our Beloved Shoghi Effendi – he is already much changed and developed and is showing the greatest judgement and wisdom in all that he does.'[281] Once, Ethel found Shoghi Effendi extremely fatigued. He had just finished translating the Tablet from 'Abdu'l-Bahá to the distinguished Swiss scientist Dr August Forel, important for its explanation of the existence of God – 'the finest (Tablet) on that particular subject,' wrote Ethel.[282]

The Guardian joined the believers on 26 February at a

memorial meeting for Helen Goodall of California who had
passed away the week before. Helen Goodall, to whom Ethel
had sent a miniature of 'Abdu'l-Bahá so many years before,
was one of the pioneer members of the American Bahá'í
community, opening her home in Oakland so that seekers
could investigate the Bahá'í teachings. Many gatherings were
held there over the years and those who knew Mrs Goodall
spoke of her sweetness and dignity, her modesty and gra-
ciousness.

For the memorial meeting the women of the household
prepared a great quantity of flat, sweet biscuits which were
piled in three dishes. The table around them was heaped with
red and pink roses. The refreshments were lovingly handed
around to everyone by Lady Blomfield, Mrs Hoagg and Dr
Ḥakím. It was, Ethel noted, a very full meeting as some ten
Persian pilgrims had recently arrived. A prayer of
Bahá'u'lláh was chanted and then Shoghi Effendi intoned
a long Tablet of the Master, revealed to Helen Goodall's
daughter, Ella Cooper, in which He mentions the passing of
Mrs Hearst and speaks of the great work done by the Disciples of Christ after His Ascension. Mrs Hoagg gave a beautiful and touching address, reminiscing about Mrs Goodall and
her unfailing devotion and great services to the Cause.

The meeting lasted a long time and Ethel, Lady Blomfield
and Laura Barney (who had recently arrived in the Holy
Land) had to leave early from the shrines of the Báb and the
Master, as they wanted to hasten home before it got dark.
It was an unusually gloomy evening owing to a heavy thun-
der storm that was brewing over the sea. The women were
frightened as they walked down Mount Carmel homewards
but got in just before the rain fell.

The situation facing the Bahá'í Cause – the loss of its
beloved Master coupled with Shoghi Effendi's apparent
youthfulness and inexperience – led some of his family and
other members of the Bahá'í community to believe it was an
opportune moment for the Universal House of Justice to be
formed. There was a belief that the young Guardian, who

refused to dress like his grandfather or follow the customs and traditions that 'Abdu'l-Bahá had kept, needed more experienced believers to guide his actions and direction. Even the Governor of Haifa thought along these lines. In a conversation with a believer, he expressed his belief that the Universal House of Justice should be formed and the Bahá'í Holy Places registered in its name, so that a firm legal basis for the religion could be established. Among those also lobbying for the House of Justice to be formed were ambitious believers such as Ávárih and Ahmad Sohrab, both prominent teachers of the Faith who secretly longed to become members of the Supreme Body.

Under such intense pressure, Shoghi Effendi took the decision to call to Haifa a number of the most capable and experienced Bahá'ís to support him and consult upon the future of the Cause. Ethel Rosenberg and Lady Blomfield were honoured to be asked to attend those historic deliberations. Added to the group were Emogene Hoagg, who had been living in Haifa for some time before the Master's passing; Laura and Hippolyte Dreyfus-Barney from France, who had arrived from Indo-China by way of Burma and Bombay; Consul and Alice Schwarz from Germany; and Roy Wilhelm, Mountfort Mills, Mason Remey and Major Tudor Pole. Ávárih and Fáḍil Mázandarání from Persia were both invited but were delayed in their arrival. Siyyid Muṣṭafá Rúmí of Burma and Corinne True and her daughter Katherine also arrived later. Mountfort Mills and Roy Wilhelm, having left the United States on 7 February, arrived on 22 February on the noon train from Cairo. Also in the Holy Land was Mrs William Randall, who suffered a bad attack of influenza on board ship but was well recovered by the time she arrived. One evening as she coming down the front steps of the Master's house from a meeting, she slipped off the lower steps, fell and sprained her ankle. The next morning an excellent German doctor was sent for, who declared that the injury was not serious but insisted that she rest entirely for a day or two.

'Mr and Mrs Dreyfus Barney arrived ten days ago,' wrote Ethel on 28 February 1922. 'Mr Mountfort Mills and Mr Roy Wilhelm came a week ago and yesterday Mrs True and her youngest daughter arrived. Mr Mason Remey is expected in a few days. Mr Tudor Pole is I am grieved to say laid up with a bad attack of influenza on his *dahabiyyah* in Cairo . . . Dr Esslemont has also had a sharp attack of flu but he has cabled that he is now convalescent. Lady Blomfield is still here. She has just been in bed for 3 or 4 days with a cold but is now quite recovered.'[283]

Mountfort Mills later shared with the American believers at their Fourteenth Annual Bahá'í Convention an inspiring description of Shoghi Effendi's strength during those difficult hours:

> We met Shoghi Effendi, dressed entirely in black, a touching figure. Think of what he stands for today! All the complex problems of the great statesmen of the world are as child's play in comparison with the great problems of this youth, before whom are the problems of the entire world . . .
> We received his joyous, hearty hand grasp and our meeting was short. A bouquet was sent to our room in the form of a young tree filled with nectarines or tangerines. It was brought by Mr. Fugeta. We awoke without any sense of sadness. That feeling was entirely gone. The Master is not gone. His Spirit is present with greater intensity and power, freed from bodily limitations. We can take it into our own hearts and reflect it in greater degrees. In the center of this radiation stands this youth, Shoghi Effendi. The Spirit streams forth from this young man. He is indeed young in face, form and manner, yet his heart is the center of the world today.[284]

A diary kept by one of the American believers recalls that 'Shoghi Effendi was occupied much of the time in consultation with Mountfort Mills, Roy Wilhelm, the Dreyfus-Barneys, Lady Blomfield, and Major Tudor-Pole, and then later when they came, the Schwarzes, about the foundation of the Universal House of Justice. I heard in a general way of the matters they discussed. It seems that before the Universal House can be established the Local and National Houses must be functioning in those countries where there are Bahá'ís.'[285]

The outcome of these discussions shows the determination of Shoghi Effendi to begin to lay the foundations for the Bahá'í Administrative Order. Wilhelm and Mills were sent to tell the American believers that their Executive Board was now to take on a legislative function. The Schwarzes returned to Germany to try to establish local bodies and a national one. The British were similarly instructed.

In his letter to the Bahá'ís of the United States of America of 5 March 1922, Shoghi Effendi urged the Bahá'ís to subordinate firmly and definitely all personal likings and local interests to the interests and requirements of the Cause of God. He called for the establishment of local spiritual assemblies in every locality where the number of adult declared believers exceeded nine. He also described the tasks and functions of the assemblies, saying that these institutions would 'in the course of time . . . evolve, with the Master's power and guidance, into the local and national Houses of Justice.'[286]

But the responsibility which had been placed upon his shoulders was beginning to weigh heavy on the young Guardian. On 5 April he left the Holy Land, seeking to restore his health, strength, self-confidence and spiritual energy in the mountains of Switzerland. The affairs of the Cause, both in Haifa and throughout the world, were left temporarily in the hands of the Greatest Holy Leaf. This significant act represents the first time in the history of the world that a world religion had been guided and directed by a woman.

The thoughts that passed through Shoghi Effendi's mind were eloquently recounted many years later by Hand of the Cause of God Leroy Ioas. Mr Ioas remembered Shoghi Effendi saying that he did not want to be the Guardian of the Cause.

In the first place, I didn't think that I was worthy. Next place, I didn't want to face these responsibilities . . . I knew what it meant. I knew that my life as a human being was over . . . I didn't want it and I didn't want to face it.

So remember I left the Holy Land, and I went up into the mountains of Switzerland, and I fought with myself until I conquered myself. Then I came back and I turned myself over to God and I was the Guardian . . . Now every Bahá'í in the world, every person in the world has to do exactly the same thing . . . Every Bahá'í must fight with himself and conquer himself. And when he has conquered himself, then he becomes a true instrument for the service of the Cause of God – and not until that.'[287]

Privileged to witness first-hand one of the most momentous and critical turning points in the history of the Bahá'í Cause, Ethel Rosenberg returned to England ready to devote the last eight years of her life to the building up of the Administrative Order of Bahá'u'lláh in her country, a land that had borne the Master's footsteps and had played such an important role in the shaping of the Faith's new Guardian.

14

The Trusted Ones of the Merciful

*The Lord hath ordained that in every city a House of
Justice be established wherein shall gather counsellors
to the number of Bahá, and should it exceed this number it does not matter . . . It behoveth them to be the
trusted ones of the Merciful among men and to regard
themselves as the guardians appointed of God for all
that dwell on earth.*[288]

Bahá'u'lláh

Before she left the Holy Land Ethel Rosenberg received
specific instructions from Shoghi Effendi to call, on her
return to England, an election for a spiritual assembly. This
assembly was to reach beyond the boundaries of London and
would, within a year, evolve into the first National Spiritual
Assembly of the British Isles.

The Guardian knew well that for the Bahá'í Movement
to survive the upheaval of losing its irreplaceable Master, and
for it to take its rightful place among the recognized, independent, divinely-inspired religious systems of the world, it
had to evolve speedily from its position as an informal mille-
narian movement based around a charismatic leader. For
Shoghi Effendi, this transformation entailed painstakingly
constructing the world-encompassing administrative order,
designed by Bahá'u'lláh and elaborated upon by 'Abdu'l-
Bahá, destined to provide the embryonic agencies for a new
world civilization. Without any question of negating or
undermining the believers' devotion to the Central Figures
of the Movement, Shoghi Effendi was faced with the task of
teaching them to transfer their obedience and allegiance

from prominent teachers and personalities to elected administrative institutions, ordained by Bahá'u'lláh Himself. The Guardian must have known that it would be a far from simple process to introduce administrative regulations, procedures and structures to individuals who had in the first instance been attracted to the Movement mainly because its leader, appropriately for that time, insisted on such an open, informal and non-restrictive approach to membership.

Ethel Rosenberg, as might be expected after more than two decades of devotion to the Cause, had little difficulty in accepting and accommodating the vision of the new Guardian into her understanding of the Bahá'í Movement. While she was still with him in Haifa, Shoghi Effendi asked Ethel to send on his behalf letters to Mrs George in London, Edward Hall in Manchester and Dr Esslemont in Bournemouth, requesting them to make lists of names and addresses of friends who wished to be considered Bahá'ís. Shoghi Effendi told Ethel that he wanted these lists prepared with a view to establishing who would vote for the spiritual assemblies. Ethel particularly asked him if she should mention to these three that the lists were being prepared for voting papers. He emphatically replied she should on no account mention this and added that the letters should be quite short, merely making the request for the lists. He added that it should be understood that Mrs George must collect all the names for London, just as Mr Hall was to collect for Manchester and Dr Esslemont for Bournemouth. Ethel immediately wrote the letters while still in Haifa and submitted them for the Guardian's approval. She posted them to England that same day in the presence of Dr Ḥakím.

As might be expected with such a new development for a community unfamiliar with formal organization, things did not go smoothly. Determining who exactly was a Bahá'í required the three recipients of Ethel's letters to make contact with other leading believers enquiring of them who amongst their own circles of friends and 'fireside' attenders were believers rather than seekers. Mother George wrote to the elderly Annie Gamble for a list of her personal friends and their addresses. After waiting some time and failing to get a reply, Mrs George wrote again. Finally Miss Gamble's list arrived and was immediately sent to Ethel in Haifa. However, Annie Gamble had inadvertently left her own name off the list.

Ethel handed the documents directly to Shoghi Effendi without taking a copy of them. Later, quite unknown to Ethel and Mrs George, Miss Gamble sent a list of additional names and addresses, including her own, directly to the Guardian. On returning to London, Ethel asked Mother George to provide her with a copy of the list of believers, and voting papers for the election were duly dispatched to all of those on the list. Mother George, of course, supplied the list she had compiled, not the list sent by Miss Gamble with additional names. When the Assembly was finally elected, the new institution and Ethel found themselves subject to bitter accusations from Miss Gamble and some of her acquaintances because none of them had received voting papers or knew of the election. Allaying the ill feelings of these friends who felt snubbed was one of the many challenges that faced the Spiritual Assembly as it set about the task of creating a truly religious community.

The first meeting of the Spiritual Assembly for London (which has also been referred to as the All-England Bahá'í Council) was held on 17 June 1922. The members of the Assembly were Ethel, Lady Blomfield, Mrs Thornburgh-Cropper, Claudia Coles, Yu'hanna Dávúd, Miss Fry, Mother George, Eric Hammond, George Palgrave Simpson and Miss Grand from London. In addition, Edward Hall represented Manchester and Dr Esslemont Bournemouth. 'I do hope that the appointment of this new Council will mark the beginning of a new and more prosperous era for the Bahá'í Movement in this country,' wrote Esslemont to his old friend, Dr Ḥakím.[289]

Sadly, Major Tudor Pole declined membership of the Assembly saying that he thought he could render more valuable service in an unofficial capacity. From that time onwards, Tudor Pole more or less distanced himself completely from the Movement, claiming that, after consultation with Shoghi Effendi, he had reached the decision that he would be more effective assisting the Cause as a non-member which would give him more weight in diplomatic circles. After this period, however, there is little mention of Tudor Pole in Bahá'í documents. It is well known that he went on to pursue other esoteric interests and gained considerable fame as a spiritual teacher in his own right, exploring his own mystical approach to Christianity. Tudor Pole may not have entirely approved of the organization of the Bahá'í Cause, for it was, to his mind, the antithesis of everything 'Abdu'l-Bahá had represented. Tudor Pole never doubted, however, the spiritual potency of the Master's life and teachings and late in his life recounted his extraordinary experiences in 'Abdu'l-Bahá's presence in his book *Writing on the Ground*, which served to introduce the Bahá'í Faith to a very large audience.

Within its first three meetings the new Spiritual Assembly formulated a number of policies to govern its functioning. Eric Hammond was elected chairman, Ethel Rosenberg secretary, Mrs Thornburgh-Cropper treasurer – Ethel remarked at the first meeting with what care and diligence Mrs Thornburgh-Cropper had filled this office in the past – and Mrs George and Miss Musgrave were appointed librarians. The Assembly decided that five ordinary general meetings should be held each year, that an extraordinary meeting could be called in an emergency at the request of three members and the secretary, and that five members present at a meeting should constitute a quorum. To enable the members to plan significantly far in advance, the five meetings were fixed for the first Saturdays of February, April, June, October and December at 3:30 in the afternoon. The option for a sixth meeting on the first Saturday in July was also recorded. In the absence of Eric Hammond, who by this time did not enjoy very good health, George Simpson was appointed acting chairman. It was in fact Simpson who chaired the first meeting as Hammond was unable to attend owing to illness.

Having a membership similar to that of the earlier Bahá'í Council meant that this new institution, rather than representing a clean break with the past, was effectively an evolution of the process that 'Abdu'l-Bahá had set in motion when He had spoken with Ethel in Paris. As before, the community's financial weakness, its public meetings and its publishing ventures were very much the most important aspects of the agenda.

Up until the formation of the Spiritual Assembly, the friends had been encouraged to pay to the central Bahá'í Fund an annual voluntary subscription of whatever amount suited them best. One of the first decisions the Assembly took was to send a letter to those believers who habitually sent more than five shillings to the Fund asking them to give an idea of the approximate amount per year they wished to donate and also what time of the year they would pay it. In this way the Assembly believed it would be able to budget and determine the scope of its activities more effectively. The letter, dated 19 September 1922, gives an interesting insight into the scope of activities in which the believers were already involving themselves.

Hitherto working expenses including those connected with Lindsay Hall, feasts (other than those given), printing, postage, stationery, etc., have amounted to approximately twenty-five pounds. This sum hitherto has been contributed at irregular intervals. In order to obviate the uncertainties arising from this method, the Council feel that the finances of the Cause should be placed on a more permanent and dignified basis, by voluntary offerings according to the Teachings.

To this end, it is suggested that each friend should send to the Treasurer, at the commencement of the financial year (Naurooz), a voluntary contribution, or promise of the same, as each feels able.

Any sum, however small, will be acceptable, and only the

total amount of all contributions for the year will be announced.

This will enable the Spiritual Assembly to allocate funds at the beginning of the year, to know the extent of their income, and to have a known and dependable fund for the expansion of the local interests of the Cause.

In this latter respect, funds for the up-keep of the Library, purchase of books, circulation of literature and information regarding the Cause are urgently needed to supply the many demands.

In order that the work of the current year may be planned for the half year ending at Naurooz, March 21, 1923, will you kindly send any contribution, or promise of such, to Mrs Thornburgh-Cropper, Mrs. George or Miss Rosenberg, who will forward all contributions received to the Treasurer every nineteen days.

Local expenses included in the General Bahai Fund are:–

Rent of Lindsay Hall.
Up-keep of Library.
Literature for free distribution to inquirers.
Nineteen-day Feasts, when not individually given.
Anniversary Feasts, such as:–
    Naurooz
    Rizwan
    Declaration of The Bab
    Fete-Day of Abdu'l-Baha
    Birthday of The Bab
    Birthday of Baha'u'llah
Memorial Anniversaries, such as:–
    The Martyrdom of The Bab.
    The Departure of Baha'u'llah.
    The Ascension of Abdu'l-Baha.
Extra meetings at which visiting Bahais may speak
    or other memorials as they occur.
Postage for secretarial work, forwarding of books,
    and mail to believers in all parts of the world.
Fund for printing of folders &c. as necessary.
Fund for the help of Bahais, or others in trouble.
Universal expenses of the Cause in which Bahais

24. Shoghi Effendi, 1922

25. Dr John E. Esslemont
whose Bahá'u'lláh and the New Era, *begun in 1916, is still a popular*
introductory book on the Bahá'í Faith.

26. George Townshend
a distinguished scholar and clergyman who, with Ethel Rosenberg,
assisted Shoghi Effendi in his translation of the Hidden Words *into*
majestic English.

27. Mountfort Mills
who delivered the Bahá'í paper at the Conference of Living Religions
within the British Empire, held in London in the autumn of 1924.

28. left: *Some of the many hundreds who gathered to receive alms after the passing of 'Abdu'l-Bahá*
29. right: *Lady Blomfield on the balcony of the old Western Pilgrim House, Haifa, circa 1921-2.*

30. Martha Root
named by Shoghi Effendi as the 'archetype of Bahá'í itinerant
teachers', the 'foremost Hand' of the Cause of God, the 'Leading
Ambassadress of His Faith' and the 'Pride of Bahá'í teachers,
whether men or women, in both the East and the West'. During her
five-month stay in Britain in 1926 she lectured in many parts of the
country.

31. Queen Marie of Rumania
whose conversion was hailed by Shoghi Effendi as a 'notable
triumph which the unbending energy and indomitable spirit of our
beloved Martha has achieved for our sacred Cause'.

32. Hetty and John Craven
shown here in Altrincham in 1935. The Cravens first learned of the
Faith in 1910.

voluntarily unite include:–
The first Mashreq'ul Azkar of the Occident
(Dr J.Esslemont, Secretary and collector of the Fund
   for England.)
The Star of the West (Bahai Magazine)
Scholarships in the Tarbiat School, Teheran (for
   Persian Orphans).
The School on Mount Carmel.
The Bab Memorial Stairway on Mount Carmel.
The Teaching Fund.
The Translation Fund.
The Publication Fund (for England).[290]

Another project supported by the Assembly was the interior decoration of a pilgrim house for Western believers in Haifa. The initial American sponsors of the pilgrim house, Mrs and Mrs Randall, appealed to the Assembly to furnish one room at a cost of thirty pounds. A new fund was opened and Lady Blomfield and Mrs Thornburgh-Cropper set the ball rolling by generously donating five pounds each.

Ethel felt strongly that the booklet entitled *The Passing of 'Abdu'l-Bahá*, compiled by Lady Blomfield and Shoghi Effendi, should be republished and she was authorized to write to the United States to find out if the believers there were thinking of reprinting it before the Assembly took any formal action. In the meantime, however, Ethel discovered that printing work could be done much more cheaply in Germany than anywhere else owing to the exchange rate. She suggested to the Assembly that it would be advisable to write to Stuttgart for an estimate of the cost of printing a thousand of the booklets for use in Britain before writing to America. This was agreed and a small sub-committee was set up to estimate the cost of reprinting. It found Germany to be a satisfactory place to print. However, concern was expressed that a book that had been printed in Germany would have very limited distribution in the United States where many of the leading stores advertised that they sold nothing made in Germany. It was decided nevertheless to have the

ETHEL JENNER ROSENBERG

booklet printed in Stuttgart. A subsequent second edition was proposed, with revisions to be made by Lady Blomfield and approved by Shoghi Effendi, which would be published in England. Ethel and Claudia Coles were also appointed by the Assembly to read and correct the remaining chapters of Dr Esslemont's book which 'Abdu'l-Bahá had been in the process of reviewing when He passed away. By the time of the Assembly's December meeting this service had been completed, the two friends having slightly modified and enthusiastically approved the text.

Thus, the meetings of the new Spiritual Assembly were proving to be very harmonious and productive.

On 9 August 1922 Ethel had the joy of hosting in her home the first Bahá'í wedding to be held in London since the passing of 'Abdu'l-Bahá, the marriage of Ḍiá'u'lláh Aṣgharzádih of 'Ishqábád to the Englishwoman Winifred Pegrim. Aṣgharzádih was born in 1880 into a Persian Bahá'í family which had moved to the Russian city when he was 15 years old. After his second pilgrimage to the Holy Land in 1920 he settled in London. At the age of 73 he became the first Bahá'í to settle in Jersey in the Channel Islands and was given the title 'Knight of Bahá'u'lláh' by Shoghi Effendi for his pioneering services. Miss Pegrim was, according to Dr Esslemont, 'a very nice looking girl who seems to be interested in the Bahai Movement, although she does not know a great deal about it yet'.[291] Aṣgharzádih proved to be an effective link between the British Bahá'ís and the very large Bahá'í community in 'Ishqábád and a loving correspondence developed between them, maintained largely by Ethel.

The Bahá'í communities in the Russian republics closest to Iran had been very prosperous. The first Bahá'í House of Worship in the world had been built in 'Ishqábád and many communities had schools and libraries. Following the Bolshevik revolution the Bahá'ís were initially allowed to continue activities without interference. However, later, under Stalin, the community's activities were increasingly frowned upon and opposition and persecution arose.

The London Bahá'ís felt this wedding of East and West
to be so important that Claudia Coles sent a report to *Star
of the West* saying,

> As a proof of the power of the revelation of Baha'Ullah to
> bring the East and the West together, the unity of the
> representatives of the diverse nationalities and religions in
> the little group gathered for the religious ceremony is so
> significant of the future, that I am sending an account of the
> happening, for it seems a part of the spiritual history of
> these early days of the new era, and of interest as a matter
> of record.[292]

Gathered at Ethel's house, in the room where 'Abdu'l-Bahá
had spoken in 1911, were: Ethel, Miss Musgrave and the
bride's mother representing England; 'Abdu'l-Vahab
Bajkiroff – the son of a martyr of Yazd and the President of
the 'Ishqábád House of Spirituality; Haji Ahmad Alieff, also
of Yazd and a member of the House of Spirituality; the
bridegroom's brother from Beirut; a host of friends from
'Ishqábád just returning from pilgrimage to the Holy Land;
and a believer from Turkey. Yu'hanna Dávúd, whose own
marriage had been blessed by the presence of 'Abdu'l-Bahá
whilst He was in London, was also in attendance.

With Ethel's permission, Claudia Coles placed a photograph of 'Abdu'l-Bahá on a cushion in the chair He had used
in Ethel's upper room and on the cushion at the foot of the
picture she placed a pink rosebud. Prayers followed and the
'spirit seemed like a flood of light'.[293] Dávúd chanted the
words of Bahá'u'lláh on marriage and then translated them
into English. Then the President of the 'Ishqábád House of
Spirituality rose and joined the hands of the bride and groom
and they repeated the Bahá'í marriage vow in Persian. When
the ceremony was over, Ethel led all of the guests upstairs
for the wedding feast and the cutting of the cake.

For Ethel and her friends the presence of the believers
from 'Ishqábád seemed to be a link in a great plan. For more
than a year these believers had tried to make the pilgrimage

to 'Abdu'l-Bahá but could not get permission from the Soviet government to leave Russia for Haifa. Finally, after months of work and writing, the necessary leave was obtained from the government and they were free to start upon the long journey. Arriving in Tehran, they heard the news of the Master's passing but nonetheless chose to continue onwards to pay their respects to the new Guardian, arriving in Haifa only to discover that he had gone to Switzerland. From Palestine they finally departed for England. 'From the ends of the earth,' Claudia Coles wrote, 'link after link in the chain of existence, seem to have been woven to bring together that little group of eleven in that upper room and link after link of the chain of existence, such unity is being forged by the Greatest Name wherever the hearts of the firm meet in worship.'[294]

Throughout these months, the weekly Wednesday meetings at the Lindsay Hall continued but were poorly attended. Some members of the Assembly believed that advertising of meetings had brought very little result. One action that the Assembly did take, however, to improve the situation was to insist that the meetings start promptly at eight o'clock rather than allowing a quarter of an hour's grace for latecomers.

Outside of the meetings Ethel proved to be a continuing source of inspiration to her co-workers, particularly to Edward Hall, who had to endure a terribly long journey travelling south from Manchester for the Assembly meetings. After the second meeting on 7 October 1922, Hall spent 'a beautiful evening . . . in the company of Miss Rosenberg who . . . read extracts from her many Tablets from 'Abdu'l-Bahá' and described interesting incidents which occurred during her visits to 'Akká and Haifa in the Holy Land.'[295]

On Saturday 28 October the Spiritual Assembly held its first emergency meeting, called out of concern at another potential wave of persecution of the Bahá'ís in Mashhad. News of the dangers reached London via one of the Persian believers, Mr Froughi, and the Assembly invited Dr Ḥakím as well as Mr Aṣgharzádih to join the consultation. The general feeling was that nothing could be done by the British authorities during that period when relations with Persia were so poor. Dávúd suggested that the best actions could be taken by France and America. After a full discussion it was decided that in case of emergency the Spiritual Assemblies in the United States should be contacted so that pressure could be brought to bear upon the American government authorities and official action could be taken to protect the Persian believers.

At its next scheduled meeting on 2 December 1922 the Assembly was forced to deal with the complaints levelled at it that its election had not been fairly conducted. The situation, of course, had arisen because Ethel had not known that additional names had been forwarded to Haifa. Regardless of who was to blame, the Assembly had to find a way to persuade the friends who felt aggrieved to lay their grievances directly before the Assembly and to refrain from perpetual discussion of the matter in private. Dr Esslemont calmly offered to solve the problem, saying that he was speaking at Miss Gamble's Sunday meeting the following day and that he would talk to her, explain the matter fully and try to persuade her not to discuss it further once it had been resolved.[296]

This whole incident raised an issue which was to be a bone of contention for the Bahá'í Assemblies for several years into the future: whether or not there should be some manner of formal registration or membership so that someone who identified himself with the Bahá'í Movement could enjoy administrative rights. Mother George and Mr Simpson supported the idea of preparing a document which friends newly joining could be asked to sign. Dr Esslemont, on the other hand, proposed a process whereby two members of the Assembly would interview a potential believer in a simple and informal way to explain what was regarded as necessary to be accepted by members of the movement and what a new member's responsibilities would be, should he or she decide to join. Claudia Coles, Mr Asgharzádih and Yu'hanna Dávúd found the whole notion of a written declaration undesirable, saying the Master had not allowed it. The Assembly favoured Dr Esslemont's suggestion but the issue was by no means resolved.

Before the end of 1922 the Assembly was blessed with two letters from Shoghi Effendi – now returned from his prolonged absence – written on consecutive days, 16 and 17 December. In the first letter the Guardian informed the members that 'the thought, so often comforting and sustaining, that in the counsels of my British co-workers of that land, I shall find spontaneous and undiminished support as well as wise and experienced assistance, is surely one of those forces which will hearten me in the midst of my future labours for the Cause'.[297] Shoghi Effendi was delighted to hear the news of the formation of the Assembly and assured them of the splendid and unique opportunities that were theirs. Already the Guardian was directing and prompting this new institution with prayers that it might 'smooth speedily and definitely all differences that may arise, may promote the all-important work of Teaching, may widen the sphere of its correspondence and exchange of news with the distant parts of the Bahá'í world, may secure through its publications a dignified and proper presentation of the Cause to the enlightened public, and may in every other respect prove itself capable of distinct and worthy achievements'.[298]

The second message from the Guardian was written in reply to a letter from Ethel – the first letter to reach Shoghi Effendi from the West – 'bearing the joyful news of the safety, the unity and the happiness of my British friends across the seas! I read it and re-read it with particular pleasure and felt a thrill of delight at the welcome news of the harmonious and efficient functioning of your Spiritual Assembly.[299] Shoghi Effendi informed the Assembly that 'an able and experienced teacher recently arrived from Persia'[300] was about to visit Britain and that they should make full use of his great learning and experience. His name was 'Abdu'l-Ḥusayn Ávaríh.

Ávaríh was an outstanding scholar of the Faith who had won his way into the hearts of the friends all over the world. His visit to Britain was described as 'wonderful, inspiring, quickening, genial and harmonizing'.[301] He was perhaps the first Bahá'í teacher of international stature to visit the north of England, spending ten days in Manchester. Included in his visit was a tour of the Linotype Works where two thousand people were employed. Its management was most impressed with their oriental guest and took the Bahá'í delegation to tea. E.T. Hall described Ávaríh as an 'incomparable teacher'.[302] His tour also took him to the south coast and Brighton. On 24 February 1923 he was the guest of Elizabeth Knight, a Bahá'í, and many Bahá'ís and inquirers heard him speak. He also addressed the Brighton Theosophical Society. Under Ávaríh's direction two new Spiritual Assemblies were formed – in Manchester on 24 March 1923 and in Bournemouth on 11 April. However, as had happened with some other prominent Bahá'í teachers before him, Ávaríh inwardly hoped that his prominence in the community would at some point enable him to be recognized as a leader. He despised the fact that the young Shoghi Effendi had been appointed Guardian and shortly after his visit to Britain he began to stir up mischief and to try to win allegiance away from the Guardian. Subsequently, after years of warnings, Shoghi Effendi had no choice but to cast Ávaríh out of the community, later describing him as the 'most shameless, vicious, relentless apostate in the annals of the Faith, who, through ceaseless vitriolic attacks recorded in voluminous writings and close alliance with its traditional enemies, assiduously schemed to blacken its name and subvert the foundations of its institutions'.[303]

At its meeting on 24 March 1923 the Spiritual Assembly studied a long and detailed letter from the Guardian on the organization and election of Spiritual Assemblies. It proved to be a great struggle for the members to understand the guidance which Shoghi Effendi had given. The chief problem they were unable to resolve was his insistence that the

224 ETHEL JENNER ROSENBERG

Assemblies should be re-elected annually on the first day of
Riḍván. The Assembly felt that there was a 'grave possibility'
of the work and the progress of the Cause being retarded by
'such frequent re-election', as the period of time for which
the Assemblies existed – one year – was 'hardly long enough
to get them working efficiently and if there were to be such
frequent introductions of new and untrained members it
might form a serious hindrance of the work of the Bahá'í
Movement which was going forward...'[304]

One month later the Assembly called an emergency
meeting to discuss Shoghi Effendi's reply. It had come addressed to Ethel, was written on Shoghi Effendi's behalf and
contained very important guidance. Shoghi Effendi told them
that the election at Riḍván would and should automatically
dissolve the present Assembly. He hoped that the result could
be announced on the first day of Riḍván – 21 April – but that
this was not absolutely necessary. However, he wrote, it
would be quite in place to have the polling prior to the first
day of Riḍván and the results declared on that day. Shoghi
Effendi emphasized strongly that every single believer was
eligible to serve on the Assembly and that its members
should number no more and no less than nine.

The Assembly unanimously agreed to carry out the
Guardian's instructions. It resolved to call an immediate
election for the London Spiritual Assembly and then in
collaboration with the new Spiritual Assemblies of
Bournemouth and Manchester to arrange for the election of
the first National Spiritual Assembly. Ethel was authorized
to produce a complete list of all declared Bahá'ís and to have
it printed with instructions on how to vote. The ballots,
which when completed were to be returned to Mr Simpson,
appeared as in Figure 1.

VOTING PAPER
for the
Election of
NINE MEMBERS
- of the -
LONDON SPIRITUAL ASSEMBLY

INSTRUCTIONS TO VOTERS.

1. Underline NINE names or a less number, but NOT MORE. If more than NINE are underlined the voting paper will be rejected on the count.
2. Those persons whose names are marked with a cross x would be unable to serve owing to distance from London or other causes.
3. Do not write anything on the paper.
4. Place in addressed envelope and post at latest on Wednesday 9th April.
5. If envelope is left unfastened ½d stamp suffices; but if fastened down 1½d stamp must be affixed.

Afnan, Mr. Ruhi
Ainslie, Miss
Arnoup, Miss
Asgarzadeh, Mr. Z.
Asgarzadeh, Mrs.Z.

Baldaro, Miss
Bedingfield, Mr. E.
Bedingfield, Mrs. E.
Bevan, Miss
Blomfield, Lady
Brodsky, Mr.
Brown, Mrs. Arthur
Buckle, Miss E.
x Buckton, Miss A
Bull, Mr. S.

x Cather, Miss
Cather, Miss A.
Champion, Mrs.
Chaudri, Mrs.
x Cheape, Miss
Cole, Mr. C. S.
Coles, Mrs. Claudia

Darab, Prof.
Dawud, Mr. J.
Draper, Miss

Fforde, Comder. T. R.
Fforde, Mrs. T. R.
Froughi, Mr.
Fry, Miss Isobel

Gamble, Miss
x Garrard, Miss
George, Mrs.
Ginman, Mrs.
Gladish, Miss
Grimshaw, Miss
x Grimwood, Mr.
x Grimwood, Mrs.
x Nochougati, Mr. El.
Hakim, Mr. M. S.
Hakim, Mrs. M .S.
Hall, Mrs. Basil
x Hammond, Mr. E.
x Hammond, Mrs. E.
Haybittel, Miss
Herrick, Miss

Irwin, Miss B.

Kellgren, Mrs. E.
x Knight, Mrs. R. D.

Lane, Mr. Scott
Lay, Miss
Lay, Miss
Lea, Miss E.

Mackeith, Miss
x Marshall, Mr. J. L.
x Marshall, Mrs. J. L.
Maule, Mrs. Carteret
Morris, Mr. Carey
Morris, Mrs. Carey
Musgrave, Miss N.

x Platt, Miss P.

x Rabbani, Miss R.
Redfern, Mrs.
Roberts, Mrs.
Rosenberg, Miss E.

x Scaramucci, Mrs
x Schepel, Miss
Slade, Mrs.
Slade, Miss
Simpson, Mr. G. P.

Tanner, Mrs
Thornburgh-Cropper, Mrs.
Tovey, Mrs.

Valentine , Miss

Wellard, Mr.
Wellard, Mrs.
Woods, Miss A.

Yandell, Miss M.[305]

Figure 1: Replica of original voting sheet. United Kingdom Bahá'í Archives.

At its next meeting on 19 May the outgoing Spiritual Assembly gathered to receive the result of the election. Of the 80 papers sent out, 66 were returned. One of those was blank and four were spoilt. The highest possible vote was thus 61. The nine members elected were, as follows:

Lady Blomfield – 55 votes
Mrs Thornburgh-Cropper – 50
Mrs George – 45
Miss Rosenberg – 45
Mr Hammond – 43
Mrs Coles – 42
Mr Simpson – 41
Miss Herrick – 33
Mr Aṣgharzádih – 32.

Ethel was authorized by the Assembly to write to Manchester and Bournemouth to enquire how soon they could be ready to proceed with the election of delegates who would chose the members of the National Spiritual Assembly. It was assumed that of the nine members of the National Assembly, six would be from London to be elected by delegates from that city only, two would come from Manchester and one from Bournemouth, elected by representatives from those communities alone.

On 12 June 1923, Ethel wrote to the Bahá'ís in 'Ishqábád sending greetings and love from the London Spiritual Assembly. She informed them of the three Local Spiritual Assemblies now formed in London, Manchester and Bournemouth, stating that there were many other believers in different places but nowhere in sufficient numbers to establish Assemblies of their own. She enthusiastically shared with them news that the National Spiritual Assembly was shortly to be elected and that Dr Esslemont's book as well as the first publications of Shoghi Effendi's translations would soon be available.

Dr Esslemont's ground-breaking work *Bahá'u'lláh and the New Era* was eagerly anticipated. Shoghi Effendi had told

Esslemont he thought it 'the finest presentation that has so far been given of the Cause, and I am confident that it will arouse immense interest.'[306] Elizabeth Herrick had also been working on an introductory text about the Cause entitled *Unity Triumphant*. Ethel read the first draft and offered a number of suggestions to Miss Herrick, such as the possibility of including a number of 'Abdu'l-Bahá's talks in London. The book was published in 1923 by Kegan Paul, Trench, Trubner and Co. Ltd. of Carter Lane and ended with a statement that it had been 'unanimously approved by the London Baha'i Spiritual Assembly',[307] following a precedent set in the American community of having publications officially recognized by the Bahá'í administrative body responsible.

Thus the stage was set for the election of the first National Spiritual Assembly of the Bahá'ís of the British Isles. Along with the National Assemblies established for Germany and India, it was one of the first three such administrative bodies in the world.

15

A Firm Foundation

You, surely, have laid a firm foundation for the future development of the Cause in those regions, and my hope is that the National Assembly of Great Britain may, by full, frequent, and anxious consultation, protect the Cause, maintain and promote harmony amongst the friends, and initiate and execute ways and means for the diffusion of its spirit and the promotion of its principles.[308]

Shoghi Effendi

On Saturday 13 October 1923 eight believers gathered at Ethel Rosenberg's home at 74a Sinclair Road, Kensington, for the historic, first meeting of the 'Bahá'í National Spiritual Assembly'. The institution had been elected by postal ballot. London believers elected six members from among their own number; two seats on the Assembly were given to the Manchester believers to fill from their locality and the remaining seat was allocated to Bournemouth. The National Spiritual Assembly consisted of Eric Hammond, Mrs Thornburgh-Cropper, Ethel Rosenberg, George Palgrave Simpson, Lady Blomfield and Mother George, all from London; Edward Hall and Jacob Joseph from Manchester; and Dr Esslemont from Bournemouth. Ethel was pleased to welcome to her home for that signal gathering Dr Esslemont, Mr Hall, Mr Joseph, Mrs George, Mr Simpson and Mrs Thornburgh-Cropper. The minutes note that John Craven from Manchester was also present at the table, by request of Mr Joseph, to assist with any language problems which may have arisen.

Reflecting on the momentous event that took place in Ethel Rosenberg's house, it is tempting to believe that it must have been a powerful and spiritually charged moment, its participants filled with a profound awareness of its historical importance. The Assembly's minutes, however, suggest otherwise. As might realistically be expected, the first session began with the members determined to work out the basic running of the Assembly. A lengthy discussion took place on who should be 'president'. Mr Simpson proposed Dr Esslemont. Mrs George and Ethel Rosenberg proposed Mr Simpson. Considerable discussion followed on the necessary qualifications for the office. Mr Hall then proposed that Ethel should be president. Ethel expressed her appreciation of the proposal but stated that she did not feel able to occupy the position. After further discussion, Simpson withdrew his initial suggestion of Esslemont and was subsequently elected president himself.

Following on from this drawn-out debate, Dr Esslemont was elected vice-president and Mrs Thornburgh-Cropper treasurer. When it came to electing secretary, Ethel was unanimously chosen. She, however, pointed out that the correspondence with other Assemblies would entail a considerable amount of work and that she would like some help. Mr Simpson was therefore appointed to assist with clerical duties.[309]

The Assembly was prompt to record its 'Rules of Debate'. These were unanimously adopted with the recommendation that while due attention should be paid to them, it would be left to the discretion of the chairman of the meeting to relax them in moderation. The rules were 1) that all observations be addressed to the chair and not to individuals; 2) that members speak in rotation in the order which they were seated; 3) that any member wishing to speak a second time had to obtain permission to do so.[310] The question was raised whether it was permissible to canvass electors at elections to the Assembly, or to give advice about persons to whom votes should be given. The Assembly resolved that canvassing of electors was not permissible but that if advice were to be sought by an elector, the enquirer could justifiably be informed of the desirable qualifications for service which the person being enquired about might have.

With the formal details of functioning finalized, the Assembly turned its attention to the national picture, with each member presenting a brief summary of the conditions of his or her own locality. Mr Hall told the Assembly that there was a receptivity in Manchester and that good progress was being made. The friends had difficulty in meeting regularly because they were widely scattered around the suburbs but special meetings had been held. Great help had been given by two Unitarian ministers – one allowed the sale of Bahá'í literature in his church and the other lent his school room for meetings on Sundays as well as having gatherings in his church. Mr Hall said that the Manchester Assembly had encountered some difficulties by allowing newer adherents to the cause to 'push to the front over the heads of those whose service in the Cause could be counted by many years'.[311] Though not a member of the Assembly, John Craven reported how in Altrincham where he was secretary of the Works Committee of the Linotype Company, he had been able to introduce Bahá'í principles not only to the workers but to the foremen and manager. He was circulating copies of *Star of the West* magazine and the manager had agreed that, in the future, Dr Esslemont could address the 1,450 men and women workers during their dinner hour.

For Bournemouth's contribution, Dr Esslemont reported that it was now eight years since regular weekly meetings had been started and that the Nineteen Day Feast had been celebrated since December 1920. Some difficulties were being encountered chiefly owing to a lack of harmony among the members of the Assembly, but, said Dr Esslemont, thanks to the 'opportune resignation of one member',[312] that particular stumbling block had been removed. The Bournemouth Spiritual Assembly had recently formulated a resolution that in the future, before any person was accepted as a member

of the community, his or her name had to be proposed in the
Spiritual Assembly and duly seconded before acceptance. The
two proposers would have to ascertain beforehand that the
applicant had a sufficient knowledge of what membership
of a Bahá'í group entailed and that he or she was apparently
sincere in the intention to live in accordance with the teachings. Under these arrangements, Dr Esslemont told the
Assembly that five new members would shortly join. This
subject of what constituted a 'believer' and how such a
registration could be formally introduced occupied much
consultation time of the British Bahá'ís in the years to come.
Dr Esslemont added that in the meantime, one of the
Bournemouth believers, Sister Challis, had established her
own nursing home at West Moors and had set apart one
room especially for the use of the believers. Reporting on
events in London, Mr Simpson told how the friends had
suffered a great loss with the return of Dr Ḥakím to his
native Persia.

Despite the Assembly's obvious lack of experience and
maturity, Shoghi Effendi was full of praise for the members
of the newly-formed institution. In a letter of 29 November
1923, he wrote to them saying, 'I feel happy and encouraged
to learn that those few, yet earnest and promising, servants
of Bahá'u'lláh in that land are, despite the vicissitudes and
obstacles that confront the rapid rise of the Movement,
wholeheartedly striving and co-operating for the fulfilment
of His divine Promise.'[313] Shoghi Effendi particularly welcomed 'the active participation of our beloved sister, Mrs.
Thornburgh-Cropper, in the affairs of the Cause' and felt
'confident that her wisdom, her experience, her influence,
and her unparalleled opportunities for the service of the
Movement will pave the way for the wholesome growth of the
Cause in that land'.[314]

Undoubtedly, the outstanding and main event that was
to occupy a large proportion of the National Assembly's time
and attention during its earliest months was an important
conference on 'Living Religions within the British Empire',

arranged to run alongside the British Empire Exhibition at
Wembley. The conference was organized for the autumn of
1924 under the auspices of the University of London School
of Oriental Studies and the Sociological Society. Its purpose
· was to promote the various faiths which then prevailed in the
Eastern and Western dominions of the British Commonwealth. The National Assembly was pleased to find out that
one of the members of the conference's organizing committee
– possibly the Orientalist Sir E. Denison Ross – personally
knew Shoghi Effendi and hoped to see him during a forthcoming visit to Syria. The Guardian believed that the conference offered a great opportunity for a wide proclamation of
the Bahá'í teachings and carefully began to select representatives from India and America to represent the Cause at the
meeting. Shoghi Effendi also generously allocated funds to
the National Assembly to provide for the expenses of the
Bahá'í representatives.

Critical to the impact which the Bahá'í delegation would
make on the conference was the high standard and accuracy
of the community's presentation. The Guardian called upon
the American national Bahá'í body to commission a comprehensive article from a special committee for presentation at
the gathering. It was hoped that Shoghi Effendi himself
would be able to attend the conference and give the paper.
Indeed, in a letter of 11 June 1924 received by George
Simpson, the Guardian's secretary wrote that he had informed the Conference organizers that Shoghi Effendi
sincerely hoped to deliver the address in person. The National Assembly was delighted at the prospect and also
decided to invite the distinguished Canadian Bahá'í lawyer
Mountfort Mills to attend. The euphoria with which the news
of Shoghi Effendi's attendance at the conference was met
was, however, short-lived. The young Guardian, over burdened by his heavy workload was once again forced to with-
draw from the Holy Land for much-needed spiritual and
physical recuperation. Mountfort Mills delivered the paper
prepared by the special committee composed of himself,

Horace Holley and Agnes Parsons. The paper was subsequently revised by some members of the British National
Assembly, which had been authorized by the Guardian to
undertake corrections in case his absence made it impossible
for him to make them himself. Having studied the document,
the Assembly came to the conclusion that it would be desirable to elucidate more fully the practical applications of the
teachings and to this end a short supplementary paper was
prepared and presented by Shoghi Effendi's cousin Ruhi
Afnan on the 'Bahá'í Influence on Life'.

On 23 September 1924 the Guardian cabled the National
Assembly saying 'MAY WEMBLEY (SIC CONFERENCE) FULFIL
YOUR FONDEST HOPES PRAY CONVEY AUTHORITIES MY SINCERE
REGRET AT INABILITY TO BE PRESENT I WISH THEM FULL SUC-
CESS IN THEIR NOBLE ENDEAVOURS. SHOGHI'[315] In fact, unfore-
seen circumstances caused the event to be moved from
Wembley to the Imperial Institute in South Kensington. It
took place between 22 September and 3 October. Mountfort
Mills's presentation ended with these words:

> None can claim that he is a follower of Bahá'u'lláh until, in
> spirit, he is a follower of every Messenger who has bright-
> ened earth with the 'glad tidings' of the victory of God. None
> can claim that he is a follower of Bahá'u'lláh who conceives
> any portion or aspect of life as non-religious, non-contribu-
> tive to the eternal ascent of the soul. None can claim that
> he is a follower of Bahá'u'lláh whilst secret intolerance
> separates him from any fellowman. Above all, none can
> claim that he is a follower of Bahá'u'lláh whose heart re-
> mains barren, fearful or indifferent in this present age – the
> day which is witness to the overthrow of the foundations of
> materialism, and the kindling of human hearts with the
> spirit of universal knowledge and love.[316]

Three days after the Bahá'í presentations, Dr Walter Walsh,
leader of the Free Religious Movement, gave an address at
the Steinway Hall in London where he openly expressed his
reverence and admiration for the teachings of Bahá'u'lláh.
Shoghi Effendi was extremely pleased by Walsh's response.
'Dr Walsh's sermon is astonishingly good,' he wrote to

George Simpson. 'I wish you would send me about fifty copies of the same.'[317]

The conference was generally considered by those who arranged it to be a great success. The organizers reported that the large attendance was 'most gratifying'[318] and in excess of anything they had been led to expect, especially taking into account that nothing had been spent on advertising. Widespread publicity had been received in the press particularly in relation to the arrival at the conference of the Khalifat-ul-Masih, head of the Ahmadiyya movement. The gathering also attracted the attention of the British prime minister Ramsay MacDonald who wrote a message:

> Many religions and many creeds live in amity within our Empire, each by their own different way leading our peoples onwards towards some ultimate light. I welcome cordially the objects of the Conference and the knowledge which it spreads amongst us that our peoples, in the aspirations of the Spirit, 'walk not back to back but with an unity of track'.[319]

The Bahá'í community's main influence was felt away from the main conference platform. A comprehensive selection of literature was displayed at a book stall and a new catalogue of Bahá'í publications was compiled for delegates, funded by a generous gift from Mr Asgharzádih. Lady Blomfield made a unique contribution by personally hosting a well-attended reception for dignitaries and delegates at Claridge's for which she was warmly thanked. Shoghi Effendi wrote that her 'idea of a reception was undoubtedly inspired and was admirably executed. It has indeed rejoiced my heart. My love and my gratitude for her wise, patient and fruitful efforts.'[320] A photograph of that gathering shows the wide variety of nationalities and creeds represented, the guests resplendent in a dazzling range of exotic robes and head-dresses.

The high profile of the representatives of the Ahmadiyya movement posed a particular problem for the Bahá'ís, who found themselves under verbal attack from these delegates.

The Ahmadiyya are followers of the Indian-born Mirza Ghulam Ahmad who had advanced claims of prophethood at about the same time as Bahá'u'lláh. Particularly upsetting to the English Bahá'ís were the attempts made by the Ahmadiyya representatives to discredit Bahá'u'lláh's character, particularly by pointing out that Bahá'u'lláh had more than one wife. Ethel and other friends who had the experience and knowledge to answer this question firmly stated that it was true but all of Bahá'u'lláh's marriages had been contracted before His Declaration in Baghdad and were simply in keeping with the Persian and Islamic cultural milieu in which He had been raised.

On a brighter note, one of the most significant outcomes of the conference for the future of the British Bahá'í community was the introduction of the Bahá'í Faith to a young man named Richard St Barbe Baker. He had been serving as Assistant Conservator of Forests in Kenya since 1920 and delivered a paper at the conference on the African tribal religious beliefs that he had encountered. At the conclusion of his talk, Claudia Coles rushed up to him and said, 'You are a Bahá'í.'[321] Many of the believers gathered around him to thank him for his presentation, and a few days later Claudia presented him with his first Bahá'í literature. Subsequently St Barbe, as he became known, founded the internationally renowned organization the Men of the Trees, now known as the International Tree Foundation, with Shoghi Effendi as its first life member. For 12 consecutive years the Guardian sent an official message to the World Forestry Charter gatherings initiated by St Barbe and attended by ambassadors and dignitaries from scores of countries. While St Barbe did not formally declare himself to be a Bahá'í until 1935, he frequently acknowledged the influence of the teachings on his life and work in the period immediately following the conference in London.

Since the First World War religious groups in Britain had been suffering a crisis of authority. The churches, and particularly the non-conformist chapels which had become beacons of morality during the Victorian era, experienced a fall in membership, declining funds and reduced influence. The message propounded by the Church of England was seen to be increasingly ineffective and the impact of Christianity was clearly waning among the post-war generation. The General Strike of 1926 dealt another blow as Britain fought to maintain its unity. With hindsight, it is easy to think that such a state of affairs could well have been capitalized upon by the Bahá'í community but its numbers were too few and its struggle to develop a distinctive identity prevented it from making any real impact on the life of the country.

Teaching the Cause during this critical period was an important item on the National Spiritual Assembly's agenda but the believers' understanding of the spiritual process of teaching was extremely limited. The Assembly considered appointing a special Teaching Committee to be responsible for propagating the Bahá'í message. The idea was initially proposed by Mr Aṣgharzádih but following consultation the Assembly resolved not to appoint such a committee. It felt the number of believers was not sufficient nor were there opportunities to assemble classes on the subject. It was further thought that the handful of Local Spiritual Assemblies could better deal with this question in their own centres.

Shoghi Effendi made it abundantly clear to the Assembly that success in teaching required more than simply having a greater number of teachers or accurate presentations of the teachings. On his return from Switzerland to the Holy Land, he wrote to the entire British community, outlining the necessary qualities for success in teaching. 'Humanity,' he wrote, 'through suffering and turmoil, is swiftly moving on towards its destiny; if we be loiterers, if we fail to play our part surely others will be called upon to take up our task as ministers to the crying needs of this afflicted world.'

Not by the force of numbers, not by the mere exposition of a set of new and noble principles, not by an organised campaign of teaching – no matter how worldwide and elabo-

rate in its character – not even by the staunchness of our
faith or the exaltation of our enthusiasm, can we ultimately
hope to vindicate in the eyes of a critical and sceptical age
the supreme claim of the Abhá Revelation. One thing and
only one thing will unfailingly and alone secure the un-
doubted triumph of this sacred Cause, namely, the extent
to which our own inner life and private character mirror
forth in their manifold aspects the splendour of those eternal principles proclaimed by Bahá'u'lláh . . .

And now as I look into the future, I hope to see the
friends at all times, in every land, and of every shade of
thought and character, voluntarily and joyously rallying
round their local and in particular their national centres of
activity, upholding and promoting their interests with
complete unanimity and contentment, with perfect understanding, genuine enthusiasm and sustained vigour. This
indeed is the one joy and yearning of my life, for it is the
fountain-head from which all future blessing will flow, the
broad foundation upon which the security of the Divine
Edifice must ultimately rest. May we not hope that now at
last the dawn of a brighter day is breaking upon our beloved
Cause?[322]

The community of Bahá'u'lláh's followers in Britain was
however about to lose one of its brightest and most capable
adherents. Dr Esslemont's breathing problems had worsened
during the first few months of the National Spiritual Assembly's existence and by the summer of 1924 he was forced to
leave the south of England to spend three months in his
native Scotland. His extended stay in his homeland was
nevertheless crowned with success in the teaching arena and
a woman declared her faith in Bahá'u'lláh – the 'first one in
Scotland so far as I know to become a professed Bahá'í'.[323]
Dr Esslemont resigned from the National Assembly and the
friends in Bournemouth duly elected Sister Challis to represent them in his place.

Shoghi Effendi, concerned for Esslemont's health, extended an invitation for the doctor to come to Haifa for the
winter. Esslemont arrived on 21 November 1924. Exactly

one year later, having rendered invaluable assistance to the Guardian in all manner of secretarial duties, he passed away after suffering three consecutive strokes. Shoghi Effendi stayed up with Esslemont for the whole of his last night on earth. On 23 November George Simpson received Shoghi Effendi's grief-stricken cable:

BELOVED ESSLEMONT PASSED AWAY, COMMUNICATE FRIENDS AND FAMILY DISTRESSING NEWS URGE BELIEVERS DEDICATE SPECIAL DAY FOR UNIVERSAL PRAYER AND REMEMBRANCE. SHOGHI.[324]

Earlier, immediately following Dr Esslemont's resignation from the National Spiritual Assembly, George Palgrave Simpson appears to have experienced some great difficulties which led him to question the effectiveness of his service to the nascent Bahá'í administration. In a letter of 25 October 1924 Shoghi Effendi promised Simpson his 'assurance and sympathy in view of the heavy burden of responsibility that rests on your shoulders in these difficult and trying times. My fervent and increasing prayer is that 'Abdu'l-Bahá may show you the way that will enable you to continue your splendid pioneer work effectually, peacefully, free from every earthly care and anxiety.'[325] Just ten days later another letter from the Guardian encouraged Simpson to 'take all necessary measures against a slacking in our pace and it is truly unfortunate that just when the individual endeavours of every single member is most needed and necessary, age and earthly cares deprive us of some of our experienced and able co-workers.'[326] Whatever prompted Simpson to offer his resignation from the National Spiritual Assembly and London Spiritual Assembly, by mid-November 1924 his thoughts had changed. Shoghi Effendi's secretary wrote that the Guardian was 'very happy to know that even the thought of it [resignation] has totally vanished. The hopes that he cherished in you are far too many to permit you a more quiet part in Bahá'í activities in England, and the hopeful signs of progress in the past year has made the prospects of the coming

year very bright and it all depends upon the efforts of the
friends in England and the guidance of our Master from on
high just how bright it shall turn out to be.'[327]

In fact, the community found itself increasingly being
called upon to support the efforts of like-minded organizations and institutions. A Mr Wren of the League of Nations
Union attended the National Spiritual Assembly meeting of
4 July 1925 to explain the workings of the League's Religious
and Ethics Committee. The Committee had originally been
an independent League of Religions but had subsequently
joined forces with the Union. The fundamental principles on
which the Committee acted were righteousness and the
prevention of war. It hoped that rather than to bring politics
into religion, religion could be brought into politics. Heads
of religions and congregations were being invited to join as
corporate members. In the ensuing discussion, while all the
Assembly members were in favour of individuals joining the
Union, it was felt that there was a risk of the Assembly
becoming involved in political matters – which is forbidden
in the teachings – if the Assembly joined as a corporate body.
Mr Wren reassured the Assembly members on this point and
there was a unanimous vote to join the Union under the
auspices of the Religious and Ethics Committee provided that
by so doing it was understood that the Assembly would take
no part in any political measures or activities.

The National Spiritual Assembly was also keen to investigate the benefits of constituting the Bahá'í community into
a corporate body with the aim of attaining a permanent
status under English law. There were three ways in which
this could be done: 1) by registration as a Friendly Society,
2) by registration as a Provident Society and 3) by registration as a Limited Company which allowed the omission of the
word 'Limited' in special cases. The first two methods involved performing a number of onerous obligations to the
authorities and covered many activities which the Assembly
considered undesirable to undertake. On the other hand the
incorporation of the community as a limited company with

a nominal capital of five pounds, constituted by one hundred shares of a shilling each, was deemed simpler and allowed greater latitude in the Memoranda and Articles of Association by which the company would be bound, as well as obviate much of the official supervision attached to registration under the first two categories. The members of the Assembly were united in their views that it was most desirable to secure a legal status in the way suggested. Hipployte Dreyfus Barney from Paris – who was present as a guest at this particular meeting – said that he considered it essential to obtain such status from the point of view of possible bequests which might be made for Bahá'í purposes. He added that in the United States such a step had been contemplated for some time but had not yet been achieved. George Simpson took it upon himself to investigate the matter further.

Ethel harboured a particular worry about the number of believers who were unable to attend National Assembly meetings owing to ill health, old age or geography. She wrote to Shoghi Effendi wondering if it would be possible to co-opt additional members to serve on the Assembly. The Guardian replied that it would be permissible to ask two additional believers to attend the meetings and even take part in the discussion. In the event of one or more of the nine being unable to attend the meetings, these believers could act as substitute members of the Assembly with power to vote. Except when acting as substitutes for absent members, they were not to take part in the voting. Shoghi Effendi believed that some of the more capable and trustworthy of the group members outside of the Assembly should have the opportunity of familiarizing themselves with the work of the institution so that they might be better fitted to take up the work when some of the older members had to retire. Shoghi Effendi left it to the National Assembly to decide how this ought to be done. Strong opposition to this idea was expressed by Edward Hall and Ruhi Afnan, the latter believing that the procedure would be entirely contrary to the democratic constitution of the Bahá'í Cause which provides that

the members of the governing body should be elected by the
believers. As a compromise, the Assembly agreed that when
the delegates elected the nine regular members of the National Assembly each year they should also elect an equal
number of substitute members who in the absence of the
regular members could attend the meetings and have the
right of speaking and voting. This method was adopted for
the postal election of the National Spiritual Assembly at
Riḍván 1926. Thus, for example, the London believers, who
only voted for London representatives on the National
Spiritual Assembly, elected Ethel, George Simpson, Mr
Aṣgharzádih, Lady Blomfield, Claudia Coles and Mother
George. In addition, as substitute members, they elected Mrs
A. Brown, Mrs Thornburgh-Cropper, Mrs Ginman, Mary
Basil Hall, Mr R. R. Jackson, Miss Musgrave and Mrs Slade.
Manchester elected Jacob Joseph and John Craven as mem-
ber, with Edward Hall and Albert Joseph as reserves.
Bournemouth elected Sister Challis with a Miss Kilford as
substitute. Shoghi Effendi was clearly concerned with the
way this system of substitutes would work and urged the
National Spiritual Assembly to consult with its counterpart
in the United States to find out how it ensured a regular
quorum at its meetings. The Guardian wrote that he realized
'the special and peculiar difficulties that prevail in London
and the nature of the obstacles with which the [the believers]
are confronted. I feel however that an earnest effort should
be made to overcome them and that the members must
arrange their affairs in such a way as to ensure their prompt
attendance at 9 meetings which are held in the course of the
year. This surely is not an insurmountable obstacle.'[328]
    The first gathering of the incoming National Spiritual
Assembly in 1926 was blessed by the presence of the outstanding Bahá'í teacher Martha Root, Mountfort Mills – who
had come from Paris to discuss a further outbreak of persecutions in Persia with Martha – and Annie Romer. Martha
Root had arrived in England early in June 1926 and spent
five months in the country as the guest of Mrs Romer and

her husband Harry, a journalist, from New York who had
settled on the outskirts of London. Martha was named by
Shoghi Effendi as the 'archetype of Bahá'í itinerant teachers', the 'foremost Hand' of the Cause of God, the 'Leading
Ambassadress of His Faith' and the 'Pride of Bahá'í teachers,
whether men or women, in both the East and the West'.[329]
She was the first believer to respond to the call made by
'Abdu'l-Bahá in His Tablets of the Divine Plan and travelled
four times around the world over a period of 20 years. Far
from being seen as exhausting and taxing journeys for a
woman in poor physical health, Root's travels have been
hailed by Bahá'ís ever since as enormous victories for the
Cause, the crowning triumph of which was Martha's introduction of Queen Marie of Rumania into the Faith of
Bahá'u'lláh.

During Martha Root's five-month stay in Britain she
travelled around the country extensively, giving talks and
lectures, meeting the believers, stirring up press interest in
the Persian situation and organizing the Bahá'í programme
for an eight-day Esperanto conference in Edinburgh. One
thousand delegates from 39 countries attended the Congress
and the Bahá'í sessions took place in the same building
where 'Abdu'l-Bahá had spoken more than a decade before.
After the Congress, Lady Blomfield accompanied Martha to
Manchester where six lectures had been arranged. Returning
to London, Martha received an invitation to stay from Mrs
Thornburgh-Cropper but she declined, preferring to live
among people who were not yet Bahá'ís. Her visit caused a
great stir and not since the visit of 'Abdu'l-Bahá had the
community enjoyed such a high profile among the thinkers
and outstanding personalities of British life. The Spiritualist
Church, of which Sir Arthur Conan Doyle was president,
invited Martha to conduct a Sunday morning service. Visits
to Oxford, Cambridge, Brighton and Birmingham followed.
Her voice was heard all over Britain when she spoke to the
BBC radio about her impression of the British dominions.
Martha's presence on British shores inspired other promi-

nent believers to join the whirlwind of teaching that was
sweeping the country. In addition to Mountfort Mills, George
Townshend arrived from Dublin, the Dreyfus-Barneys came
from Paris, Mrs Schopflocher arrived from Montreal, Louise
Gregory visited on her way to Budapest and Vienna, and
Ahmad Yazdi arrived from Port Said. Julia Culver arrived
with the granddaughters of 'Abdu'l-Bahá to see London
before they returned to Haifa.

The damp and cold weather in London suited Martha's
health and she liked the city immensely. However she was
quick to notice that the English were conservative and slow
to take up the message of Bahá'u'lláh. But she had great
faith in the nation's abilities and potential and said that
when 'the English get these teachings they will take them
to China and other lands with the same calibre, stick-to-
itiveness, and efficiency with which they have taken Christianity.'[330]

Martha's wisdom and experience was a great help to the
National Spiritual Assembly although it appears that her
manner and style raised a few eyebrows, as it did everywhere. The Assembly had resolved to encourage all the Local
Assemblies to circulate their latest news to each other once
every 19 days. At Martha's suggestion, Ethel proposed that
the distribution of the 19-day letters should be extended to
include Bahá'í friends who lived at a distance from the
several centres so that they might be kept informed of the
progress of the Cause nationally. Thus the foremost international teacher of the Bahá'í community helped the new
institution to expand its vision to include every soul in every
locality who might benefit from receiving the latest news.

Five years had now elapsed since that fateful November
night in 1921 when 'Abdu'l-Bahá had passed away. The
British Bahá'í community had clearly come a long way since
His Ascension, struggling as it now was to establish its
administrative roots and to formalize its activities, nurtured
and sustained by the continuing sacrificial efforts of its most
experienced members including Ethel Rosenberg, Lady

Blomfield and Mrs Thornburgh-Cropper, all of whom had been taught at the Master's own table. Their advancing age and poor health were obviously not conducive to the dynamic functioning of the new institution, yet what they lacked in physical energy they made up for in wisdom, knowledge and good judgement. On 28 November 1926 the London Spiritual Assembly addressed a letter to the believers nationally commemorating the fifth anniversary of 'Abdu'l-Bahá's passing. It ends,

> With Bahá'í love, renewed faith, and deeper reverence, may we attain to severance from all save God, then, free from the subtle serpent of the mind, the ego, we shall be of those who move forward to service free from self-deception, because we are severed from all save God. That which we seek in truth, we shall sow in truth. 'God causes things to grow.' 'Abdu'l-Bahá is the witness of this![331]

Earlier in the year Ethel Rosenberg had received a letter from Shoghi Effendi inviting her to return to the Holy Land. The Guardian greatly valued her abilities and wished her to assist him with translations. Thus, in the final months of 1926, shortly after entering her sixty-eighth year, a quarter of a century after her first visit, Ethel was called once again to the World Centre of her Faith. Despite the long years of painful illness that slowed down her selfless service to the Cause, Ethel's capabilities were still engraved on Shoghi Effendi's heart and mind. He who had relied heavily on his family to carry out his work and correspondence since the passing of Dr Esslemont requested that his dear Rosa return to Haifa to help him carry his heavy load.

Preparing for the last time to make the long and physically gruelling voyage to the Holy Land, Ethel, in her typically practical manner, wrote to the Guardian stating that she would need a new pair of glasses and some dental work before the journey. This he provided for her. In a letter written on behalf of Shoghi Effendi dated 29 November 1926, the Guardian's secretary recorded that they were 'eagerly awaiting to meet Miss Rosenberg and Mrs. [Isobel] Slade to obtain a first hand information of the condition of the Cause in England and the extent to which Mr. Mills and Miss Root have succeeded to improve it'.[332] Ethel was no doubt equally eager to see once again the Guardian whom she had befriended as a student at Oxford and his blessed Great Aunt, the Greatest Holy Leaf. As a fitting conclusion to her life of dedication and devotion, Ethel was about to render signal services to Shoghi Effendi in the preparation of his masterly English translation of one of Bahá'u'lláh most important works.

16

Inestimable Services

Nothing but the abundance of our actions, nothing but the purity of our lives and the integrity of our character, can in the last resort establish our claim that the Bahá'í spirit is in this day the sole agency that can translate a long cherished ideal into an enduring achievement.[333]

Shoghi Effendi

Shortly after inviting Ethel Rosenberg to Haifa to assist him in his translation work, Shoghi Effendi received a letter from Ireland written by the distinguished clergyman George Townshend. Although Townshend did not resign from the church until 1947, he counted himself a Bahá'í and worked hard for the Bahá'í Cause. As well as corresponding with the Guardian, Townshend wrote prolifically about the Bahá'í Faith. Townshend's letter of 27 February 1926 reads:

> I have been told that you invited Miss Rosenberg to Haifa to help in translating work, though (as I believe) she knows little or no Persian. I am encouraged by this to offer now my services, such as they are, in this kind of work. Having myself no knowledge of Persian and being a clergyman resident in Ireland, my help can not be anything better than advice as to English idiom and grammatical structure.[334]

Townshend suggested that the Guardian might send him 'the proposed English rendering of certain passages when not judged quite satisfactory'.[335] Shoghi Effendi's immediate response was to send Townshend the first part of his new translation of the *Hidden Words*, encouraging the clergyman to 'alter and revise it with all freedom, for I have great appreciation of your literary taste and attainments'.[336] By the time Ethel Rosenberg arrived in Haifa, a steady flow of correspondence was passing between the Guardian and George Townshend and draft translations of the *Hidden Words* were being sent backwards and forwards, surely representing the most unique and unusual collaboration in the history of any religion. Shoghi Effendi wrote to George Simpson on 16 July 1926, informing him of his correspondence with Townshend. The Guardian told Simpson that he had received Townshend's second letter containing suggestions for translations and that he hoped to revise the translation of the *Hidden Words* when his correspondence with Townshend was over. Shoghi Effendi urged the British National Spiritual Assembly to postpone reprinting the book until the revisions were completed.[337]

When Ethel Rosenberg once again set foot in the Holy Land, three significant events in the Bahá'í world were particularly occupying Shoghi Effendi's mind. The first was the resumption of the appalling persecutions of the Bahá'í community in Persia which resulted in the martyrdom of a number of believers. The Guardian called upon the British National Assembly to do its utmost to gain wide and effective publicity in the British press about the atrocities.

The second event, of remarkable significance, was the positive response of Queen Marie of Rumania to the Bahá'í message when presented to her by Martha Root. In 'language of exquisite beauty', the Queen had written a heart-felt testimony to the 'power and sublimity of the Message of Bahá'u'lláh' which the Guardian hoped the believers would publish throughout the world. The conversion of the Queen was hailed as a 'notable triumph which the unbending energy and indomitable spirit of our beloved Martha has achieved for our sacred Cause'.[338] With the testimonies of the Queen widely available, Shoghi Effendi anticipated a transformation in the attitudes of many 'to a Faith the tenets of which have often been misunderstood and sorely neglected. It will serve as a fresh stimulus to the enlightened and cultured to investigate with an open mind the verities of its message, the source of its life-giving principles.'[339]

The third event that concerned the Guardian was the violation of the House of Bahá'u'lláh in Baghdad by a 'relentless enemy'. The House, the Guardian wrote, had been converted into a rallying centre for the 'corrupt, the perverse, and the fanatical'.[340] High-level negotiations were underway to restore the House to Bahá'í ownership so that it could be maintained as a site of pilgrimage.

Shoghi Effendi had high hopes of Ethel's visit which he thought in the long term would assist and aid the work in Britain as well as prove beneficial to the Cause in general. 'I feel that the opportunities now open to the friends,' he wrote, 'are greater than ever before and I will pray that the measures they undertake will redound to the glory, the power and effectiveness of the Cause. The utterances of the Rumanian Queen should be given the fullest possible publicity and be fully utilised as I feel they are of great significance and value. More power to your elbow!'[341]

Perhaps because of her failing health and weakened physical condition, Ethel invited another believer, Isobel Slade, to accompany her to the Holy Land. Mrs Slade had first heard of the Bahá'í Faith shortly before the passing of 'Abdu'l-Bahá. She had planned to visit the Master but never met Him in person. After her pilgrimage with Ethel, she became known as a stalwart member of the British Bahá'í community, serving for 14 years on the National Spiritual Assembly and holding all possible offices during that time. In 1948 she helped to establish the first Local Spiritual Assembly in Edinburgh. She eventually passed away in 1972 at the extraordinary age of 98, prompting the Universal House of Justice to hail her as an 'outstanding believer'.[342]

In an unpublished recollection of their visit, Isobel Slade recorded that life in Haifa as she and Ethel found it in 1926 was much as it must have been at the time of the Master. Mountfort Mills and Ethel's dear friend Laura Dreyfus-Barney were also staying in the Holy Land at that time. The pilgrim house was being looked after by the Australian believer Effie Baker and by 'Abdu'l-Bahá's Japanese helper, Saichiro Fujita. Ethel and Mrs Slade were amused and astonished by the way that the tiny Fujita spoke about his relationship with the Master. Fujita had frequently been told by 'Abdu'l-Bahá to return to Japan, an instruction which the devoted servant stubbornly refused to obey. Mrs Slade recorded how she was surprised to hear that anyone would dare to disobey an instruction of the Master!

Ethel particularly enjoyed the bounty of once again being received by 'Abdu'l-Bahá's sister, the Greatest Holy Leaf. When the women arrived in Haifa they went almost immediately to the Master's House to be received by her - 'a wonderful gracious figure with a white fleecy shawl and a white veil on her head,' wrote Mrs Slade. 'A beautiful face with dark blue eyes, a face lined with suffering that had been her lot in life. She might have been any nationality and though unable to speak any English, one felt her understanding and knew that she was the rock on which the youthful Guardian depended so much in those early days.'[343]

Bahíyyih Khánum told Ethel and Isobel that Bahá'u'lláh had been asked why He had not given her a husband to protect her. He had replied that no man was worthy of her. She herself had always begged Bahá'u'lláh to let her devote herself to Him and 'Abdu'l-Bahá. Until the very end of her life she was an invaluable source of comfort and guidance to her youthful great nephew as he rose to manage the heavy burden which had been placed upon his shoulders.

Shortly after their arrival, Mrs Slade received news that her mother had been taken ill in England and she was forced to return earlier than she had expected. Her brief pilgrimage included visits with Ethel to the Riḍván garden, the house of 'Abdu'lláh Páshá and the prison where Bahá'u'lláh had been incarcerated, as well as to the environs of the Shrine of Bahá'u'lláh. Unfortunately they were unable to visit all of the buildings associated with the Faith as 'Abdu'l-Bahá's faithless half-brother Muḥammad-'Alí still occupied the Mansion of Bahjí.

Her initial pilgrimage ended, Ethel set about her task of answering correspondence on behalf of the Guardian. As well as the letters of encouragement she was asked to write to believers throughout the world, Ethel had the task of conveying the Guardian's elucidations on the development of the Faith's institutions to the many believers who were trying hard to build the administrative order. Ethel found great joy in renewing correspondence with those scores of believers whom she had personally encountered in her many travels over the years.

Ethel wrote one such letter to a believer on 26 December 1926. It records how much she was interested to read a reference to Mrs Helen Cole of New York City who Ethel believed had shared her first pilgrimage way back in 1901. Her age and failing memory, however, got the better of her and she wondered whether it might not have been on her second visit in 1904 that the two had met. 'At any rate I knew and loved her', is her conclusion, dismissive of the failing of memory.[344]

Ethel deeply enjoyed and appreciated the opportunity of being with the Holy Family once again. To Ethel, the Holy Family may have been something of a replacement for the children and husband she never had. However, her brother George was never far from her mind. George lived for three years in Rockhampton in Queensland, Australia after leaving Cambridge University to teach science and mathematics in a grammar school. Ethel was particularly pleased to hear that one of the believers who wrote to Shoghi Effendi had visited Rockhampton. Ethel wrote to the correspondent saying that the school authorities greatly desired that George remain in Rockhampton but that their mother was in very poor health and he had faithfully promised to return to England at the end of three years.

The wide variety of correspondence which Ethel undertook on Shoghi Effendi's behalf is an indication of the spread of the Bahá'í Faith in the years since Ethel's last visit to the Holy Land. On 11 January 1927 she replied to a letter from

Amy Dewing in New Zealand which had been received by the Guardian just one day previously. In it Ethel conveyed Shoghi Effendi's pleasure at hearing of Dewing's activities in New Zealand and promised that the Guardian would 'pray earnestly that your sincere efforts to make Bahá'u'lláh's Revelation widely known will bring forth much fruit and have a great result. In the newer countries minds are more open, and the people are more ready and willing to receive this Great Message.'[345] Ethel informed Amy Dewing of the importance Shoghi Effendi had given to the testimonials of Queen Marie of Rumania, particularly the one in which she acknowledged Muḥammad as a true Prophet of God. This, Shoghi Effendi said, had great importance for the East, particularly Persia.

Another duty given to Ethel was to forward money from Evelyn Watkin, a believer in New Zealand, to help the believers in Persia. Ethel assured the donor that the Persian friends 'will be very much pleased at receiving this kind remembrance and help from far distant New Zealand!'[346]

During the precious hours spent with Shoghi Effendi, Ethel was able to gain firsthand knowledge of the evolving administrative order of the Faith of Bahá'u'lláh and learned how aspects of it should be practised. Ethel conveyed this guidance from the Guardian to the friends in England through letters written by her on his behalf. Ethel was extremely anxious that every detail of the Guardian's vision for the healthy growth of these institutions should be observed. It is interesting to detect her own surprise at some of Shoghi Effendi's utterances. For example, in January 1927, George Simpson wrote to Shoghi Effendi about a number of matters. Ethel answered at the Guardian's request. She wrote:

> He says that in one way we are not quite correct in the way we manage our elections for the National Assembly – Shoghi Effendi says that the intention is, that when once the 19 delegates have been elected by the friends of the respective centres in the proportions you mention, i.e. 12 delegates

from among the London friends, five from the Manchester
friends, and two from the Bournemouth group, that then,
these 19 delegates assembled should choose by secret ballot
from the whole body of the believers in Gt. Britain and
Ireland, the nine friends they consider most suitable as
members of the National Assembly. Heretofore, as I understand it, it has rather been our practice that the 12 London
delegates elected six from the London friends – the Manchester five delegates elected two from Manchester and the
Bournemouth delegates elected one from Bournemouth.
But, Shoghi Effendi says, all the 19 delegates must clearly
understand that they must select from the whole body of the
believers in Gt. Britain and Ireland those 9 whom they
consider the most fit and suitable members to constitute the
National Assembly. Therefore it will be necessary to supply
each of the 19 delegates with a complete list of all those
believers in Gt. Britain and Ireland. From that complete list
of course must be eliminated all those who from one cause
or another are unable to serve on the National Assembly.
Also – Shoghi Effendi says that those 19 elected delegates
should if possible meet during the Feast of Ridvan in London thus forming as it were a baby Convention! I had not
realised before that the annual Baha'i Convention in the
U.S.A. consists solely of those delegates who had been
chosen by their respective Centres in order that they may
elect the 9 to form the National Assembly of that country.
Did you understand this? I certainly did not. As Shoghi
Effendi points out – it is quite possible that – e.g. in the
future – 7 members might be elected from the Manchester
friends and only two from London! On the other hand – it
is quite possible that all nine members chosen by the 19
delegates might be from the London group. Of course, on
reflection one sees clearly that the proceedings must be as
now described because in the future there may be 21 or 53
separate local Assemblies in Gt. Britain just as is now the
case in the U.S.A. – and it would obviously be impossible for
each of these Assemblies to elect one of their number to sit
as their representative on the National Assembly. No doubt
I ought to have understood this before – but I must confess
I did not! . . .[347]

Shoghi Effendi also clarified the catchment area of the London community. He suggested it would save trouble if a circle was drawn widely enough to include believers on the periphery of the capital rather than use the postal area but this decision he left to the London Assembly. The Guardian, through Ethel, also urged the National Assembly to select the date that the 19 delegates should be in London during the Riḍván period for the election.

This letter was just one of many which Ethel exchanged with George Simpson while she served as Shoghi Effendi's secretary between December 1926 and April 1927. As a result of this letter in particular, which outlined the principles for the election of the National Spiritual Assembly and prescribed the Riḍván period as the date for the national convention, 13 delegates attended the next convention and four voted by post. However, the believers in their naivety elected ten members onto the National Assembly as two believers had received an equal number of votes for the ninth place. In a later letter to Simpson, Shoghi Effendi patiently suggested that the following year, the number of members should be strictly confined to nine, a second ballot being 'quite proper and justified'.[348] Interestingly, among those elected was one Reverend Biggs who had, it appears, wavered on the edge of Bahá'í activity for some time. Shoghi Effendi wrote that he trusted that the choice of Reverend Biggs signified 'his unreserved acceptance of the Faith in its entirety – a condition that we must increasingly stress in the years that come'.[349]

During the early part of her stay in Haifa, Ethel caught the influenza which swept through the whole of the Guardian's household but by late January she had almost recovered. She learned, too, that Mrs Thornburgh-Cropper was seriously ill and the friends in Haifa gathered to pray for her recovery.

With the arrival of manuscripts from George Townshend with his suggestions for adjustments to the Guardian's translation of the *Hidden Words*, Ethel and Shoghi Effendi set about preparing the final version. Ethel's understanding of Persian was by now very good and she and the Guardian sat together comparing Townshend's suggestions word by word with the original text and wherever possible accepting his emendations. On 7 March 1927 Townshend sent to the Guardian his suggestions on the last pages of the translation of the *Hidden Words*. Townshend wrote, 'I have done my utmost . . . I hope fervently that the result of all this combined effort may be as little unworthy as possible of the great opportunity and that the British public will now note and acclaim this exalting and unparalleled monument of religious and literary genius.'[350]

Shoghi Effendi's gratitude to both Ethel and George Townshend was enormous. He wrote to Townshend,

> I am glad to inform you that at last I have managed to devote the necessary time to the consideration of your splendid suggestions in connection with the revision of the Hidden Words. Miss Rosenberg and myself (I wish you were with us also!) have carefully altered the text in the light of your suggestions and I trust that it will soon be published in London. The assistance you and Miss Rosenberg have rendered will be acknowledged and I wish to thank you from the bottom of my heart for your unique and invaluable collaboration.[351]

Ethel wrote to Townshend saying that she would be bringing the revised text back to London for publication by the National Spiritual Assembly. She noted that on the title page Shoghi Effendi had added, after his own name as translator, ' . . . revised with the Assistance of G. Townshend and E. J. Rosenberg.'[352] Townshend sent Shoghi Effendi an urgent message in response, requesting that his name not to be placed on the title page as he believed it would associate him too intimately with the Bahá'í Revelation and would endanger his plan to influence his colleagues in the church with a less direct approach. The Guardian responded that he well understood Townshend's concerns and would comply with

his wishes. To this day the title page reads, 'Translated by
Shoghi Effendi with the assistance of some English
friends'.[353] Ethel presumably did not much favour the idea
of having her name by itself beneath that of the Guardian.
Shoghi Effendi had made his first translation of the
Hidden Words in 1923, sending it to the American Bahá'í
community for publication and to the Bahá'ís in England for
their use. The British National Spiritual Assembly had
published this revised translation by January 1924. A year
later, when the American National Spiritual Assembly
informed the Guardian of the immense demand for the book,
he told them that it was of urgent importance that the
English text be revised, hence his collaboration with the two
distinguished British believers. A brief glance at but one of
Bahá'u'lláh's verses translated in three versions will suffice
to demonstrate what that unique collaboration achieved. An
early translation of one of the verses published in London
in 1909 reads:

> O Son of man! In My Ancient Eternity and in My Eternal
> being, was I hidden. I knew My Love in thee, therefore I
> created thee; upon thee I laid my Image, and to thee re-
> vealed My Beauty.[354]

Shoghi Effendi's first translation is a tremendous improvement on that rather rough and unpoetic effort:

> O Son of Man! Veiled in my immemorial Being and in the
> ancient eternity of My Self, I felt My love for thee; hence,
> I created thee, have engraven on thee the Image of My
> Likeness and revealed to thy sight the beauty of My Counte-
> nance.[355]

The Guardian's final version, taking into account the suggestions of George Townshend and Ethel Rosenberg, is more
poetic yet resounds with a subtle potency:

> O Son of Man! Veiled in my immemorial being and in the
> ancient eternity of My essence, I knew My love for thee;
> therefore I created thee, have engraved on thee My image

and revealed to thee My Beauty.[356]

Ethel's free hours, when not engaged in letter-writing, were spent with the pilgrims and visitors to Haifa. She relished their company and the insights they gave into the rapid growth of the Faith and the great challenges it faced throughout the world. One guest whom she found particularly interesting was a Dr Habíb of Kirmánsháh who visited Shoghi Effendi in January 1927 along with his wife and little girl. Dr Habíb told Ethel and the assembled believers of the continued fanaticism of the Muslims in Persia and how during two periods of the year especially – the fast month and the eight-week period of Muḥarram – the 'fanatical Mullahs preach against the Bahá'ís from their pulpits – saying to the ignorant "No matter what evil things you have done during your life, or what sins you have committed, if you kill a Bahá'í who is an enemy of Islam, or even if you take his property or severely injure him, all your own sins will be wiped out and forgiven for the sake of this good deed of destroying an enemy of the Faith!!"'[357] Dr Habíb reported that the Bahá'í teachings were spreading rapidly amongst the more educated classes but that it was difficult to teach the very poor and ignorant fanatical people, although when they did become believers 'they are very strong and faithful'.[358]

A particularly special correspondence began to develop at this time between Ethel and the American believer Louise Waite. Mrs Waite was nine years younger than Ethel and had grown up in Baltimore and Washington DC. A strong Episcopalian upbringing left her with a desire to express her devotion to God in song and she is perhaps best remembered as the composer of many Bahá'í hymns commonly sung in the meetings of the early American Bahá'í communities.

Louise Waite's life was filled with tragedy. In the course of just one year, she lost her mother, brother, husband and daughter. Traumatized, she left Baltimore for Chicago where she first heard of the Bahá'í Movement in 1902. She accepted it almost immediately and began a regular correspondence with 'Abdu'l-Bahá, receiving more than 40 Tablets from Him. By the mid-1920s, Louise, now known as Shahnaz, was recognized as one of the outstanding workers for the Cause in the United States and was in demand as a travelling teacher, both in California where she had moved with her second husband in 1915, and further afield.

It is clear from the correspondence between Ethel and Shahnaz Waite that both women shared a devotion to the Holy Family and felt very close to them. Shahnaz, it seems, was always keen to receive mementoes of the family and it was Ethel's task on a number of occasions to answer her requests or to forward less than positive replies. On 14 January 1927 Ethel wrote on behalf of the Greatest Holy Leaf to Shahnaz, who had written to Bahíyyih Khánum requesting permission to cover prayer books with materials taken from garments worn by members of the Holy household. Ethel's task was gently to warn Shahnaz against doing such a thing. In her response Ethel mentions that the Greatest Holy Leaf had spoken with Shoghi Effendi about the request and that in view of 'Abdu'l-Bahá's wishes they considered it 'not advisable to cover the little prayer books in the manner you propose. Our beloved 'Abdul-Bahá deprecated and discouraged the use of materials worn by members of the Holy household, regarding them as especially sacred and our dear Guardian thinks that if such practices were to be adopted it would eventually lead to superstition. Therefore she [the Greatest Holy Leaf] is not sending you one of her dresses.'[359] This stern and direct response was counterbalanced by an offering of love. 'Because she loves you very much on account of your constant services, as for yourself personally, she will be pleased to send you one of her headcoverings for your use.'[360]

Further correspondence developed between Ethel and Shahnaz, Ethel answering a number of requests on behalf of the Greatest Holy Leaf. On 19 March 1927 Ethel records that the Greatest Holy Leaf 'is very glad that her head covering has given you so much happiness and she is most

pleased to give it to you.'³⁶¹ Another request was granted:
'With regard to the Candles you wish for from the Holy
Shrine, the Beloved Khanum says these shall be sent to you
direct, the burial stone she will send to you by post also.'³⁶²
Ethel informed Mrs Waite that she hoped to be back in
London by about 6 May and that future correspondence
should not be directed to Haifa.

Later Mrs Waite wrote with another request which Ethel
at once answered on behalf of the women of 'Abdu'l-Bahá's
family:

My dear Bahá'í Friend Shahnaz,
    Ever since your request to me so many weeks (months?)
ago – I have been doing my best to collect these precious
writings for you! You see the whole of the family are so busy
always - and if you get one of them to write then it is quite
difficult to catch the others – one by one – at a leisure
moment! But now I am thankful to say they are completed
just 2 or 3 days before I leave for England. Khanum's eyes
are too weak now to allow her to write that is why her
writing is not included but the dear holy mother took much
pleasure in writing for you.
    Mr Sohrab – or better Ali Kuli Khan or some other of
your Persian friends will make translations for you of the
three which are in Persian. I have written in pencil on the
back the names so that you can rub it out easily.
    You will notice what extremely beautiful writing is our
dear Tooba Khanum's. I will send these precious writings
to you by registered mail and I know you will treasure and
value them. With the best of good wishes and Bahá'í love
to you,
    Ever your sincere friend,
    Ethel J. Rosenberg

No matter how long one's visit the parting and leaving this
dear place is always a great sadness. Pray for me my dear
friend that I may be able to serve our Beloved Cause as the
dear Master would wish.³⁶³

Ethel recorded that she felt it to be a great blessing to have

been in Haifa throughout the winter. She also found that her
health was wonderfully improved. On 6 May 1927 Ethel told
a correspondent that she would leave early the following day
for Port Said en route for England. 'Pray for me,' she wrote,
'that I may have the opportunity and power to serve the
beloved Cause.'[364] Before she left, Shoghi Effendi entrusted
Ethel with a precious gift to the British Bahá'í community.
Densely wrapped in tissue paper and protected by a solid
cardboard box, was a robe worn by Bahá'u'lláh, given by the
Guardian of the Bahá'í Faith to his dear and precious Rosa.

With her departure from Haifa, Ethel Rosenberg may well
have realized that it would be the last time that she would
ever lay eyes on the lofty heights of God's Holy Mountain
and the beautiful young face of the beloved Guardian.

17

The Messenger of Joy

O Lord! My bones are weakened, and the hoar hairs
glisten on My head . . . and I have now reached old age,
failing in My powers' . . . No strength is there left in Me
wherewith to arise and serve thy loved ones . . . O Lord,
My Lord! Hasten My ascension unto thy sublime
Threshold . . . and my arrival at the Door of thy grace
beneath the shadow of Thy most great mercy . . .[365]

'Abdu'l-Bahá

Spiritually revitalized by her experiences in Haifa although
no doubt exhausted by the effects of the gruelling journey on
her frail constitution, Ethel Rosenberg returned to England
only to discover her colleagues serving on the embryonic
Bahá'í institutions continuing to struggle to function effectively. Theirs was understandably a formidable task and
their duties were not made easier by their frustration at the
apparent lack of spiritual receptivity among the British
people. Even Shoghi Effendi, in a letter written on his behalf
of 8 February 1928, was moved to comment:

> It is strange that the English Bahá'ís have really contrib-
> uted a great deal to the Cause, and in the form of books and
> publications given us works of real and permanent value –
> perhaps proportionately more than America, and yet it is
> such a Herculean affair to bring in new fellow-workers.
> Perhaps just that difficulty is a sign of their merit – staunch
> and unflinching adherence once they believe in some-
> thing.[366]

Ethel was never again able to contribute her experience and

knowledge through service on the National Spiritual Assembly but in her final years she tried her best to keep up active participation on the London Assembly. After her return from Haifa she decided to move out of central London and took up residence with her brother George in an attractive terraced house at 82 Lambton Road in West Wimbledon. It was during this period that Ethel became particularly friendly with an American Bahá'í living close to her whose name was Louise Ginman, also known as Madame Charlot.

Mrs Ginman had become a Bahá'í in Burlingame, California around 1910 and had moved to England with her daughter, Alma, late in 1919. During 'Abdu'l-Bahá's visit to America, Mrs Ginman travelled from town to town trying to see the Master but every time she arrived she discovered that the Master had just left. She served on the London Spiritual Assembly for a period and later 'pioneered' to Oxford and Bristol. Ethel's visits to the Ginman home were filled with delight for the young Alma to whom she paid special attention. Alma – later surnamed Gregory – recalled with great fondness the early days of the Faith and how Ethel Rosenberg took her under her wing. While Alma did not formally register as a Bahá'í until 1942, she became a distinguished pioneer, first to Northampton where she helped form the first Local Spiritual Assembly, then moving to Liverpool in 1949 for the same purpose. Alma herself served as a member of the National Spiritual Assembly between 1948 and 1956. At the time of writing Alma still remains, despite her advanced years, at her remote pioneer post of Stornoway in the Western Isles off the coast of Scotland.

Alma Gregory remembers Ethel Rosenberg in this period as slim, small and upright with grey hair and a deep voice. Her chest complaint required her to take a lot of medication. The London suburb where Ethel and her brother set up home was in those days still quite unspoilt and isolated from the hustle of the city. Because George was not a Bahá'í, Ethel preferred not to have meetings in her own home but went out to them, travelling everywhere on buses. Alma loved to

sit next to Ethel and hear her talk about the Bahá'í Faith
and her two other passions, art and gardening. It seems that
one of the reasons Ethel spent so much time at the Ginmans'
home was because she loved their garden so much. Ethel's
own house had only a very small garden and she enjoyed
sitting on the Ginmans' balcony looking down the long lawn
to the tennis court while Alma sat beside her chatting and
sketching. Alma admired a number of Ethel's portraits of
Lady Blomfield's daughters which Ethel displayed in her
drawing room. It was Ethel who encouraged the young
Alma to go to the London School of Arts and Crafts in
Southampton Row.

Shortly after Ethel returned from Haifa Alma and her
mother received a telephone call from her, inviting them to
visit her immediately. When they arrived, Ethel sat them side
by side on the settee and then produced a cardboard box from
which she took sheet after sheet of tissue paper. She then
lifted from the box the robe of Bahá'u'lláh that Shoghi
Effendi had given her and laid it gently across their knees.
The robe is now kept in the British Bahá'í Archives and was
displayed to some three thousand believers who gathered
at the Resting Place of Shoghi Effendi in London in May
1992 to commemorate the Centenary of the Passing of
Bahá'u'lláh.[367]

With Ethel back from her extended absence, the London
Spiritual Assembly promptly set about defining its terms of
reference for the coming administrative year. It agreed that
it would hold nine meetings each year at 2:30 p.m. on the
first Saturday of every month except August, September and
January. Five members would constitute a quorum and
notices of motions would be sent to Ethel – once again elected
secretary of the Assembly – ten days before the meeting at
which the motion was to be made. Extraordinary meetings
could be called on the demand of three members and the
secretary.

One of the Assembly's major preoccupations was the spirit
– or lack of it – at the community gathering known as the

Nineteen Day Feast as well as at the commemoration of Holy Days. At one Assembly meeting, held at the home of Claudia Coles in Warwick Gardens, consultation centred around the quality of a recent Holy Day celebration. Mr Aṣgharzádih voiced his concern that the meetings were not sufficiently joyful. He quoted from the writings of Bahá'u'lláh about the importance of the Bahá'ís enjoying themselves while taking care not to overstep the bounds of good taste. He explained that the Bahá'ís in 'Ishqábád had introduced features into the Feasts to enhance the pleasure of the believers and that Shoghi Effendi had said that both spiritual and material happiness should be encouraged. Aṣgharzádih's translator Mr Hafezi, who was also present, subsequently joined in the consultation, mentioning a theatrical play that the friends in Beirut had been encouraged by the Guardian to perform. He added that in Persia, where he said the believers were more fanatical than in England, there were only two short prayers said at the Feast, one at the beginning and one at the end of the meeting. Outsiders were also welcomed into the Feast, which was primarily a social event. He felt that there were too many prayers and long Tablets recited at the London Bahá'í gatherings. Mr Aṣgharzádih agreed and expressed his concern that what the believers did now would set a precedent for the future of the Cause. He believed that in the future the Bahá'ís would have much more practical work to do and people would not have so much time for prayer. A very long discussion ensued where a wide variety of views were shared. Isobel Slade, for one, felt that the meetings were unspiritual and not peaceful enough.

At this point, Ethel interjected her opinion. She strongly felt that the spiritual content of a meeting was intended to create joy and did not accept the prevalent feeling that spirituality was necessarily equated with dullness. Ethel suggested that the spiritual programme might be limited to about half an hour during which time there would be readings and prayers. The rest of the meeting, she hoped, might be given over to refreshments and socializing, stressing especially the necessity of promoting unity and fellowship among the Bahá'ís.

The London Spiritual Assembly frequently returned to this matter. Over the next few meetings, opinions were variously expressed about the underlying purpose of any Bahá'í gathering. Some cared particularly about showing hospitality rather than about formal procedures. Others favoured holding the Feasts unofficially and keeping them flexible. It was not until two years later that the Assembly members, after reading the words of 'Abdu'l-Bahá, arrived at a common understanding of the institution of the Feast and realized that it was only in its earliest stages and that eventually its format would become fixed. The Assembly resolved to note the dates of the Nineteen Day Feasts for the whole Bahá'í community and to encourage the Bahá'ís to show hospitality where possible on the first day of every Bahá'í month.[368]

It is clear that these Assembly meetings were not the easiest aspect of Bahá'í life for the early administrators of the Cause. The strength of their personalities and their reluctance to let go of their own ideas placed a great strain on the process of consultation and limited its effectiveness. Alma Gregory recalls the stormy relationship between Ethel Rosenberg and George Simpson, who apparently were always at loggerheads. On one occasion Alma was seated beside Ethel at a meeting when Simpson was talking. Ethel turned to the young girl and whispered into her ear, 'My dear, isn't he ponderous?'[369]

Simpson, for his part, became increasingly disillusioned with his own services to the Bahá'í administration and on 16 May 1928 penned a letter to the National Spiritual Assembly announcing his resignation.

> Such a decision was not the result of any sudden impulse due to the occurrences at that meeting [12 May] which did but constitute the culminating point of an intention present in my mind for a considerable length of time.
>
> This intention originated from the fact that I have recognized that in the past I have been too prone to conduct the

business of the Assembly on material lines whereas I am
convinced that, more especially now, spiritual ideas should
inspire the views of the members and the conclusions at
which the Assembly as a whole may arrive in matters affect-
ing the progress and efficient working of the Bahá'í Cause
in this country.

Whilst therefore I relinquish a task, which I feel I am not
spiritually fitted to carry on, I am willing and indeed should
rejoice, to continue to attend to the material side of the
Assembly's business, for which I may have some aptitude,
by acting as Treasurer, should the Assembly so desire; but
of course without any power of voting on propositions
brought forward for decision.[370]

The British Assemblies also had to grapple again with the
perennial issue of what actually constituted a fully-fledged
member of the Bahá'í community. The London Spiritual
Assembly forced itself to consider the matter after receiving
guidance from the Guardian that three conditions were
necessary for an individual to be accepted as a new believer:
first, that the person accepted the station of Bahá'u'lláh;
second, that he or she agreed to abide by the conditions of
the Will and Testament of 'Abdu'l-Bahá; and third, that the
newcomer accepted the present administration of the Cause
throughout the world.

Initially the Assembly felt it reasonable to embody the
three conditions into some form of membership statement
and ask those who wished to join the Cause to sign it. This
suggestion opened up a hornet's nest of conflicting views and
understandings of the nature of enrolment into the community. The fundamental question facing the Assembly was how
it could best determine that these requirements had been
fulfilled before adding the enquirer's name onto the voters'
roll. One suggestion was that a formal declaration might be
drawn up to be signed by those who desired to join. This
course of action was, however, strongly opposed by Mr
Asgharzádih who had been absent from the meeting at which
the decision had been made. In a letter to the Assembly he

said that although he believed wholeheartedly in Bahá'u'lláh and was, he hoped, willing to make any sacrifice that was necessary in support of his faith, he would definitely have refused to sign any document had he been asked to do so. He claimed that the Master had previously rejected the suggestion that a written obligation of any description be taken as proof of a person being a Bahá'í. The Bahá'í community, Asgharzádih said, was a family of friends joined spiritually together by their faith and love. Written undertakings, he warned, were absolutely against Bahá'í principles of free brotherhood and faith. Mother George and Ethel sympathized with Asgharzádih's viewpoint and expressed their aversion to anything that might narrow the movement to the extent that it became regarded as a form of creed. Three other members of the Assembly – Elizabeth Herrick, Claudia Coles and Isobel Slade – as well as the chairman, were opposed to the idea of a formula declaration being made available for signing.

By rejecting the idea of formal registration procedures, the Assembly was now faced with the decision of how to go about placing newcomers on the voting list. Previously it had decided that a new believer should be vouched for by one or two Assembly members. It was now recommended that, in addition to this, enquirers should be enrolled only after they voluntarily expressed a desire to be registered; it was undesirable that any pressure should be put upon them to do so. It was suggested that if one member of the Assembly was convinced that a person accepted the three vital points laid down by Shoghi Effendi, it should be enough for that member to bring the name before the Assembly which would then welcome the new believer. Discussion ensued on whether more than one opinion should be received on such an important a question as mistakes had been made in the past and persons placed on the electoral roll who speedily withdrew themselves for different reasons. The Assembly believed that while an inquisition should be avoided, it was necessary for anyone going on to the electoral roll to be sufficiently informed of the teachings and in full agreement with the requirements laid down by the Guardian. Finally, the resolution was drafted that any person wanting to join in the service of the Bahá'í Cause and enrolling on the voter's list must be proposed by one member of the Assembly and seconded by another. The resolution was carried by a majority vote.

The decision, however, failed to satisfy Mr Aṣgharzádih who protested by letter at the meeting saying that the Bahá'í community was not like a club or company in which guarantees of social position and financial standing were necessary. That, he wrote, was a matter for the conscience of the person who asked to join and he reiterated that written or verbal declarations must be avoided. The chairman warned the Assembly that the letter would reopen the discussion on an issue which had already been voted upon and that it was within the power of the Assembly to refuse further discussion. The Assembly, however, wished Aṣgharzádih to express his views further. Following further consultation and heated exchanges, the resolution was recorded that there was indeed no question of making any decision about who should be called a Bahá'í, rather such a decision related only to a person's inclusion on the voters' list. It had always been the practice of the Assembly to revise the list of voters annually at its March meeting and it was customary at that time to bring forward any new names for enrolment. After further consultation, the resolution was amended to read that any person desiring to be enrolled on the voters' list should have his or her name brought to the notice of the Assembly by one of its members at the time of the revision of the list. This was agreed.

Aṣgharzádih was worried that the decision recorded by the Assembly would stand for the whole duration of the Cause, which would be hundreds of years, and reiterated his feelings that it was necessary to be very careful to keep the teachings simple. Mrs Slade was quite upset that the whole debate had been reopened. She pointed out that the decision arrived at by the Assembly did not entitle any member to adopt an attitude of criticism and that it was far from anyone's mind that others should be judged as to whether or not they had a right to be called Bahá'ís.[371]

The strain of such extended debates and arguments could have done little to relieve Ethel's anxiety at her waning physical condition. Shoghi Effendi was saddened to learn of her debilitating health problems. In a beautiful letter, written on 22 October 1927, he expressed his deepest sentiments towards her:

> My dear and precious Rosah:
> I grieve to learn of your failing health and mental restlessness. How much I miss you this year! I will most assuredly pray for you from the bottom of my heart. Your past services are engraved upon my heart and mind, and I trust that you will be guided and strengthened to render still more service to the sacred Threshold. Much love to your brother and the friends whom I always remember. Shoghi.[372]

Ethel's precarious physical condition and the increasing difficulty which she, Lady Blomfield and Mrs Thornburgh-Cropper had in attending meetings, either as a result of health or other commitments, led to an interesting discussion regarding the three women's membership of Bahá'í institutions. On 17 March 1928 Elizabeth Herrick proposed the following motion to an extraordinary meeting held jointly between the London Assembly and National Spiritual Assembly:

> That subject to the approval of the Guardian and their own willingness, our devoted and valued friends of the Bahá'í Cause Mrs Thornburgh-Cropper, Miss Ethel J. Rosenberg and Lady Blomfield – herein named in their chronological order of their service to the Bahá'í Cause – who have from the commencement of the Bahá'í organisation been almost invariably elected to serve on the National and London Spiritual Assemblies and who nevertheless find it either impossible or extremely difficult to attend Assembly meetings regularly, and in order that their valued services may

be retained as much as possible, as well as in the common
interest of the Cause be recommended by the joint Assemblies and the Guardian for appointment as permanent
honorary members of both Assemblies, entitled to attend
the meetings for the purpose of assisting in consultations
and discussions provided always that the 9 elected members
of each Assembly alone have the right to vote.[373]

For once the Assemblies displayed an unusual maturity in
dealing with this motion and, while valuing the sentiments
behind it, the members were almost unanimous in rejecting
it, saying it could lead to the creation of a spiritual hierarchy,
which was against the teachings. The Assemblies also resolved not to bother Shoghi Effendi with the matter.

More critically, there was an increasing lack of understanding between the believers in London and their co-
workers in Manchester. The details of this crisis are not fully
retrievable but it appears that Edward Hall had become
progressively disaffected with the decisions of the National
Spiritual Assembly and tensions reached a head at the end
of 1928. As a result Shoghi Effendi delivered one of his
shortest and pithiest messages to the British community,
which read in its entirety, 'Not until harmony and concord
are firmly established among the friends of London and
Manchester will the Cause advance along sound and progressive lines. May they be guided and inspired to do His Will and
achieve His purpose.'[374]

Towards the end of 1928 Ethel was saddened to hear of
the death, after a slow and painful illness, of her French
counterpart Hippolyte Dreyfus-Barney, whose 'distinctive
and inestimable services', according to Shoghi Effendi,
achieved for him 'a standing which few have as yet
attained'.[375]

Just one year later one of the English community's
staunchest supporters, Elizabeth Herrick, also passed away.
She had been identified with the Movement from its earliest
days and was remembered as reliable, zealous, enthusiastic
and indefatigable, particularly in her work on behalf of the

suffering and oppressed. Apart from publishing her introductory book on the Faith, *Unity Triumphant*, she had devoted a great deal of time to studying and spreading Esperanto.

However tragic these deaths were for the community, equally sad were instances of Bahá'ís turning away from the Covenant. Ethel's great experience and knowledge were once again called upon when attempts to challenge the authority of Shoghi Effendi were brought to the attention of the London Spiritual Assembly.

The Assembly received a pamphlet published by the American believer Ruth White questioning the recent organization of the Cause and the validity of the Will of 'Abdu'l-Bahá. White was vehemently opposed to any form of Bahá'í administration and, believing that she was guided by higher powers, concluded that 'Abdu'l-Bahá's Will was a forgery – a notion which even the unfaithful members of the Holy Family found unconvincing however much they despised Shoghi Effendi's position of authority. At the fortieth meeting of the London Spiritual Assembly, held on 2 February 1929 at the home of Annie Romer, Ethel was requested to give an account of the reading of the Master's Will, at which she had been present. The Assembly believed Ethel's recollection of the event would guide them in their deliberations about Mrs White's pamphlet.

Ethel was not unduly concerned by the appearance of the pamphlet. She had, after all, firsthand experience of the opponents of the Cause and knew that they were ultimately powerless to cause any lasting damage to the Bahá'í community. The only danger she foresaw was that Mrs White might find support among the Persian Covenant-breakers which would inevitably cause heartache for the Guardian.

Ethel told the Assembly how the Will had been sealed in a packet and addressed in 'Abdu'l-Bahá's own handwriting to Shoghi Effendi. She said there was not the slightest question as to the validity of the document, as she herself had examined it and saw that it was old and had been stained from the damp inside the strongbox where 'Abdu'l-Bahá had hidden it. Ethel vividly recalled that solemn meeting in Haifa at which the Will had been read. There had been several 'old grey-headed men present who had been in the Movement for many years'[376] and had there been the slightest doubt as to the authenticity of the Will, they would have known it. Ethel told the Assembly that Hippolyte Dreyfus-Barney had told her that a Persian believer who had been with the Master around the time He was writing the Will had thought how much everything depended on 'Abdu'l-Bahá and wondered who would succeed Him. At that exact moment 'Abdu'l-Bahá had called aloud 'Shoghi Effendi' and the little nine-year-old boy had come running very quickly to the Master. The Master had said to His grandson, 'Here is a friend who very much wishes to see you.' The Assembly was convinced by Ethel's account of events and decided that no action need be taken regarding the pamphlet.[377] It is interesting to consider how the Assembly might have dealt with the situation had Ethel not been present to share her valuable experiences.

Ruth White arrived in London to gain support for her campaign and later claimed to have met nearly all of the believers in the city. She also claimed to have witnessed great disunity among those serving on the National Spiritual Assembly, stating that Lady Blomfield had told her that there was practically no longer a Bahá'í Cause in England. Were these claims to be believed, they would undoubtedly have added to White's conviction that the Bahá'í Movement could and should not be organized. However, as with every attempt to undermine the authority of the Central Figures of the Faith, White's campaign came to nothing. She eventually, in old age, left the Faith and diverted her interests and allegiance to the guru Meher Baba.

In contrast to the trouble stirred up by the likes of Ruth White, the believers in London saw the visits of the American Bahá'í teacher Mary Hanford Ford as a spiritual benediction. Many people first learned of the Bahá'í Cause during her stays in the capital. She spoke at a number of well-attended meetings at Lindsay Hall and gave inspiring lectures to the

International New Thought Conference, three Unitarian churches, the Fellowship of Faiths and a peace meeting. Mrs Ford also ventured further afield, to York and Liverpool where she lectured to interested audiences and talked with many individual seekers.

While such meetings were successful, the National Assembly strongly felt it was time to invest in their own Bahá'í Centre. This would allow them the freedom to host events as and when they pleased without the difficulty of renting halls.

The believers hoped that the Centre would not only provide a home for the regular meetings of the London Bahá'ís but would also provide a permanent headquarters for the community. The idea was to keep the Centre open from ten o'clock until six every day. Bahá'í literature would be available and someone would be in attendance to give information to seekers.

Suitable premises were found at Walmar House in London's Upper Regent Street, close to Oxford Circus, and the Centre opened on the evening of 19 September 1929. A large number of believers gathered to celebrate what was to many a direct answer to their prayers in the previous year that the Movement might spread. Shoghi Effendi was invited to attend the opening but he was unable to do so. The Greatest Holy Leaf cabled his response: 'GUARDIAN WIRES DEEPLY REGRETS INABILITY PARTICIPATE PERSONALLY DEDICATION GATHERING OVERJOYED BRIGHT PROSPECTS LOVING GOOD WISHES, SHOGHI. BAHÁ'ÍYYIH.'[378] At the opening ceremony, the Master's former secretary Dr Yúnis Khan Afrúkhtih spoke a few words and chanted 'Abdu'l-Bahá's Tablet of Visitation.

Shoghi Effendi's hopes for the progress of the British community were encouraged by the purchase of the Centre. On 29 November 1929, a message written on his behalf states that he was 'much hopeful of your new centre in Regent Street . . . and he trusts that it will mark a turning point in the history of the Cause in England - from happy tea-parties at individual homes, into a group of less personal but eager, active and thoughtful workers co-operating in a common service. It is a basis upon which healthy progress is possible.'[379] Early in 1930 Shoghi Effendi again wrote, this time through Claudia Coles, saying he would pray at the Holy Shrines for the Centre's progress: 'Kindly assure my dear English friends of my heartfelt appreciation of their staunchness, their renewed activity, their self-sacrificing endeavours. I will continue to pray for their individual, as well as their collective efforts, from the bottom of my heart.'[380] But the Guardian warned the believers that they should not think that with a permanent centre their events would be automatically more successful: 'We should, however bear in mind that no matter how important the hall may be – the talks given and the unity manifested are of far greater significance.'[381]

In April 1930 the British Bahá'ís gathered for the first annual National Convention to be held at Walmar House. On the afternoon of 26 April, when the Feast of Riḍván was over, delegates from all over the country met together and elected the National Spiritual Assembly. Those elected were Mr Aṣgharzádih, Sister Challis (chairman), Claudia Coles (secretary), John Craven, Mother George, Albert Joseph, Annie Romer, Isobel Slade and Alfred Sugar (from Manchester). The overwhelming mood of rededication is tangibly expressed in a letter written by Claudia Coles which appeared in the *Bahá'í Newsletter* in July 1930:

Dear Friends, we have entered upon a new year of work with a sense of deep thankfulness for all the blessings of the past year and of gratitude to God for his unspeakable mercy and love to us. But as we look forward we realise how tremendous are the opportunities and responsibilities lying before us – opportunities which we can never cope with until we obey more consistently the teachings of the Master – responsibilities which we can never adequately fulfil until we avail ourselves of the mighty Power of the Holy Spirit ever ready for the assistance of every obedient faithful soul.[382]

The new Assemblies, Claudia, wrote, were taking up their work 'realising that they are not leaders, but servants. Theirs is no easy task and they approach it humbly, for the responsibilities are great. The spirit of co-operation and readiness to put individual views aside at the will of the majority are not easily acquired.'[383]

The opening of the permanent Bahá'í Centre in Upper Regent Street must have brought great satisfaction to Ethel Rosenberg as she began to accept that her life was rapidly slipping away. When Ethel had been born, more than seven decades before, into the celebrated Rosenberg artistic dynasty in the city of Bath, Bahá'u'lláh had not yet announced to His closest confidants that He was the Promised One of all ages, the Manifestation of God for the age of human maturity. Now His Movement, His Cause, His Faith was spreading throughout the planet, touching the hearts of thousands of souls who longed to play their part in ushering in the long-promised Golden Age of world unity and universal peace that His revelation made possible. The early years of the Formative Age of the Bahá'í Faith demanded that its followers be particularly staunch, active and self-sacrificing – the very qualities Shoghi Effendi said distinguished the English Bahá'ís – because it was on their shoulders alone that the monumental task of establishing the Bahá'í Cause in the world was placed. Ethel Jenner Rosenberg was outstanding amongst such followers.

Despite her failing powers, Ethel struggled to remain active in her Bahá'í work until the end of her days. Only at the very last did she become housebound, when her deteriorating health completely prevented her from going out.

Ethel Rosenberg passed away peacefully in her sleep on 17 November 1930 at the age of 72.

In a cable to the National Spiritual Assembly of the Bahá'ís of the British Isles, Shoghi Effendi, the Guardian of the Bahá'í Faith to whom Ethel had proved herself such a faithful co-worker and dedicated supporter, praised her exemplary life of devotion, service and unquestioned loyalty to the Cause of Bahá'u'lláh:

DEEPLY GRIEVED PASSING ROSENBERG ENGLAND'S OUTSTAND-
ING BAHÁ'Í PIONEER WORKER. MEMORY HER GLORIOUS SERVICE
WILL NEVER DIE 'ABDU'L-BAHÁ'S FAMILY JOIN ME IN EXPRESS-
ING HEARTFELT CONDOLENCES HER BROTHER RELATIVES URGE
FRIENDS HOLD BEFITTING MEMORIAL SERVICE. SHOGHI[384]

The Spiritual Assembly of Ṭihrán also sent a cable: 'DEEPLY
GRIEVED ROSENBERG PASSING. CONDOLENCE FAMILY,
FRIENDS.'[385] The London Spiritual Assembly decided to send
this on to Ethel's brother and placed a copy of it on the
Bahá'í Centre notice board. A message of thanks was sent
to the Assembly in Persia.

Ethel Rosenberg was buried three days after her passing
at the Gap Road Cemetery in Wimbledon, a short distance
from the house she shared with her brother. The young Alma
Gregory, attending her first funeral service, was among the
many friends and believers who came to pay their final
respects to a woman who was widely regarded as the mother
of their community. Among the mourners was Claudia Coles,
herself with only six months to live, seen by Alma walking
out from the graveyard supporting and comforting George
Rosenberg.

On 20 November the London Bahá'ís arranged special
services of remembrance and a dignified memorial meeting
was arranged at Walmar House as an appropriate expression
of the love which the believers held for their long-time friend
and counsellor. Recognition was given to Ethel's clear understanding of the Bahá'í Cause and to her lucid, authoritative
expositions of it.

The National Spiritual Assembly sent the news of Ethel's
passing around the Bahá'í world. In a letter to National
Assemblies, penned by Claudia Coles, Ethel's last moments
were described as 'peaceful, and all who loved her felt that
the release from the body of her ailments was a Bounty
vouchsafed to her, and a rejoicing to her aspiring spirit'.[386]
Claudia recalled how with Ethel's failing health 'her joy in

the love of Shoghi Effendi comforted her heart, and from the first moment of her belief in the Glory of God manifest, to her last breath, her faith and the clarity of her teachings, blessed those who heard her.'[387]

A warm tribute to Ethel's life and services was published in the December edition of the British *Bahá'í Newsletter*. The article noted that recently:

> ... she had been prevented by illness from taking an active part in the work of the Movement, but older believers can estimate the value of the pioneer work done by her. She was inspired by her great personal devotion to the Master who accorded to her the great privilege of much intimate intercourse with him.
>
> One who has known her during the years she has worked for the Cause writes:
>
> 'With the passing of Miss Ethel Rosenberg a large circle of Bahá'í friends have lost one of the most indefatigable workers for the Cause. During 25 years she devoted herself wholeheartedly to the teaching of Bahá'u'lláh's Message, and never spared her strength, nor purse, to send out the precious Word. She made several journeys to Akka and Haifa, staying as a guest for long periods in 'Abdu'l-Bahá's family, where she was an earnest student, besides giving her services for secretarial work.
>
> 'The Meetings held in her own house many years ago were a real inspiration to the seekers after Bahá'í truth. These she taught the great value and beauty of the Message.
>
> 'An old student of those days remarked quite recently that she had never forgotten Miss Rosenberg's remarkable teaching nor her wide cultured outlook on life.'
>
> Ethel Rosenberg had an unusual gift for imparting knowledge to others and it is the strength of this gift that she leaves on our memories today, the indelible work of her personal contribution to the Bahá'í Cause.[388]

At its meeting on 1 December 1930 Annie Romer reported to the London Spiritual Assembly that flowers to the value of one pound had been purchased for Ethel's brother and the Assembly agreed to contribute fifteen shillings from its funds towards the cost of the bouquet. Claudia Coles and Annie Romer told the Assembly about the funeral service and the actions they were taking to secure information about Ethel's life and work for *Star of the West*. The Assembly noted that it had received a letter of thanks from George Rosenberg and put it on file.

A year later the Assembly saw to it that all of Ethel's papers were carefully removed from George's house, as they had been left to the Assembly. Shoghi Effendi sent George a special letter of thanks in October 1931 for his help in making available his sister's possessions. The robe of Bahá'u'lláh, Ethel's pilgrims' notes, some photographs and her miniature painting of the Greatest Holy Leaf were among the precious items left to the Assembly. The robe was placed in a bank vault in the name of the London Bahá'í Fund.

Claudia Coles did her utmost to look after George Rosenberg following his sister's death. However, never physically strong at the best of times, Claudia herself grew steadily weaker from that time on. Although she still remained anxious to attend meetings, it became increasingly difficult for her to travel the long distance between her home and the Bahá'í Centre. On 23 May 1931, on the Anniversary of the Declaration of the Báb, Claudia joined her devoted friend Ethel in the realms on high. Her funeral took place at noon on 27 May at her home in Warwick Gardens which, according to one report, became that day like a garden of flowers.[389] The mourners, including Lady Blomfield, Mary Hanford Ford and Beatrice Irwin, then travelled to a country cemetery on Bled-Low Ridge near Claudia's daughter's cottage where Claudia's remains were interred.

The loss of Ethel Jenner Rosenberg and Claudia Coles within a six month period was an especially cruel blow to the British Bahá'ís. On 24 July 1931, Shoghi Effendi's secretary wrote to them:

> Although this year has been on the whole very disastrous because of the terrible loss which the English friends have

suffered by the passing of Miss Rosenberg and Mrs Claudia Coles, yet the Guardian hopes that the believers far from being discouraged will be enabled to unite their efforts and to carry on a successful campaign of teaching. He wishes the friends to follow the example of our two distinguished Bahá'í sisters who have recently passed away and to never cease to deliver the Holy Message by every means at their disposal.[390]

Obituaries for both women were written for *Bahá'í World*, the international record of Bahá'í activity. On 8 October 1931 the Guardian sent guidance to those preparing the memorial tributes, saying that he heartily approved 'the idea of having an article regarding Miss Rosenberg. A brief reference to her life before her conversion is surely very advisable, but special stress should be laid on her journeys and work during the early days of the Cause in the West. She rendered so many inestimable services when workers were very few that a sketch of her life will attract great interest.'[391] Ethel's obituary, along with a picture, can be found in *Bahá'í World*, volume 4 (1930-1932).

Ethel Rosenberg's grave is marked by a tall, grey granite Celtic Cross, intricately carved with a traditional decorative motif and bearing the simple inscription 'Ethel Jenner Rosenberg 1858-1930'. The Gap Road Cemetery is now within the jurisdiction of the London Borough of Merton and Ethel's grave remains to this day in remarkably good condition.

Now, at the distance of almost seven decades since Ethel's passing, one can only speculate how this distinguished and experienced soul might have looked back on her varied life, filled as it was not only with such momentous meetings and pioneering achievements but also with the greatest of material and physical tests. How might she have anticipated her 'going home'? It is reassuring to think that she took comfort in a message she received from her Master in 1909. In this Tablet, translated by Ethel herself from the Persian original, 'Abdu'l-Bahá perhaps gave her a foretaste of the eternal delights yet to come:

> To the attracted maid servant of God, Miss Rosenberg. Upon her be Baha'u'llah Abha!
>
> Oh you who are attracted to the Kingdom of Abha! . . . Do not be sad and be sure of the blessings of God, for you are accepted in the Kingdom and are mentioned in this heavenly gathering.[392]

Appendix

Afterwards

With the passing of Ethel Jenner Rosenberg, an era unique in the history of the British Bahá'í Community began to draw to a close, a period when the believers enjoyed the privilege of close communion with 'Abdu'l-Bahá. While subsequent generations had the inestimable bounty of meeting Shoghi Effendi and participating in his far-reaching plans for the expansion of the Cause and the consolidation of its institutions, that special link with the Heroic Age of the Faith was more or less broken in England by the end of the 1930s. Within nine years of Ethel's death her two closest and most distinguished co-workers also passed away. Mrs Thornburgh-Cropper died on 15 March 1938. The infirmity of her declining years prevented her from actively associating with the Bahá'ís but she was believed to be a staunch and loyal supporter until the end. It is thought that for some reason her remains were cremated. Lady Blomfield passed away peacefully on the last day of 1939 at the age of 80. At the end of her life she recorded her priceless memories in the book *The Chosen Highway*. Her grave has recently been rediscovered in the London borough of Hampstead.

The death of Ethel Rosenberg, while a blow to the British Bahá'í community, failed to deter it from its commitment to continue its many activities. Perhaps it is a sign of the firm foundations that Ethel had laid that the community in London and around the whole country wholeheartedly rededicated itself to activity.

Shortly after Ethel's death the London community joyfully welcomed 'Abdu'l-Bahá's granddaughter Miriam Jalal to its fold, and Mr Dehkan, a student from Beirut who enthusiastically contributed his services as a speaker at the Wednesday

33. Mary Basil Hall (Blomfield), left, *with Isobel Slade in 1945.
Standing behind is Mrs Constance Langdon-Davies. Ethel met Mary
Basil Hall, the daughter of Lady Blomfield, in Paris in 1907. Isobel
Slade accompanied Ethel on her journey to the Holy Land in 1926.*

34. Bahá'í group, taken at the home of Elizabeth Herrick, 38 North Side, Clapham, London SW4, probably at Riḍván 1922. Some of the individuals can be identified:

1. George Palgrave Simpson
7. Elsie Lee
10. Winifred Asgardzadeh
12. Mr Cole
18. Claudia Coles
22. Miss Cacher?
31. Miss Maud Yandell
34. Mary Virginia Thornburgh-Cropper
35. Ethel Rosenberg
38. Alice Gamble
39. Mrs Ginman (Madam Charlot)
48. Elizabeth Herrick
50. Mary Basil Hall
52. Victor Audigier
53. Mr Foroughi

35. Conference on 'Some Living Religions within the Empire', 22 September – 3 October 1924, held at the Imperial Institute, South Kensington, London. Lady Blomfield is seated centre. Ethel Rosenberg appears in the third row, eighth from the left.

36. *Bahá'ís in London, 1923. Taken at 'Heathfield', 21 West Side, Clapham Common, London. Ethel is in the second row from the front, fourth from the left.*

37. *Bahá'ís in London, April 1923.*

38. *Bournemouth Bahá'ís in 1924, with Martha Root, centre, and Sister Grace Challis to her right.*

evening meetings in London. A long time close enquirer Mrs Ruth Hall registered her belief in Bahá'u'lláh at this time and other friends from Australia and Canada joined the slowly swelling ranks of the community. Around this time, at Shoghi Effendi's request, Lady Blomfield, Mrs Thornburgh-Cropper and Mother George began to prepare an article on 'The Beginnings of the Cause in England'. The Guardian advised the London Spiritual Assembly to appoint a committee for the task.

The Wednesday evening meetings at Walmar House continued with outside speakers and a small number of new faces who joined the audience. The meetings were advertised with printed notices pinned to notice boards and mailed out to individuals. The community consolidated contacts with other organizations including the Overseas Club, the English Speaking Union, New Thought, the American Women's Club and the Fellowship of Faiths. This last organization distributing considerable amounts of Bahá'í literature. A sale held by the Fellowship of Faiths attracted more than 50 people with a keen interest in the Cause.

Monday afternoon prayer meetings were held consistently at four o'clock, regardless of the numbers present, and prayers were read every day at the Bahá'í Centre for the friends around the world, for Shoghi Effendi, for those who were in trouble or ill and for the spread of the Cause. Mother George continued her Sunday meetings with good results. Many people who attended remarked on the spirit of friendliness and hospitality and appreciated the opportunity for discussion. The Young People's Study Class also met regularly, Holy Days were commemorated, and informal afternoon teas included addresses from Lady Blomfield and Sister Challis.

The room at Walmar House was kept open throughout the year at great sacrifice and effort and became known throughout the Bahá'í world. The community was excited to read an article mentioning the Cause in *The Times* newspaper by the orientalist Sir E. Denison Ross which was widely seen. Mary Hanford Ford spent more of her summers in England and gave the Message to thousands of souls.

Indeed, the British Bahá'í community recognized, in the months immediately following the passing of its pioneer worker, that attitudes towards their Cause were definitely changing. A report of their activities in *Bahá'í World*, volume 4, states:

> The Bahá'í Cause is steadily progressing in Britain. It is little use troubling ourselves about the rise and fall of the wavelets in our activities; the tide is coming in – and it is the tide that matters. It is not a long time since there were no friends of the Cause of Bahá'u'lláh in Britain; the Bahá'í Glad Tidings of the Kingdom were unknown, unvoiced, even unimagined – but today scores of earnest souls are alive to the subject, voicing it, loving it, magnifying it, awakening people to the Glory of the coming era; and it is true to say that thousands of people in Britain have now heard the first faint but certain notes of the sweet call of the Abha Kingdom. In fact, the *Call for the Unification of the World in the Glory of God* is being more and more definitely heard by the people through the efforts of a steadily increasing number of friends.[393]

The interested reader may well wonder what happened to the many other believers and acquaintances with whom Ethel Rosenberg had shared her life of devoted service and who lived on to serve further. The extraordinary achievements of **Shoghi Effendi** are, of course, well documented. Seven years after the passing of Ethel Rosenberg, the Guardian married Mary Maxwell, the daughter of the distinguished Canadian architect William Sutherland Maxwell and May Bolles Maxwell, who opened the first Bahá'í centre in Paris at the turn of the century. During Shoghi Effendi's 36-year ministry, he built the Bahá'í administrative order throughout the world, establishing his great-grandfather's Faith as a world religion through coordinated plans of global expansion. Shoghi Effendi's remarkable and prolific achievements include his magnificent translations of the major writings of Bahá'u'lláh into matchless English, thousands of letters of guidance elucidating and interpreting the Bahá'í sacred texts and the development of the World Centre of the Faith in the Holy Land. He passed away prematurely at the age of 60 while visiting England in 1957 and his resting place in north London is now a place of pilgrimage for Bahá'ís from all over the world.

Despite suffering from constant ill health, **May Bolles Maxwell** travelled ceaselessly for the Faith for another decade. Her final trip was to Argentina in 1940 where she passed away aged 70. Shoghi Effendi awarded her the 'priceless honour' of 'a martyr's death'.[394]

'Abdu'l-Bahá's sister, Shoghi Effendi's beloved great-aunt, **Bahíyyih Khánum** outlived her brother 'Abdu'l-Bahá by a full decade, passing away on 15 July 1932 at the age of 86. Hers was 'a saintly life which history will acknowledge as having been endowed with a celestial potency that few of the heroes of the past possessed'.[395] Her tomb is situated in the Monument Gardens on Mount Carmel and forms the central focus of the far-flung Arc around which stand the buildings of the Bahá'í Faith's world administrative headquarters. The Master's widow, **Munírih Khánum**, died six years later, aged 96. William Sutherland Maxwell who met her in the last year of her life described how 'the rigours of a life in which great sufferings and hardships had been experienced side by side with her beloved 'Abdu'l-Bahá, had failed to dim the sweetness of character and sympathetic personality of this noble woman'.[396]

As we have seen, most of the opposition to Shoghi Effendi's plans came from the closest members of his own family. Abdu'l-Bahá's daughters, with whom Ethel had enjoyed such close companionship, in time threw in their lot with the Covenant-breakers and Shoghi Effendi had no choice but to excommunicate them from the community along with most the other members of his immediate family who rejected his leadership and authority. Among those whom he was forced to brand enemies of the Cause were his cousin **Ruhi Afnan** who had served as his secretary. Meanwhile, the Guardian's sister **Rúḥangíz**, who had studied in London, married a Covenant-breaker, forcing Shoghi Effendi to disassociate himself from her. 'Abdu'l-Bahá's merciless half-brother, **Mírzá Muḥammad-'Alí**, the arch-breaker of the Covenant of Bahá'u'lláh, died in 1937, 'his hopes shattered, his plottings frustrated, the society of his fellow-conspirators extinguished'.[397] **Charles Mason Remey**, one of the outstanding itinerant teachers of the Faith in its early years, was honoured by Shoghi Effendi with the title Hand of the Cause of God and was appointed president of the International Bahá'í Council. However, his attempts in old age to usurp for himself the title of Guardian after the passing of Shoghi Effendi resulted in his inevitable expulsion from the Cause. He died at the age of one hundred in Florence, Italy, abandoned by his followers and buried without religious rites. The Universal House of Justice cabled, 'History pitiable defection by one who had received great honours from both Master and Guardian constitutes yet another example futility all attempts undermine impregnable Covenant Cause Bahá'u'lláh.'[398]

Of the faithful believers encountered by Ethel Rosenberg, the Master's secretary, **Dr Yúnis Khán Afrúkhtih**, lived into his eighties, passing away in Ṭihrán on 28 November 1948 after a prolonged illness. His final decades were spent travelling extensively, teaching the Cause and deepening the understanding and knowledge of the believers in America and Europe before settling back in Iran where he served with great distinction on the National Spiritual Assembly and the Ṭihrán Spiritual Assembly. **Dr Luṭfu'lláh Ḥakím** returned to England in 1950 after marrying in Persia. In 1951 he was summoned to serve in Haifa and was later appointed to the first International Bahá'í Council. In 1963 he was elected to the Universal House of Justice but was forced to resign owing to ill health. He died in 1968. **Ḍiá'u'lláh Aṣgharzádih** continued his business in London as a carpet merchant until 1953 when he became the first Bahá'í to pioneer to Jersey during Shoghi Effendi's Ten Year Crusade.

He was a member of the National Assembly of Great Britain for various periods between 1925 and 1941. His pioneering efforts earned him the title 'Knight of Bahá'u'lláh'.

Laura Dreyfus Barney continued to serve the Cause selflessly and to work in influential circles until ill health prevented her from continuing into old age. She died at the age of 95 in 1974. Throughout her life she was awarded great distinctions in recognition of her work in the fields of international peace, women's rights and education. She is buried in the heart of Paris, her grave situated close to that of the composer Debussy and in the shadow of the Eiffel Tower.

One of Ethel Rosenberg's most consistent correspondents, **Julia Culver** served the Bahá'í community unstintingly for 47 years. In the 1920s she travelled for five years in Europe with Martha Root and undertook outstanding teaching work in connection with Esperanto Congresses. She was a generous sponsor of teaching projects all over the world and took full financial responsibility for the running of the Bahá'í International Bureau in Geneva after 1927, devoting much energy to its development. 'Her exemplary spirit, unshakable loyalty, generous contributions unforgettable' wired Shoghi Effendi when she passed way at the age of 89.[399]

Mary Hanford Ford died on 2 February 1937 at the age of 80 after a lifetime of distinguished service teaching the Faith in the United States, Italy, Switzerland, France and Great Britain. She taught 'unceasingly, attracting thousands of people through her devotion, and her objective, brilliant, well-stocked mind'.[400] Shoghi Effendi paid tribute saying her 'unique and outstanding gifts enabled her to promote effectively the best interests of the Faith in its new-born and divinely-conceived institutions . . . Her services will always be remembered and extolled.'[401] **Mother George** lived until the age of 91, passing away on 4 November 1950. Distinguished for her pioneering work in the field of children's education, Shoghi Effendi described her 'notable meritorious services' as 'unforgettable'.[402]

Ella Goodall Cooper lived until 1951 when she passed

away just four days after her husband at the age of 81. Hers was an 'enchanting spirit of exquisite grace, whose gentleness, warmth and generosity were showered continuously on all peoples'.[403] **Marion Jack** the 'immortal heroine . . . greatly-loved and deeply-admired by 'Abdu'l-Bahá' as a 'shining example' to pioneers of present and future generations surpassed in 'constancy, dedication, self-abnegation' and 'fearlessness by none except [the] incomparable Martha Root'[404] passed away in Sofia, Bulgaria on 25 March 1954 where she had been living for 24 years as a Bahá'í pioneer.

Mountfort Mills died in 1949 after 43 years of active service to the Cause. The first chairman of the National Spiritual Assembly of the United States and Canada, his appeal in the case of the House of Bahá'u'lláh at Baghdad is remembered as his most heroic act. **Harry Romer** died on 13 April 1935 aged 64 after holding important posts in the Associated Press. He served on the London Spiritual Assembly between 1933 and 1934. His wife, Annie, lived until 1955. **Edith Sanderson**, one of the first pioneers of the Faith in France, had been taught by May Bolles and is remembered for her heroic services in France during the two World Wars. She passed away in the late 1950s. **George Palgrave Simpson** passed away in 1934. The news of his death deeply grieved Shoghi Effendi. The Guardian prayed that he would be fully rewarded for all his services and particularly for the active part he took in establishing the administration in Britain in its early days. **Louise Waite** died on 27 May 1939. Shoghi Effendi described her as a 'beloved pioneer' the record of whose outstanding services was 'imperishable'.[405] **Wellesley Tudor Pole** lived until the age of 84, passing away in September 1968. On hearing of his death, one friend recalled, 'Everyone who came into contact with him was raised in consciousness and like all great men – W. T. P. was one of the greatest – he had his lighter side and a most remarkable sense of humour. W. T. P. was undoubtedly one of the most spiritually evolved men of our time.'[406]

Bibliography

'Abdu'l-Bahá. *Paris Talks*. London, Bahá'í Publishing Trust, London, 1967.
— *The Promulgation of Universal Peace*. Wilmette, Ill.: Bahá'í Publishing Trust, 1982.
— *Selections from the Writings of 'Abdu'l-Bahá*. Haifa: Bahá'í World Centre, 1978.
— *Some Answered Questions*. Wilmette, Ill.: Bahá'í Publishing Trust, 1981.
— *Tablets of the Divine Plan*. Wilmette, Ill.: Bahá'í Publishing Trust, 1977.
— *The Will and Testament of 'Abdu'l-Bahá*. Wilmette, Ill.: Bahá'í Publishing Trust, 1971.
'Abdu'l-Bahá in London. London: Bahá'í Publishing Trust, London, 1987.
Armstrong-Ingram, R. Jackson. *Music, Devotions, and Mashriqu'l-Adhkár*. Los Angeles: Kalimát Press, 1987.
Bahá'í World, The. vols. 1-12, 1925-54. rpt. Wilmette, Ill.: Bahá'í Publishing Trust, 1980.
Bahá'í World, The. vol. 16. Haifa: Bahá'í World Centre, 1978.
Bahá'u'lláh. *Gleanings from the Writings of Bahá'u'lláh*. London: Bahá'í Publishing Trust, 1978.
— *The Hidden Words*. Wilmette, Ill.: Bahá'í Publishing Trust, 1979.
— *The Kitáb-i-Aqdas*. Haifa: Bahá'í World Centre, 1992.
— *Tablets of Bahá'u'lláh revealed after the Kitáb-i-Aqdas*. Haifa: Bahá'í World Centre, 1978.
Balyuzi, H. M. *'Abdu'l-Bahá*. Oxford: George Ronald, 1971.
— *Bahá'u'lláh, The King of Glory*. Oxford: George Ronald, 1980.
— *Edward Granville Browne and the Bahá'í Faith*. Oxford: George Ronald, 1970.
Benét, William Rose. *The Reader's Encyclopedia*. London: A & C Black, 1965.
Blomfield, Lady. *The Chosen Highway*. London: Bahá'í Publishing Trust, 1940.

Boase, Frederick. *Modern English Biography*. vol. 3 (R-Z). London: Cass, 1901 & 1965.

Browne, Edward G. 'Introduction', *A Traveller's Narrative*. Cambridge: Cambridge University Press, 1891.

Chase, Thornton. *In Galilee*. Los Angeles: Kalimát Press, 1985.

Cherry, Deborah. *Painting Women*. London: Routledge, 1993.

Clifford, Derek. *Collecting English Watercolours*. London: John Baker, 1970.

Ellet, E. *Women Artists in All Ages and Countries*. London: Bentley, 1859.

Esslemont, John E. *Bahá'u'lláh and the New Era*. London: Bahá'í Publishing Trust, 1974.

Compilation of Compilations, The. vols. 1 and 2. Australia: Bahá'í Publications, 1991.

Fisher, Stanley. *A Dictionary of Watercolour Painters 1750-1900*. London: Foulsham & Co., 1972.

Foskett, Daphne. *A Dictionary of British Miniature Painters*. London: Faber, 1972.

— *Miniatures Dictionary and Guide*. London: A & CC, 1987.

Gail, Marzieh. *Arches of the Years*. Oxford: George Ronald, 1991.

— *Summon up Remembrance*. Oxford: George Ronald, 1987.

Garis, M. R. *Martha Root: Lioness at the Threshold*. Wilmette, Ill.: Bahá'í Publishing Trust, 1983.

Gillet, Paula. *The Victorian Painter's World*. Gloucester: Alan Sutton, 1990.

Graves, Algernon. *A Dictionary of Artists 1760-1893*. London: Kingsmead Press, 1901.

— *The Royal Academy of Arts: A Complete Dictionary of Contributors and their Work from its Foundation in 1769-1904*. London: Henry Graves & Co, 1906.

Haddon, John. *Portrait of Bath*. London: Robert Hale, 1982.

Hall, E. T. 'A Brief Narrative of My Life', unpublished manuscript.

— *Early Days of the Bahá'í Faith in Manchester*. Manchester: Bahá'í Assembly, 1925.

— *Poems by Edward Theodore Hall (1879-1962)*. Published by his daughters, undated.

Hall, Mary Basil. *Sitarih Khánum (Sara, Lady Blomfield), A Brief Account of Her Life and Work by Her Daughter, Mary Basil Hall*. United Kingdom Bahá'í Archives.

Hammond, Eric. *The Splendour of God*. London: John Murray, 1909.

Herrick, Elizabeth. *Unity Triumphant*. London: Kegan Paul, Trench, Trubner & Co., 1923.

Hofman, David. *George Townshend*. Oxford, George Ronald, 1983.

Hollinger, Richard. 'Ibrahim George Kheiralla and the Bahá'í Faith in America'. *Studies in Bábí and Bahá'í History*, vol. 3. Los Angeles: Kalimát Press, 1984.

Holy Bible. King James Version. London: Collins, 1839.

Hubbard, Hesketh. *A Hundred Years of British Painting 1851-1951*. London: Longmans, Green & Co, 1951.

Hunt, Simon. *A Bath Camera 1850-1950*. London: Dovecote, 1983.

Hutchinson, Sidney C. *The History of the Royal Academy 1768-1986*. London: Robert Royce Ltd., 1968.

ITN Factbook. London: Guild Publishing, 1990.

Jacobs, Michael and Warner, Malcolm. *Phaidon Companion to Art and Artists in the British Isles*. London: Phaidon, 1980.

Johnson, J. and Grentzner, A. *The Dictionary of British Artists 1880-1940*. London: A & CC, 1987.

Khursheed, Anjam. *The Seven Candles of Unity*. London: Bahá'í Publishing Trust, 1991.

Lambourne, L. and Hamilton, Jean. *British Watercolours in the Victoria and Albert Museum*. London: Sotheby Parke Bernet, 1980.

Lee, Sidney. *Dictionary of National Biography*. vol. 49. London: Smith Elder Co, 1897.

— *The Concise Dictionary of National Biography*. Oxford: Oxford University Press, 1903.

Loftus Hare, William. *Religions of the Empire*. London: Duckworth, 1925.

Mallalieu, H.L. *Dictionary of British Watercolour Artists up to 1920*. London: A & CC, 1986.

Maude, Constance. *Sparks Among the Stubble*. London: Philip Allan, 1924.

Maxwell, May. *An Early Pilgrimage*. Oxford: George Ronald, 1969.

McKechnie, Sue. *British Silhouette Artists and their Work 1760-1860*. London: Sotheby Parke Bernet, 1978.

Momen, Moojan. *The Bábí and Bahá'í Religions, 1844-1944. Some Contemporary Western Accounts*. Oxford: George Ronald, 1981.

— *Dr. John Ebenezer Esslemont*. London: Bahá'í Publishing Trust, 1975.

— *Selections from the Writings of E. G. Browne on the Bábí and Bahá'í Religions*. Oxford: George Ronald, 1987.

Momen, Wendi. *A Basic Bahá'í Dictionary*. Oxford: George Ronald, 1989.

Morgan, Kenneth. *The Sphere Illustrated History of Britain 1789-1983*. London: Sphere, 1985.

Petteys, Chris. *Dictionary of Women Artists*. Boston: G. K. Hall & Co.

Phelps, Myron H. *The Master in 'Akká*. Los Angeles: Kalimát Press, 1985.

Power of the Covenant, The. Part 2. New Delhi: Bahá'í Publishing Trust, 1979.

Rabbaní, Rúhíyyih. *The Priceless Pearl*. London: Bahá'í Publishing Trust, 1969.

Roget, John Lewis. *A History of the Old Watercolour Society*. London: Longmans, 1891.

Rosenberg, Ethel. *Behaism*. London: R. F. Hunger, 1905.

— *A Brief Account of the Bahai Movement*. London: Priory Press, 1911.

Rutstein, Nathan. *Corinne True*. Oxford: George Ronald, 1987.

— *He Loved and Served*. Oxford: George Ronald, 1982.

Shoghi Effendi. *Arohanui*. Suva: Bahá'í Publishing Trust, 1982.

— *Bahá'í Administration*. Wilmette, Ill.: Bahá'í Publishing Trust, 1974.

— *God Passes By*. Wilmette, Ill.:Bahá'í Publishing Trust, 1944.

— *Messages to the Bahá'í World*. Wilmette, Ill.: Bahá'í Publishing Trust, 1958.

— *The Passing of 'Abdu'l-Bahá*. With Lady Blomfield. Stuttgart: Heppeler, 1922.

— *The Unfolding Destiny of the British Bahá'í Community*. London: Bahá'í Publishing Trust, 1981.

Skrine, Francis H. *Bahaism*. London: Longmans, Green and Co., 1912.

Smith, Peter. *The Bábí and Bahá'í Religions*. Cambridge: Cambridge University Press, 1987.

Smith, Phillip R. 'The Development and Influence of the Bahá'í Administrative Order in Great Britain, 1914-1950'. *Community*

Histories. (Studies in the Bábí and Bahá'í Religions), vol. 6. Los Angeles: Kalimát Press, 1992.

— 'What was a Bahá'í? Concerns of British Bahá'ís, 1900-1920'. *Studies in the Bábí and Bahá'í Religions*, vol. 5. Los Angeles: Kalimát Press, 1988.

Star of the West. rpt. Oxford: George Ronald, 1978, 1984.

Taherzadeh, Adib. *The Covenant of Bahá'u'lláh*. Oxford: George Ronald, 1992.

— *The Revelation of Bahá'u'lláh*. vol. 4. Oxford: George Ronald, 1987.

Thomson, David. *England in the Nineteenth Century*. London: Penguin, 1950.

Tudor Pole, Wellesley. *A Man Seen Afar*. Saffron Walden: C. W. Daniel, 1988.

— *My Dear Alexias*. London: Neville Spearman, 1979.

— *The Silent Road*. London: Neville Spearman, 1965.

— *The Writing on the Ground*. London: Neville Spearman, 1968.

Universal House of Justice. *Synopsis and Codification of the Kitáb-i-Aqdas*. Haifa: Bahá'í World Centre, 1973.

Villiers, Oliver G. *Wellesley Tudor Pole: Appreciation & Valuation*. Canterbury: Oliver Villiers, 1977.

Washington, Peter. *Madame Blavatsky's Baboon*. London: Secker, 1993.

Whitehead, O.Z. *Some Bahá'ís to Remember*. Oxford: George Ronald, 1983.

— *Some Early Bahá'ís of the West*. Oxford: George Ronald, 1976.

Whiteman, Yvonne. *Bath City & Countryside*. London: Sidgwick & Jackson, 1983.

Williamson, George C. *The Miniature Collector*. London: Herbert Jenkins, 1920.

Wood, Christopher. *Dictionary of Victorian Painters*. London: A & CC, 1978.

Youth Can Move the World. Florida: Palabra, 1992.

Notes and References

Chapter 1:
The Rosenbergs of Bath

1. Swinburne, 'Verse about Bath', quoted in Hadden, *Portrait of Bath*, p. 122. Algernon Charles Swinburne (1837-1901) was an English poet and man of letters.
2. Pepys, quoted in Whiteman, *Bath City and Countryside*, p. 6. Samuel Pepys (1633-1703) was an English politician, best known for his diary.
3. Advertisement in Bath *Chronicle*, 11 October 1787.
4. Advertisement in Bath *Chronicle*, 1 November 1792.
5. Note on the life of Charles Christian Rosenberg, Bath Museums Service.
6. Advertisement in Bath *Chronicle*, 12 February 1796.
7. Advertisement in Bath *Chronicle*, 25 October 1798.
8. Notes on the life of Charles Christian Rosenberg, Bath Museums Service.
9. Advertisement in Bath *Chronicle*, 11 April 1798.
10. Advertisement in Bath *Chronicle*, 25 April 1804. The verse is by James Thomson (1700–48), the Scottish-born poet known as the forerunner of romanticism.
11. McKechnie, *British Silhouette Artists*, p. 563.

Chapter 2:
A Most Valued Citizen

12. Bahá'u'lláh, *Tablets*, p. 36.
13. Obituary of George Frederick Rosenberg, Bath *Chronicle*, 23 September 1869.
14. See Roget, *History of the Old Watercolour Society*.
15. ibid.
16. Prospectus of Grosvenor College, Bath Museums Service.
17. ibid.

18. This statement of Ethel Rosenberg was noted by Florence George in her unpublished recollection of the early days of the British Bahá'í community. United Kingdom Bahá'í Archives. See also Whitehead, *Some Early Bahá'ís of the West*, p. 55.
19. See Roget, *History of the Old Watercolour Society*.
20. ibid.
21. Obituary of George Frederick Rosenberg, Bath *Chronicle*, 23 September 1869.
22. ibid.
23. Ellet, *Women Artists*, p. 2.
24. *Art Journal*, 1868, p. 46.
25. *Englishwoman's Review*, April 1885, p. 160.
26. Cherry, *Painting Women*, p. 46.

Chapter 3:
The Young Artist in London

27. Bahá'u'lláh, from a Tablet translated from the Persian, in *Compilation*, vol. 1, p. 3.
28. Fore, 'The Slade', *Motif*, no. 4, March 1960, p. 34.
29. Poynter's inaugural lecture, 'Systems of Art Education', 2 October 1871, quoted in ibid.
30. Thornton, cited in Forge, 'The Slade', *Motif*, no 4, March 1960.
31. See Gillett, 'Painting and the Independent Woman' and 'Progress and Obstacles', *The Victorian Painter's World*.
32. ibid.

Chapter 4:
The Bahá'í Movement

33. Bahá'u'lláh, *Gleanings*, VII, p. 10.
34. E. G. Browne, quoted in Balyuzi, *King of Glory*, p. 372.
35. ibid. pp. 379-80.
36. Cited in Blomfield, *Chosen Highway*, p. 235.
37. ibid.
38. ibid. pp. 235-6.
39. Whitehead, *Some Early Bahá'ís of the West*, p. 16.

40. Maxwell, *Early Pilgrimage*, pp. 29-30.
41. ibid. p. 30.
42. Hearst, cited in 'Two Letters of Mrs. Phoebe A. Hearst', *Bahá'í World*, vol. 8, p. 801.
43. ibid. pp. 801-2.
44. ibid. p. 801.

Chapter 5:
Afire with the Love of God

45. 'Abdu'l-Bahá, Tablet to Ethel Jenner Rosenberg, *Selections*, pp. 172-5.
46. Rosenberg, *Brief Account of the Bahá'í Movement*, p. 21.
47. Maxwell, 'Letter from Mrs. May Maxwell to Mr. Charles Mason Remey', *Star of the West*, vol. 5, no. 19 (2 March 1915), p. 298.
48. Maxwell, 'A Brief Account of Thomas Breakwell', *Bahá'í World*, vol. 8, p. 707.
49. ibid.
50. Breakwell, cited in Maxwell, 'Letter from Mrs. May Maxwell to Mr. Charles Mason Remey', *Star of the West*, vol. 5, no. 19 (2 March 1915), p. 298.
51. Afrúkhtih, *Memories of Nine Years in 'Akká*, pp. 180-7.
52. ibid.
53. Maxwell, 'A Brief Account of Thomas Breakwell', *Bahá'í World*, vol. 8, p. 710.
54. Afrúkhtih, *Memories of Nine Years in 'Akká*, pp. 180-7.
55. ibid.
56. Funeral card of Thomas Breakwell. Author's collection.
57. Afrúkhtih, *Memories of Nine Years in 'Akká*, pp. 180-7.
58. Chase, *In Galilee*, pp. 22-4.
59. Ford, cited in 'The House of 'Abdu'lláh Páshá', *Bahá'í World*, vol. 16, p. 106.
60. 'Abdu'l-Bahá, quoted in Shoghi Effendi, *God Passes By*, p. 275.
61. Luke 12:4-5.
62. Recorded in 'Notes taken at Haifa by E. J. Rosenberg, February and March 1901', p. 5. United Kingdom Bahá'í Archives.
63. ibid. p. 14.

64. ibid. p. 1.
65. Shoghi Effendi, *God Passes By*, p. 108.
66. The book was *Views of Acca, Haifa, Mount Carmel and Other Holy Places*, published between 1900 and 1902 in Chicago. United Kingdom Bahá'í Archives.

Chapter 6:
Questions and Answers

67. 'Abdu'l-Bahá, *Some Answered Questions*, p. 79.
68. Letter from Munavvar Khánum to Ethel Rosenberg, 7 October 1902. United Kingdom Bahá'í Archives.
69. ibid.
70. Undated letter from Munavvar Khánum to Ethel Rosenberg. United Kingdom Bahá'í Archives.
71. ibid.
72. ibid.
73. Letter from Countess de Canavarro to Ethel Rosenberg, 22 September 1902. United Kingdom Bahá'í Archives.
74. Letter from Countess de Canavarro to Ethel Rosenberg, 29 October 1902. United Kingdom Bahá'í Archives.
75. Marzieh Gail, 'Familiar 'Akká Voices', in Phelps, *The Master in 'Akká*, pp. xix-xx.
76. Letter from Ethel Rosenberg to Helen Goodall, 14 October 1903. United States Bahá'í Archives.
77. Letter from Ethel Rosenberg to Helen Goodall, 16 November 1903. United States Bahá'í Archives.
78. Letter from Munavvar Khánum to Ethel Rosenberg, 23 November 1903. United Kingdom Bahá'í Archives.
79. 'Abdu'l-Bahá, cited in *Synopsis and Codification*, p. 61.
80. Unauthorized translation of an unpublished Tablet of 'Abdu'l-Bahá to Ethel Rosenberg. See Research Department, *Ethel Jenner Rosenberg*, p. 3.
81. Authorized translation of an unpublished Tablet of 'Abdu'l-Bahá to Ethel Rosenberg in reply to her questions about the Tablet of Wisdom. Research Department, Bahá'í World Centre.
82. Letter from Munavvar Khánum to Ethel Rosenberg, 2 September 1903. United Kingdom Bahá'í Archives.

83. ibid.
84. Letter from Dr Yúnis Khán Afrúkhtih to Ethel Rosenberg, 3 October 1903. United Kingdom Bahá'í Archives.
85. Habíb Táhirzádeh, 'Dr. Youness Afrukhtih', *Bahá'í World*, vol. 12, p. 680.
86. Laura Clifford Barney, 'Preface to First Edition', *Some Answered Questions*, p. xvii.
87. 'Abdu'l-Bahá, cited in 'Love is the foundation of everything', *Star of the West*, vol. 7, no. 11, p. 108.
88. Notes made by Ethel Rosenberg in 'Akká, 29 April 1904. United Kingdom Bahá'í Archives.
89. Bahá'u'lláh, *Tablets*, p. 145.
90. Authorized translation of unpublished Tablet of 'Abdu'l-Bahá to Ethel Rosenberg in reply to her questions about the Tablet of Wisdom. Research Department, Bahá'í World Centre.
91. Undated letter from Munavvar Khánum to Ethel Rosenberg. United Kingdom Bahá'í Archives.
92. Letter from Munavvar Khánum to Ethel Rosenberg, 10 April 1906. United Kingdom Archives.
93. Letter from Thornton Chase to Ethel Rosenberg, 11 May 1906. United States Bahá'í Archives.

Chapter 7:
Encountering Lady Blomfield

94. Bahá'u'lláh, from a Tablet translated from the Persian, in *Compilation*, vol. 2, p. 358.
95. All of the stories and events relating to Lady Blomfield's life are taken from *Sitarih Khánum (Sara, Lady Blomfield), A Brief Account of Her Life and Work by Her Daughter, Mary Basil Hall*. United Kingdom Bahá'í Archives.
96. The story of Lady Blomfield's encounter with the Bahá'í Movement is recounted in Blomfield, *Chosen Highway*, pp. 1-2.

39. The inscription on the back of this photograph reads:

Presentation copy to "The Bahá'í Magazine." Star of the West. Celebration of the Feast of Riḍván, "Heathfield", 21 West Side, Clapham Common, London S.W.4. Under the auspices of the London & National Bahá'í Assemblies, April 21st, 1928. From Elizabeth Herrick.

Ethel is in the back row, fifth from the left.

40. *Ethel's home at 74 Sinclair Road, West Kensington, as it appears today in a somewhat run-down state. Many major Bahá'í events took place in this house, including the first meeting of the National Spiritual Assembly of the British Isles in 1923.*

41. Sinclair Road, West Kensington, as it appears today. Ethel's home at number 74 is right of centre, with the wholly white facade.

42. The white house in the centre is the last home occupied by Ethel, at 82 Lambton Road, Wimbledon. She passed away here on 17 November 1930.

43. *Ethel's grave is marked by a tall, grey granite Celtic Cross,*
intricately carved with a traditional decorative motif.

44. Detail from Ethel's grave stone, showing the carving of the Celtic Cross.

45. *Detail from Ethel's grave, which bears the simple inscription 'In Memoriam Ethel Jenner Rosenberg 1858-1930'.*

46. *Ethel's grave in the Gap Road Cemetery, Wimbledon, a short distance from the home she shared with her brother George on Lambton Road. Ethel's grave remains to this day in remarkably good condition.*

Chapter 8:
The Opening of the Way

97. Bahá'u'lláh, *Tablets*, p. 142.
98. Letter from Thornton Chase to Ethel Rosenberg, 19 January 1908. United States Bahá'í Archives.
99. ibid.
100. Gail, *Summon Up Remembrance*, p. 114.
101. Letter from Thornton Chase to Ethel Rosenberg, 3 March 1908. United States Bahá'í Archives.
102. Letter from Thornton Chase to Ethel Rosenberg, 5 September 1908. United States Bahá'í Archives.
103. From Ethel Rosenberg's notes, *Bahaism: Its Ethical and Social Teachings*. United Kingdom Bahá'í Archives. The talk was later published in *International Congress for the History of Religions (3rd), Transactions*, vol. 1, pp. 321-5. A modern translation of the passage of 'Abdu'l-Bahá may be found in *Some Answered Questions*, p. 159.
104. ibid.
105. ibid.
106. ibid.
107. ibid.
108. See Rosenberg, 'Love is the foundation of everything', *Star of the West*, vol. 7, no. 11, pp. 107-8.
109. ibid. p. 108.

Chapter 9:
A Brief Account of the Bahá'í Movement

110. Bahá'u'lláh, in *Compilation*, vol. 2, p. 407.
111. Rosenberg, *A Brief Account of the Bahai Movement*, p. 1.
112. ibid. p. 3.
113. ibid. pp. 3-4.
114. ibid. p. 4.
115. ibid. p. 5.
116. ibid. p. 6.
117. ibid. p. 11.
118. ibid.
119. ibid. p. 12.
120. ibid. p. 14.

121. ibid.
122. ibid. p. 16.
123. ibid. p. 17.
124. ibid. pp. 17-18.
125. ibid. p. 19.
126. ibid.
127. ibid. p. 21.

Chapter 10:
A Community Evolves

128. Bahá'u'lláh, *Gleanings*, V, p. 7.
129. *Bahai News*, vol. 1, no. 6, pp. 12-13.
130. Villiers, *Wellesley Tudor Pole*, p. 6.
131. Tudor Pole, *Writing on the Ground*, p. 141.
132. This story is recounted by Tudor Pole in *The Silent Road*, pp. 77-9.
133. *Bahai News* (*Star of the West*), vol. 1, no. 18, p. 6.
134. Hall, *Bahá'í Dawn – Manchester*, pp. 2-3.
135. Letter from Sarah Ann Ridgeway to E. T. Hall, 12 November 1910. Quoted in Whitehead, *Some Bahá'ís to Remember*, p. 31.
136. Hall, *Bahá'í Dawn – Manchester*, pp. 4-5.
137. ibid. p. 5.
138. Hall, 'To Him We Love – Late Prisoner in Acca', *Poems by Edward Theodore Hall*, p. 6.
139. *Star of the West*, vol. 2, no. 2, p. 2.
140. 'Abdu'l-Bahá, in *Star of the West*, vol. 2, no. 5, p. 6.
141. *Star of the West*, vol. 2, no. 2, p. 2.
142. *Star of the West*, vol. 2, no. 5, p. 7.
143. Momen, *Bábí and Bahá'í Religions*, p. 324.
144. Tudor Pole, 'The First Universal Races Congress', *Star of the West*, vol. 2, no. 9, p. 3.
145. 'Abdu'l-Bahá, in ibid. p. 4.
146. ibid. p. 6.

Chapter 11:
'Abdu'l-Bahá in the West

147. 'Abdu'l-Bahá, *Tablets of the Divine Plan*, p. 39.
148. Shoghi Effendi, *God Passes By*, pp. 279-80.
149. Blomfield, *Chosen Highway*, pp. 149-50.
150. *'Abdu'l-Bahá in London*, p. 53.
151. Hall, *Sitarih Khánum*, pp. 9-11.
152. Blomfield, *Chosen Highway*, p. 165.
153. ibid. pp. 150-1.
154. Letter from Ethel Rosenberg to Albert Windust, 20 September 1911. United States Bahá'í Archives.
155. Blomfield, *Chosen Highway*, p. 153.
156. *'Abdu'l-Bahá in London*, pp. 44-5.
157. Letter from Ethel Rosenberg to Albert Windust, 20 September 1911. United States Bahá'í Archives.
158. Letter from Tudor Pole to *Star of the West*, vol. 2, no. 15, p. 11.
159. Florence George, unpublished recollections of the early days of the British Bahá'í community. United Kingdom Bahá'í Archives.
160. Momen, *Bábí and Bahá'í Religions*, p. 326.
161. Report in *The Christian Commonwealth*, 13 September 1911.
162. ibid.
163. *'Abdu'l-Bahá in London*, p. 20.
164. Letter from Charles Mason Remey, *Star of the West*, vol. 2, no. 12, p. 10.
165. Report in *The Christian Commonwealth*, 20 September 1911.
166. *'Abdu'l-Bahá in London*, p. 24.
167. ibid. p. 78.
168. ibid. p. 79.
169. ibid. p. 40.
170. ibid. p. 41.
171. ibid. p. 33.
172. ibid. p. 34.
173. ibid. pp. 38-9.
174. Shoghi Effendi, *God Passes By*, p. 286.
175. 'Abdu'l-Bahá, *Paris Talks*, p. 29.
176. Hall, *Sitarih Khánum*, p. 14.

177. Notes taken by Ethel Rosenberg in Paris, 19 November 1911. United Kingdom Bahá'í Archives.
178. *'Abdu'l-Bahá in London*, p. 122.
179. *Star of the West*, vol. 2, no. 16, p. 14.
180. Skrine, *Bahaism*, p. 66.
181. *Star of the West*, vol. 3, no. 13, p. 14.
182. *Star of the West*, vol. 3, no. 19, p. 4.
183. *Star of the West*, vol. 3, no. 17, p. 7.
184. *Star of the West*, vol. 3, no. 18, pp. 8-9.
185. For an excellent account of 'Abdu'l-Bahá's visit to Scotland, see Khursheed, *Seven Candles of Unity*.
186. Blomfield, *Chosen Highway*, pp. 176-7.
187. Shoghi Effendi, *God Passes By*, p. 294.

Chapter 12:
Years of Darkness

188. 'Abdu'l-Bahá, *Tablets of the Divine Plan*, pp. 53-4.
189. 'Abdu'l-Bahá, *Promulgation*, p. 376.
190. Morgan, *Sphere Illustrated History*, p. 116.
191. This was a commonly expressed hope of the period, see *ITN Factbook*, p. 901.
192. 'Abdu'l-Bahá, in *Star of the West*, vol. 5, no. 16, pp. 244-5
193. Tablet of 'Abdu'l-Bahá to the Bahá'ís in London, who had sent Him a New Year's greeting on 21 March 1914. United Kingdom Bahá'í Archives.
194. 'Florence George: A Tribute by Alfred Sugar', *Bahá'í World*, vol. 12, p. 697.
195. These deliberations are recorded in the minutes of the Bahai Committee and Council kept by Ethel Rosenberg. United Kingdom Bahá'í Archives.
196. Hall, *Sitarih <u>Kh</u>ánum*, p. 17.
197. Quoted in Momen, *Bábí and Bahá'í Religions*, p. 421.
198. Memorandum from Laurence Oliphant, 6 May 1915. Quoted in ibid. p. 423.
199. Letter from Dr Esslemont to Luṭfu'lláh Ḥakím, 23 May 1925. United Kingdom Bahá'í Archives.
200. Tablet of 'Abdu'l-Bahá to John Craven, 30 July 1914. Quoted in Hall, *Bahá'í Dawn – Manchester*, pp. 10-11.

201. Letter from Ethel Rosenberg, *Star of the West*, vol. 5, no. 19, p. 293.
202. Letter from Daniel Jenkyn to Luṭfu'lláh Ḥakím, 22 November 1914, in ibid.
203. Tablet of 'Abdu'l-Bahá to Daniel Jenkyn, in ibid. p. 295.
204. Letter from Dr Esslemont to John Craven, quoted in Whitehead, *Some Bahá'ís to Remember*, p. 49.
205. Letter of Edward Hall, *Star of the West*, vol. 7, no. 16, p. 161.
206. Hall, 'A Brief Narrative of My Life', pp. 31-2.
207. Hall, 'The Woods of Blavincourt', *Poems by Edward Theodore Hall*, pp. 7-8.
208. Tablet of 'Abdu'l-Bahá to E. T. Hall, quoted in ibid. p. 7.
209. Minutes of the Bahai Council, 19 February 1916. United Kingdom Bahá'í Archives.
210. See Smith, 'The Development and Influence of the Bahá'í Administrative Order in Great Britain, 1914-1950', *Community Histories*, p. 158.
211. Letter from Ethel Rosenberg to Helen Goodall, 23 November 1917. United States Bahá'í Archives.
212. Tudor Pole, *Writing on the Ground*, p. 152. Tudor Pole's own account in this book does not exactly tally with the evidence of his own letters of the time. For example, he states that it was March 1918 that he learned of 'Abdu'l-Bahá's situation, but he had already written to Sir Mark Sykes MP about it in December 1917. See Momen, *Bábí and Bahá'í Religions*, pp. 333-7. Other elements of this story may also be somewhat inaccurate.
213. Momen, *Bábí and Bahá'í Religions*, p. 333.
214. Quoted in ibid. p. 334.
215. Letter from Ethel Rosenberg to Roy Wilhelm, May Maxwell and Helen Goodall, 28 March 1919. United Kingdom Bahá'í Archives.
216. Letter from Dr Esslemont to Luṭfu'lláh Ḥakím, 28 July 1918. United Kingdom Bahá'í Archives.
217. Shoghi Effendi, *God Passes By*, p. 382.
218. ibid.
219. Letter from Dr Esslemont to Luṭfu'lláh Ḥakím, 28 July 1918. United Kingdom Bahá'í Archives.

220. See Research Department of the Bahá'í World Centre, *Ethel Jenner Rosenberg*, p. 6
221. Diary of Dr Esslemont, unpublished. United Kingdom Bahá'í Archives.
222. Letter from Dr Esslemont to Luṭfu'lláh Ḥakím, 28 July 1918. United Kingdom Bahá'í Archives.
223. Rabbaní, *Priceless Pearl*, p. 38.
224. Minutes taken by Ethel Rosenberg, 22 October 1920. United Kingdom Bahá'í Archives.
225. Letter from Dr Esslemont to Luṭfu'lláh Ḥakím, 10 December 1920. United Kingdom Bahá'í Archives.
226. Whitehead, unpublished account of Claudia Coles.
227. For an excellent biography of George Townshend see Hofman, *George Townshend*.

Chapter 13:
The Heroic Age Ends

228. 'Abdu'l-Bahá, quoted in Shoghi Effendi, *God Passes By*, p. 309.
229. Shoghi Effendi, *God Passes By*, p. 309.
230. ibid. p. 311.
231. Diary of Ethel Rosenberg's visit to Haifa 1921-2. United Kingdom Bahá'í Archives.
232. ibid.
233. This conversation was reported by Ethel to Mother George in a letter of 8 December 1921. United Kingdom Bahá'í Archives.
234. ibid.
235. Shoghi Effendi, *God Passes By*, p. 277,
236. 'Abdu'l-Bahá, quoted in ibid. p. 275.
237. Letter of Ethel Rosenberg to Mother George, *Star of the West*, vol. 12, no. 19, p. 301.
238. Letter of Ethel Rosenberg to Julia Culver, 14 December 1921. United States Bahá'í Archives.
239. Letter of Ethel Rosenberg to the English Bahá'ís, 8 December 1921. *Star of the West*, vol. 12, no. 19, p. 300.
240. Letter of Ethel Rosenberg to Julia Culver, 14 December 1921. United States Bahá'í Archives.

241. Letter of Ethel Rosenberg to Mother George, *Star of the West*, vol. 12, no. 19, p. 301.
242. Letter of Ethel Rosenberg to Julia Culver, 14 December 1921. United States Bahá'í Archives.
243. Gail, *Arches of the Years*, p. 107.
244. Shoghi Effendi, *God Passes By*, p. 312.
245. Letter of Ethel Rosenberg to the English Bahá'ís, 8 December 1921. *Star of the West*, vol. 12, no. 19. pp. 300-1.
246. Letter of Ethel Rosenberg to Julia Culver, 14 December 1921. United States Bahá'í Archives.
247. Letter of Ethel Rosenberg to the English Bahá'ís, 8 December 1921. *Star of the West*, vol. 12, no. 19, pp. 300-1.
248. Ethel Rosenberg's diary of her visit to Haifa, 1921-2. United Kingdom Bahá'í Archives.
249. Letter of Abbas Adib to Zia Bagdadi, *Star of the West*, vol. 12, no. 19, p. 303.
250. Quoted in a private memorandum by Major Tudor Pole. United Kingdom Bahá'í Archives.
251. ibid.
252. *The Times,* London, 30 November 1921. Clipping in United Kingdom Bahá'í Archives.
253. *The Morning Post*, London. 1 December 1921. Clipping in United Kingdom Bahá'í Archives.
254. *The Daily Mail.* London. 1 December 1921. Quoted in a private memorandum of Major Tudor Pole. United Kingdom Bahá'í Archives.
255. *The Children's Newspaper.* London. 14 January 1922. Clipping in United Kingdom Bahá'í Archives.
256. Letter of Dr Esslemont to Luṭfu'lláh Ḥakím, 8 December 1921. United Kingdom Bahá'í Archives.
257. ibid.
258. ibid.
259. 'Abdu'l-Bahá, *Will and Testament*, p. 11.
260. ibid.
261. Ethel Rosenberg's diary of her visit to Haifa, 1921-2. United Kingdom Bahá'í Archives.
262. Blomfield and Shoghi Effendi, 'The Passing of 'Abdu'l-Bahá', *Bahá'í World*, vol. 2, p. 16.
263. *Star of the West*, vol. 13, no. 2, pp. 40-1.

264. ibid. p. 41.
265. Rabbaní, *Priceless Pearl*, p. 47.
266. *Star of the West*, vol. 13, no. 2, pp. 41-2.
267. ibid. p. 42.
268. ibid.
269. ibid. p. 44.
270. Quoted in Rabbaní, *Priceless Pearl*, p. 47.
271. Diary of Ethel Rosenberg's visit to Haifa, 1921-2. United Kingdom Bahá'í Archives.
272. ibid.
273. Undated letter of Ethel Rosenberg to the English Bahá'ís. United Kingdom Bahá'í Archives.
274. Diary of Ethel Rosenberg's visit to Haifa, 1921-2. United Kingdom Bahá'í Archives.
275. ibid.
276. ibid.
277. ibid.
278. Letter from Ethel Rosenberg to Julia Culver, 28 February 1922. United States Bahá'í Archives.
279. ibid.
280. ibid.
281. ibid.
282. Diary of Ethel Rosenberg's visit to Haifa, 1921-2. United Kingdom Bahá'í Archives.
283. Letter of Ethel Rosenberg to Julia Culver, 28 February 1922. United States Bahá'í Archives.
284. Mountfort Mills, quoted in *Star of the West*, vol. 13, no. 4, p. 68.
285. Quoted by Rabbaní, *Priceless Pearl*, p. 56.
286. Shoghi Effendi, *Bahá'í Administration*, p. 20.
287. From a talk given by Hand of the Cause Leroy Ioas, *In the Days of the Guardian*, transcribed in *Youth Can Move the World*.

Chapter 14:
The Trusted Ones of the Merciful

288. Bahá'u'lláh, *Kitáb-i-Aqdas*, para. 30.

289. Letter of Dr Esslemont to Luṭfu'lláh Ḥakím,18 June 1922. United Kingdom Bahá'í Archives.
290. Letter of the 'Council of the London Spiritual Assembly' to the 'Friends in El Baha', 19 September 1922.
291. Letter of Dr Esslemont to Luṭfu'lláh Ḥakím, 13 July 1922. United Kingdom Bahá'í Archives.
292. Letter of Claudia Coles to *Star of the West*, 13 August 1922. United Kingdom Bahá'í Archives.
293. ibid.
294. ibid.
295. Hall, *Bahá'í Dawn – Manchester*, p. 33.
296. Minutes of the Spiritual Assembly, 2 December 1922. United Kingdom Bahá'í Archives.
297. Shoghi Effendi, *Unfolding Destiny*, p. 10.
298. ibid. pp. 10-11.
299. ibid. p. 11.
300. ibid.
301. Minutes of the meeting of the Spiritual Assembly, 3 February 1923. United Kingdom Bahá'í Archives.
302. *Star of the West*, vol. 14, no. 2, p. 57.
303. Shoghi Effendi, *Messages to the Bahá'í World*, p. 53.
304. Minutes of the meeting of the Spiritual Assembly, 24 March 1923. United Kingdom Bahá'í Archives.
305. Replica of original voting sheet. United Kingdom Bahá'í Archives.
306. Shoghi Effendi, quoted in Momen, *Dr J. E. Esslemont*, p. 27.
307. Herrick, *Unity Triumphant*, p. 219.

Chapter 15:
A Firm Foundation

308. Shoghi Effendi, *Unfolding Destiny*, p. 16.
309. Minutes of the British National Spiritual Assembly, First Meeting. United Kingdom Bahá'í Archives.
310. ibid. p. 3.
311. ibid. p. 4.
312. ibid. p. 6.
313. Shoghi Effendi, *Unfolding Destiny*, p. 16.
314. ibid.

315. ibid. p. 27.
316. *Religions of the Empire*, p. 5.
317. Shoghi Effendi, *Unfolding Destiny*, p. 30.
318. *Religions of the Empire*, p. 5.
319. ibid. p. 6.
320. Shoghi Effendi, *Unfolding Destiny*, p. 30.
321. Whitehead, unpublished biography of Claudia Coles, p. 17.
322. Shoghi Effendi, *Unfolding Destiny*, pp. 28-9.
323. Esslemont, quoted in Momen, *Dr J. E. Esslemont*, p. 30.
324. Shoghi Effendi, *Unfolding Destiny*, p. 40.
325. ibid. p. 30.
326. ibid. p. 31.
327. ibid. p. 32.
328. ibid. p. 54.
329. Shoghi Effendi, *God Passes By*, p. 386.
330. Root, quoted in Garis, *Martha Root*, p. 259.
331. Circular letter from the London Spiritual Assembly to the Friends in El Baha, 28 November 1926. United Kingdom Bahá'í Archives.
332. Shoghi Effendi, *Unfolding Destiny*, p. 61.

Chapter 16:
Inestimable Services

333. ibid. p. 34.
334. Townshend, quoted in Hofman, *George Townshend*, pp. 55-6.
335. ibid. p. 56.
336. ibid. p. 57.
337. Shoghi Effendi, *Unfolding Destiny*, p. 55.
338. ibid. p. 56.
339. ibid. p. 60.
340. ibid. p. 62.
341. ibid.
342. The Universal House of Justice, quoted in biographical note on Isobel Slade, *Unfolding Destiny*, p. 471.
343. Unpublished recollections of Isobel Slade. United Kingdom Bahá'í Archives.
344. Research Department of the Bahá'í World Centre, *Ethel Jenner Rosenberg*, p. 5.

345. Letter written on behalf of Shoghi Effendi, *Arohanui*, p. 25.
346. ibid. p. 27.
347. Letter of Ethel Rosenberg, written on behalf of Shoghi Effendi, *Unfolding Destiny*, pp. 62-3.
348. Shoghi Effendi, *Unfolding Destiny*, pp. 70-1.
349. ibid. p. 71.
350. Townshend, quoted in Hofman, *George Townshend*, pp. 57-8.
351. Shoghi Effendi, quoted in ibid. p. 58.
352. ibid.
353. Bahá'u'lláh, *Hidden Words*, title page.
354. Bahá'u'lláh, *The Splendour of God*, p. 96.
355. Bahá'u'lláh, quoted in *Star of the West*, vol. 14, no. 9, p. 289.
356. Bahá'u'lláh, *Hidden Words*, Arabic no. 3.
357. Letter of Ethel Rosenberg, written on behalf of Shoghi Effendi, Arohanui, pp. 25-6.
358. ibid. p. 26.
359. Letter of Ethel Rosenberg to Shahnaz Waite, 14 January 1927. United States Bahá'í Archives.
360. ibid.
361. Letter of Ethel Rosenberg to Shahnaz Waite, 19 March 1927. United States Bahá'í Archives.
362. ibid.
363. Letter of Ethel Rosenberg to Shahnaz Waite, 22 May 1927. United States Bahá'í Archives.
364. Research Department of the Bahá'í World Centre, *Ethel Jenner Rosenberg*, p. 6.

Chapter 17:
The Messenger of Joy

365. 'Abdu'l-Bahá, quoted in Shoghi Effendi, *God Passes By*, p. 310.
366. Shoghi Effendi, *Unfolding Destiny*, p. 73.
367. From the unpublished memoirs of and personal interviews with Alma Gregory.
368. Minutes of the London Spiritual Assembly, selections 1927-9. United Kingdom Bahá'í Archives.
369. From an interview with Alma Gregory.

370. Letter of George Palgrave Simpson to the National Spiritual Assembly, 16 May 1928. United Kingdom Bahá'í Archives.
371. Minutes of the London Spiritual Assembly, 1927-9. United Kingdom Bahá'í Archives.
372. Research Department of the Bahá'í World Centre, *Ethel Jenner Rosenberg*, p. 4
373. Minutes of an extraordinary meeting held jointly by the National Spiritual Assembly and the London Spiritual Assembly. 17 March 1928. United Kingdom Bahá'í Archives.
374. Shoghi Effendi. *Unfolding Destiny*, p. 85.
375. ibid. p. 84.
376. Minutes of the London Spiritual Assembly, 2 February 1929. United Kingdom Bahá'í Archives.
377. ibid.
378. Bahíyyih Khánum, quoted in Shoghi Effendi, *Unfolding Destiny*, pp. 86-7.
379. Letter written on behalf of Shoghi Effendi, *Unfolding Destiny*, p. 87.
380. ibid. p. 88.
381. ibid.
382. *Bahá'í Newsletter*, July 1930, p. 8.
383. ibid. p. 3.
384. Shoghi Effendi, *Unfolding Destiny*, p. 90.
385. Quoted in minutes of the London Spiritual Assembly, 2 March 1931. United Kingdom Bahá'í Archives.
386. Letter of the National Spiritual Assembly to National Spiritual Assemblies around the world, 7 December 1930. United Kingdom Bahá'í Archives.
387. ibid.
388. *Bahá'í Newsletter*, December 1930, pp. 2-4.
389. *Bahá'í News*, September 1931, p. 6.
390. Research Department of the Bahá'í World Centre, *Ethel Jenner Rosenberg*, p. 4.
391. ibid. p. 5.
392. Rosenberg papers, United Kingdom Bahá'í Archives.

Appendix:
Afterwards

393. *Bahá'í World*, vol. 4, pp. 73-4.
394. Shoghi Effendi, quoted in 'May Ellis Maxwell', *Bahá'í World*, vol. 8, p. 642.
395. Shoghi Effendi, 'A Tribute by Shoghi Effendi', *Bahá'í World*, vol. 5, p. 179.
396. Maxwell, 'The Passing of Munírih Khánum, the Holy Mother', *Bahá'í World*, vol. 8, p. 263.
397. Shoghi Effendi, *Messages to America*, p. 11.
398. The Universal House of Justice, cited in *Power of the Covenant*, part 2, p. 27.
399. Shoghi Effendi, quoted in *Bahá'í World*, vol. 11, p. 509.
400. Rúhániyyih Khánum, quoted in *Bahá'í World*, vol. 7, p. 542.
401. Shoghi Effendi, quoted in ibid.
402. Shoghi Effendi, quoted in *Bahá'í World*, vol. 12, p. 697.
403. *Bahá'í World*, vol. 12, p. 681.
404. Shoghi Effendi, quoted in ibid. p. 674.
405. Shoghi Effendi, quoted in *Bahá'í World*, vol. 8, p. 661.
406. Villiers, *Wellesley Tudor Pole*, p. 8.

Index

This index is alphabetized letter by letter with hyphens, apostrophes and spaces ignored. Thus 'Indians' precedes '*In Galilee*'. The articles 'a', 'the' and 'el-' are also ignored. Thus El-Kahtib is found under 'k', while *A Brief Account of the Bahai Movement* is found under 'b'.

About the Author

Robert Weinberg was born in 1965 in Canterbury, England, and received a B.A. Honours Degree in Expressive Arts from the University of Brighton, followed by a Post-Graduate Diploma in Arts Administration from the City University, London. Professionally, he is a broadcast journalist and radio producer who has worked for both the BBC and independent radio in the United Kingdom.

Rob has served both on the Junior Youth Department and National Youth Committee of the National Spiritual Assembly of the Bahá'ís of the United Kingdom, was Treasurer of the first European Bahá'í Youth Council, and in 1991 was appointed Auxiliary Board member for Propagation of the Bahá'í Faith in south-east England. His compilation of Shoghi Effendi's letters to junior youth, *Your True Brother*, was published by George Ronald in 1991.